Communications
in Computer and Information Science 1369

More information about this series at http://www.springer.com/series/7899

Yueming Wang (Ed.)

Human Brain and Artificial Intelligence

Second International Workshop, HBAI 2020
Held in Conjunction with IJCAI-PRICAI 2020
Yokohama, Japan, January 7, 2021
Revised Selected Papers

 Springer

Editor
Yueming Wang
Zhejiang University
Hangzhou, China

ISSN 1865-0929   ISSN 1865-0937 (electronic)
Communications in Computer and Information Science
ISBN 978-981-16-1287-9   ISBN 978-981-16-1288-6 (eBook)
https://doi.org/10.1007/978-981-16-1288-6

This Springer imprint is published by the registered company Springer Nature Singapore Pte Ltd.
The registered company address is: 152 Beach Road, #21-01/04 Gateway East, Singapore 189721, Singapore

Preface

The quest for brain research is to uncover the nature of brain cognition, consciousness, and intelligence. Artificial Intelligence (AI) is committed to the realization of machine-borne intelligence. The development of these two fields is undergoing a continuous trend of crossvergence and convergence. To promote the cross-exploration and deep integration between these two important areas, thus possibly leading to ground-breaking discoveries at the frontiers of neuroscience, AI, and brain-machine interface, the International Workshop on Human Brain and Artificial Intelligence (HBAI 2020) in conjunction with IJCAI-PRICAI 2020 was organized and held online on January 7, 2021.

The key objective of HBAI is to contribute to answering the following three questions: 1) How can AI techniques help human brain research (brain computing)? 2) How can human brain research inspire the study of AI (brain-inspired computing)? 3) How can AI and brain intelligence be combined to build a more powerful one (brain-machine integration)? Thus, we encourage papers with the topics of brain-inspired computing, brain-machine interfaces, computational neuroscience, brain-related health, neuroimaging, cognition and behavior, learning and memory, neuron modulation, and closed-loop brain stimulation.

We received more than 20 papers, from which a few were withdrawn due to the undetermined program of IJCAI-PRICAI 2020 caused by COVID-19. Each paper was single-blindly reviewed by at least 3 reviewers. Finally 11 papers were accepted. Daiheng et al. proposed a spiking neural network to deal with sequential tasks. Baihan et al. presented a more general and flexible parametric framework for sequential decision making. Juyang partly answered the question by an APFGP model: can a machine be conscious? Qi et al. incorporated task-related information in dimensionality reduction for neural signals. Kai et al. explored visual encoding by an end-to-end CNN. Jintang et al. delved into graph adversarial learning from an empirical perspective. Dong et al. proposed a brain-controlled robotic arm. Chao et al. studied an automatic detection method of sleep spindles. Guoxin et al. applied multimodal physiological signals to the diagnosis of Parkinson's disease. Hongyan et al. used a multi-core tensor model for emotion recognition. Finally, Jin et al. reviewed recent studies on transfer learning.

Overall, the workshop was successfully held. During the meeting, researchers presented and discussed their research, shared their knowledge and experiences, and discussed the current state of the art and future improvements to advance the interdisciplinary field of AI and brain.

February 2021 — Yueming Wang

Organization

Program Chair

Yueming Wang   Zhejiang University, China

Program Committee

Benjamin Becker	University of Electronic Science and Technology of China, China
Xiaowei Chen	Third Military Medical University, China
Boqing Gong	Google Inc., USA
Yaoyao Hao	Baylor College of Medicine, USA
Yong He	Beijing Normal University, China
Fei He	Rice University, USA
Yong Hu	The University of Hongkong, Hong Kong, China
Wanzeng Kong	Hangzhou Dianzhi University, China
Yue Leng	University of California, San Francisco, USA
Shurong Liu	Global Biotech Inc., USA
Dan Pan	Guangzhou Dazhi Networks Technology Co. Ltd., China
Gang Pan	Zhejiang University, China
Yu Qi	Zhejiang University, China
Yiyu Shi	University of Notre Dame, USA
Aniruddha Sinha	Tata Consultancy Services, India
Xiaowei Song	Simon Fraser University, Canada
Dong Song	University of Southern California, USA
Tao Tang	Nanyang Technological University, Singapore
Yiwen Wang	Hong Kong University of Science and Technology, Hong Kong, China
Yalin Wang	Arizona State University, USA
Jimin Wang	Google Inc., USA
Juyang Weng	Michigan State University, USA
Amy Wenxuan Ding	Emlyon Business School, France
Xiaowei Xu	Guangdong Provincial People's Hospital, China
Jian Xu	Zhejiang University, China
Lin Yao	Zhejiang University, China
An Zeng	Guangdong University of Technology, China
Yang Zhan	Shenzhen Institutes of Advanced Technology of the Chinese Academy of Science, China
Qiaosheng Zhang	NYU School of Medicine, USA
Deli Zhao	Alibaba Inc., China

Contents

ARLIF: A Flexible and Efficient Recurrent Neuronal Model
for Sequential Tasks 1
   Daiheng Gao, Zhenzhi Wu, Yujie Wu, Guoqi Li, and Jing Pei

Models of Human Behavioral Agents in Bandits, Contextual Bandits
and RL 14
   *Baihan Lin, Guillermo Cecchi, Djallel Bouneffouf, Jenna Reinen,
   and Irina Rish*

Machines Develop Consciousness Through Autonomous Programming
for General Purposes (APFGP) 34
   Juyang Weng

Incorporating Task-Related Information in Dimensionality Reduction
of Neural Population Using Autoencoders 56
   Qi Lian, Yunzhu Liu, Yu Zhao, and Yu Qi

Effective and Efficient ROI-wise Visual Encoding Using an End-to-End
CNN Regression Model and Selective Optimization 72
   Kai Qiao, Chi Zhang, Jian Chen, Linyuan Wang, Li Tong, and Bin Yan

Deep Insights into Graph Adversarial Learning: An Empirical
Study Perspective 87
   *Jintang Li, Zishan Gu, Qibiao Peng, Kun Xu, Liang Chen,
   and Zibin Zheng*

Brain-Controlled Robotic Arm Based on Adaptive FBCCA 102
   Dong Zhang, Banghua Yang, Shouwei Gao, and Xuelin Gu

Automatic Sleep Spindle Detection and Analysis in Patients
with Sleep Disorders 113
   *Chao Chen, Xuequan Zhu, Abdelkader Nasreddine Belkacem, Lin Lu,
   Long Hao, Jia You, Duk Shin, Wenjun Tan, Zhaoyang Huang,
   and Dong Ming*

Diagnosing Parkinson's Disease Using Multimodal Physiological Signals. . . . 125
   *Guoxin Guo, Shujie Wang, Shuaibin Wang, Zhiyu Zhou, Guangying Pei,
   and Tianyi Yan*

Emotion Recognition Using Multi-core Tensor Learning and Multimodal
Physiological Signal 137
   Hongyan Xu, Jiajia Tang, Jianhai Zhang, and Li Zhu

A Review of Transfer Learning for EEG-Based Driving Fatigue Detection. . .   149
  Jin Cui, Yong Peng, Kenji Ozawa, and Wanzeng Kong

Author Index   163

ARLIF: A Flexible and Efficient Recurrent Neuronal Model for Sequential Tasks

Daiheng Gao[1], Zhenzhi Wu[1,2]([⊠]), Yujie Wu[2], Guoqi Li[2], and Jing Pei[2]

[1] Lynxi Technology Incorporation, Beijing, China
{daiheng.gao,zhenzhi.wu}@lynxi.com
[2] Center for Brain Inspired Computing Research, Tsinghua University, Beijing, China
wu-yj16@mails.tsinghua.edu.cn,
{liguoqi,peij}@mail.tsinghua.edu.cn

Abstract. Spiking neural networks (SNNs), stem from neuroscience, are promising for energy-efficient information processing due to the "event-driven" characteristic, whereas, they are inferior to artificial neural networks (ANNs) in real complicated tasks. However, ANNs usually suffer from expensive processing costs and a large number of parameters. Likewise, constrained to convergence speed, stability, complicated training mechanism and preprocessing setting, which is an obstacle for the SNN practitioners to expand its application scope. Inspired by the operation mechanism of human brain neurons, a brain-inspired Adaptive firing threshold Recurrent Leaky Integrate-and-Fire (ARLIF) model proposed. ARLIF and his variant ConvARLIF2D, which fuses the calculation logic of ANNs and bio-dynamic behaviors of SNNs, has a low-power dissipation since its number of weights is far less than SimpleRNN, GRU or LSTM. In this work, we present a Keras-based implementation of the layer of ARLIF and ConvARLIF2D that seamlessly fits in the contemporary deep learning framework without writing complex boilerplate code. The experiments result indicating that our ARLIF performs favorably against the state-of-the-art architectures.

Keywords: Spiking neural network · Recurrent neural network · Hybrid · Self-adjust firing threshold mechanism

1 Introduction

Spiking Neural Networks (SNNs) is viewed as the 3rd generation of neural networks [16], as it more closely mimics the mechanism of brain neurons. Since the Integrate-and-Fire model is the first neuron model was proposed by Louis Lapicque, who leads the start of the exploration in detailed behavior of neurons. With further studies and developments, a range of neuron models were proposed: Hodgkin-Huxley model [10] was the first neuron model that capable of demonstrating how the action potentials are initiated and propagated through neurons; FitzHugh–Nagumo model [7,18] produced a prototype system that simulates the excitatory/inhibitory behaviors of neurons effectively; Izhikevich [11] proposed a neuron model with both low implementation costs and biological plausibility.

Y. Wang (Ed.): HBAI 2020, CCIS 1369, pp. 1–13, 2021.
https://doi.org/10.1007/978-981-16-1288-6_1

However, SNN models are more based on continual neuronal dynamics and discrete binary spike representations, which is challenging to incorporate SNNs into high-performance deep learning frameworks and exploiting the advantages of the backpropagation learning algorithm. As many state-of-the-art works fail to deepen the network structure (only with few feature extraction layers), but in the meanwhile restrict by the speed of convergence, SNNs have merely been introduced into the category of neuromorphic computation chips. They are limited in handwritten digital recognition and other simple tasks since then.

Through the trait of brain neurons (like sparse coding, redundant noise, etc.) and the fact that RNNs could be used to imitate first-order neuro-dynamic equations, we propose the adaptive firing threshold recurrent Leaky-Integrate-and-Fire (ARLIF) model. Furthermore, we turn the fixed firing threshold in SNNs into a self-adjust manner through a novel and iterative self-learning method for f_{thres}, which independent from the training method (backpropagation through time (BPTT)), to reduce the number of parameters in ARLIF meanwhile keep a decent precision. With this fancy adaptive distribution-based f_{thres} technique, instead of suffering accuracy degradation, the test network with ARLIF could even achieve a higher accuracy under the fact that we replace 2-dim recurrent weight in SimpleRNN (SRN) with 1-dim α in ARLIF.

To verify the effectiveness of ARLIF, we conduct experiments on action recognition and object recognition. Experiments result shows that ConvARLIF2D, which performs well in the task of action recognition, is applicable to merge the feature of each timestep and maintain at a satisfactory level of accuracy compared with ConvLSTM2D, which has far more numbers of weight. Besides, as we implement ARLIF and ConvARLIF2D on Keras [5], then we encapsulated the pluggability of contemporary deep learning framework and the bio-dynamic properties into a layer (not only are the concepts same with SimpleRNN, Conv2D and other common layers but with no difference in the way of the function call). People hence no need to write boilerplate code nor puzzled with too much cryptic hyper-parameters which is common in many SNN state-of-the-art.

In summary, the major contributions of this paper are listed as follows:

1. We propose a new structure: ARLIF and ConvARLIF2D, which is the combination of the biological plausibility of SNNs and the numerical characteristics of ANNs.
2. We propose a fancy self-adjust algorithm, which is beyond the autograd mechanism of deep learning framework, design to adjust the firing threshold of ARLIF according to the data distribution of current training mini-batch.
3. The apply of ConvARLIF2D in two-stream action recognition and object recognition both show that our model of vast potential in complex real-world tasks. Furthermore, we introduce a Spatio-Temporal residual network architecture that proves our ARLIF could also work in the deep network (generally more than ten feature extractor layer).

2   Background

In this section, we do a deeper-going analysis in Leaky Integrate-and-Fire (LIF) model. Here we aim to highlight the most relevant parts to our ARLIF, which will be analyzed in more detail in the next section.

2.1 Neuron Models: Leaky Integrate-and-Fire

Neuron models are the new generation of the neural network, denote it as a subclass of Spiking Neural Networks (SNNs). Compared with Artificial Neural Networks (ANNs), SNNs incorporate the concept of time and firing mechanism into their operating model, which makes more biologically rationality.

Since Hodgkin-Huxley Neuron Model (HH model) is hard to realize large networks even for an SNN simulation due to its substantial computational overhead and complexity. For both biological rationality and computational simplicity, Gerstner [8] renews the classical Integrate-and-Fire (IF) model proposed by french neurophysiologist Louis Lapicque, which replacing the coupled nonlinear differential equations from HH model by a reset mechanism. The simplest and most common model of this class is the Leaky Integrate-and-Fire (LIF) model since it is possible to simulate extensive networks of such neurons and can be analyzed mathematically in great detail (at both neuron and network levels).

Since Leaky Integrate-and-Fire (LIF) is the most common and simple model which modeling neuron operations and some essential dynamic traits effectively with low computational costs. From a biological perspective, membrane potential $\mathbf{V}_m$ stays still at its resting value $\mathbf{E}_l$ if the absence of current stimulus $\mathbf{I}$ or synaptic input. The cell membrane, which acts as a capacitor $\mathbf{C}_m$, was changed when receiving a current stimulus. The change of the membrane potential is ($\mathbf{g}_L$ is the conductance here):

$$\mathbf{C}_m \frac{\mathrm{d}\mathbf{V}_m}{\mathrm{d}t} = -\mathbf{g}_L(\mathbf{V}_m - \mathbf{E}_l) + \mathbf{I} \tag{1}$$

Besides, with the introduction of the firing mechanism in LIF, a neuron is firing when $\mathbf{V}_m$ beyond $\mathbf{V}_t$ and its membrane potential then reset to a predefined reset potential $\mathbf{V}_{reset}$:

$$\mathbf{V}_m \rightarrow \mathbf{V}_{reset} \tag{2}$$

The major limitations of LIF and other commonly-used neuron models are they receive discrete spike trains (binary values are much less expressive than floating-point numbers) as input. Besides, the training algorithm of it represented by Spiking Time Dependent Plasticity (STDP) is not an ideal optimization algorithm because the lack of global information, to some extent, hinders the convergence of neural networks.

2.2 Recurrent Neural Network

Recurrent neural network (RNN) [19], which is naturally suitable for handling sequential data due to whose neurons are capable of sending signals to each other and capturing temporal information and the relationship between neurons is a typical class of artificial neural network.

RNN comes in many variants like Simple Recurrent neural networks (SRN), Bidirectional RNN (Bi-RNN) and etc. The most basic form of SRN, for example, can be described by

$$\widetilde{\mathbf{h}}_t = \mathbf{W}_x \cdot \mathbf{x}_t + \mathbf{b}_x \tag{3}$$

$$\mathbf{y}_t = \sigma(\widetilde{\mathbf{h}}_t + \mathbf{W}_h \cdot \mathbf{h}_{t-1}) \tag{4}$$

$$\mathbf{h}_t = \mathbf{y}_t \tag{5}$$

where $\sigma(...)$ denotes the activation function tanh, $\mathbf{b}_x$ refers to the bias term. $\cdot$ represents matrix multiplication, $\odot$ refers to the hadamard product whereas $\otimes$ refers to the convolution product. As we have seen that basic RNN has two type of weights $\mathbf{W}_x$ and $\mathbf{W}_h$, in which $\mathbf{W}_x$, $\mathbf{W}_h$ are used to do matrix multiplication separately by $\mathbf{x}_t$ and $\mathbf{h}_{t-1}$. In RNNs most general form, $\mathbf{W}_x$ (input dims × hidden units) and $\mathbf{W}_h$ (hidden units × hidden units) are both two-dimensional structure.

Due to the vanishing gradient problem [1], SRN is incapability in modeling long-term dependencies. LSTM [9], GRU [4] and other variants were invented to address this problem.

Besides, compared to LSTM and GRU, SRN has a smaller number of weights, which represents a lower computational complexity. In addition, as RNN could approximately simulate first-order neuro-dynamic equations mathematically. We internalized this concept by reducing the number of weights in ARLIF and ConvARLIF2D to maintain its lightweight structure and in the meanwhile bring the biological traits of classical neuron model into RNNs.

3   ARLIF Framework

In this section, we present the framework of the Adaptive firing threshold recurrent Leaky Integrate-and-Fire model (ARLIF) with BPTT + self-adjust f_{thres}. The main idea is to make our ARLIF more biologically plausible and achieve high computational efficiency as well. As our architecture follow by the paradigm of ANN, the general information transmitting process of discrete spikes and synapses in SNN are thus abandoned, we instead use the continuous probability distribution, which avoids the non-existence gradient phenomenon effectively.

3.1   ARLIF Model

Based on the basic Eqs. 1 and 2 of LIF, we incorporated this form into RNN then take on the newly model form

$$\mathbf{v}_t = \mathbf{W} \cdot \mathbf{x}_t + \boldsymbol{\alpha} \odot \mathbf{v}_{t-1} + \mathbf{b} \tag{6}$$

$$\mathbf{y}_t = \sigma(\mathbf{v}_t + \boldsymbol{\delta}) \tag{7}$$

if $\mathbf{y}_t \geq f_{thres}$ then

$$\mathbf{v}_t = \mathbf{v}_t - \boldsymbol{\beta} \tag{8}$$

Here, we denote x_t as the input spike signal, v_t as the membrane potential, y_t as the activation level at discrete timestep t. Moreover, α is the leakage to accumulate membrane potentials of each discrete timestep, β is the reset voltage which produces the same effect [14] like V_{reset} in Eq. 2 as to simulate the inhibitory response of neurons, δ is random activation or random noise for biological plausible, note that σ is a custom activation function or a regularized function, after which there is a novel learning algorithm (we built it into the computational graph) to adjust the firing threshold f_{thres} automatically.

3.2 Fusion of ANN and SNN

As SNNs have difficulty in retrieving the gradients due to the shape of regularized function is a step function, which make the original LIF model hard to train and converge since the gradient only exists in the place that meets the firing threshold.

To solve this, we propose a new regularized function σ with an adaptive firing threshold f_{thres}. The adaptive strategy of $f_{thres,l}$ is based on the distribution of $y_{t,l}$ with current layer l and timestep t which beyond the "auto-tape" autograd mechanism. The propose of the adaptive firing threshold aims at guaranteeing a relatively reasonable distribution of neurons excitation and inhibition, which effectively solves the problem that setting a fixed firing threshold may cause most neurons to fail in reaching the intensity of excitation. Generally, we compared the $f_{thres,l}$ with $y_{t,l}$ before firing. To facilitate understanding, we first sort the activations $y_{t,l}$ in ascending order. Then we use $thres_l$ and $thres_h$ to represent the threshold that greater than $p_1(\%)$, $p_2(\%)$ of the ordered mini-batch data. Hence, p_1 represents the lower confidence limits of the data distribution of that given mini-batch whereas p_2 represents the higher confidence limits of the data distribution of the same mini-batch. If the results show that $f_{thres,l}$ is larger than $thres_l$ and smaller than $thres_h$, the self-adjust learning algorithm for $f_{thres,l}$ would not be activated until one of these conditions is not met. Plus, the learning rate of this algorithm is denoted as lr_{thres}.

In many layer-wise SNN's methods [13, 26], there lies the fact that the input layer has the highest spike activity, and the spike activity reduces significantly as the network depth increases. The self-adjust $f_{thres,l}$ algorithm hence serves as imposing a strong constraint to the model, which indeed helps maintain a steady and smooth firing rate to train a very deep network successful with avoiding the disappearance of spike activity in deeper layers.

Since the instability of STDP, we replace it with BPTT to ensure a smooth training process. Besides, the adoption of the firing mechanism in SNN improves the robustness with less reliance on the number of parameters as we replace the matrix multiplication $W_h \cdot h_{t-1}$ in Eq. 4 with $\alpha \odot V_{t-1}$ in Eq. 6 to simulate the accumulation of membrane potential. For instance, we set SRN, LSTM and our ARLIF have the same number of neurons (1000) and the same input data dimension (3072). The number of weights of sequential model and ARLIF is compared in Fig. 1 (without constant terms).

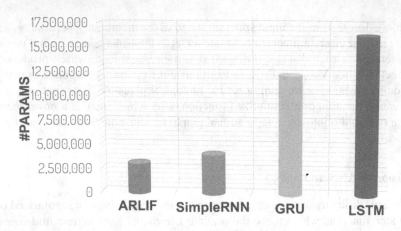

Fig. 1. The comparison of the number of weights, our ARLIF has fewer weight numbers than commonly used sequential models like SRN, GRU and LSTM.

3.3 Architecture

Define. We denote *update* as our self-adjust learning method for f_{thres}, $\mathbf{x}$, $\mathbf{v}$ and $\mathbf{y}$ as Tensor, f_{thres} as Scalar, *step* as:

$$step(a, b) = \begin{cases} 1, \, a \geq b \\ 0, \, a < b \end{cases} \tag{9}$$

and *clip* (value, LB, UB) means clip value between lower bound (LB) and upper bound (UB).

Process of Algorithm. At each time step t, ARLIF receives $\mathbf{y}_{t,l-1}$ from the previous layer as input and produces the hidden state $\mathbf{h}_{t,l}$ and then update the membrane potential $\mathbf{v}_{t,l}$ and produce current activation $\mathbf{y}_{t,l}$. Since we extent this self-adjust method for $f_{thres,l}$ to an iterative procedure, to eliminate the possibility of infinite loop, we restricted the number of iterations T_i per batch to $T_{max} = 50$, The complete updating process of f_{thres}, the most novelty part of ARLIF, is shown in Algorithm 1. Figure 2 is the detailed structure of ARLIF.

Moreover, ConvARLIF2D (inspired by ConvLSTM2D [21]), is a combination of the timing modeling capability of RNN and the engravement of local features of CNN which can further reduce the number of weights, was proposed in this paper by replacing the element-wise product of matrices with convolution in Eq. 6:

$$\mathbf{v}_t = \mathbf{W}_x \otimes \mathbf{x}_t + \boldsymbol{\alpha} \odot \mathbf{v}_{t-1} \tag{10}$$

Through Algorithm 1, more than $p_1 = 85\%$ of the neurons are de-activated; meanwhile, only a few neurons are activated in ARLIF. This phenomenon, to some extent, accords with the realistic response law of biological neurons. A noteworthy point here is that $p_1 = 85\%$, $p_2 = 98\%$ are determined by heuristic method, which means p_1, p_2 can be determined through experiment.

Algorithm 1. Forward Propagation of $l - th$ layer of ARLIF at timestep t

---

Input: $\mathbf{y}_{t,l-1}$, $\mathbf{v}_{t-1,l}$
Parameter: $\mathbf{W}_{l-1}$, $\mathbf{b}_{l-1}$, α, β, δ
Output: $\mathbf{y}_{t,l}$, $\mathbf{v}_{t,l}$
step 1: calculate hidden state $\mathbf{h}_{t,l}$.
$\mathbf{x}_{t,l} = \mathbf{y}_{t,l-1}$
$\mathbf{h}_{t,l} = \mathbf{W}_{l-1} \cdot \mathbf{x}_{t,l} + \mathbf{b}_{l-1}$
step 2: update membrane potential $\mathbf{v}_{t,l}$.
$\mathbf{v}_{t,l} = \mathbf{h}_{t,l} + \alpha \odot \mathbf{v}_{t-1,l}$
step 3: get activations $\mathbf{y}_{t,l}$.
$\mathbf{y}_{t,l} = \sigma(\mathbf{v}_{t,l} + \delta)$
step 4: update f_{thres} through adaptive learning method.
$f_{thres,l} = update(f_{thres,l})$
  1: sorted mini-batch $\mathbf{y}_{t,l}$ (ascending order),
  2: set hyper parameter $lr_{thres} = 0.001$, $p_1 = 85\%$ ($thres_l$), $p_2 = 98\%$ ($thres_h$).
  3: **while** $f_{thres,l} < thres_l$ or $f_{thres,l} > thres_h$ **and** $T_i < T_{max}$ **do**
  4:    **if** $f_{thres,l} < thres_l$ **then**
  5:      $f_{thres,l} = f_{thres,l} + lr_{thres}$
  6:    **else**
  7:      $f_{thres,l} = f_{thres,l} - lr_{thres}$
  8:    **end if**
  9: **end while**
10: **return** $f_{thres,l}$
step 5: regularized $\mathbf{v}_{t,l}$ according to $\mathbf{y}_{t,l}$ and $f_{thres,l}$.
$\mathbf{v}_{t,l} = \mathbf{v}_{t,l} - \beta \odot step(\mathbf{y}_{t,l}, f_{thres,l})$
step 6: restrict $\mathbf{y}_{t,l}$ with a changing boundaries.
$\mathbf{y}_{t,l} = clip(\mathbf{y}_{t,l}, 0, f_{thres,l})$

According to our experiments, good results could be achieved through a fixed value through every ARLIF layer in the model. However, better result could be achieved through customizing each layer with different p_1 and p_2, but it is hard to quantify the difference with the composition of the uncertain number of feature extraction layers, different combination order and type of tasks.

Therefore, people are allowed to flexibly adjust p_1 and p_2 of each ARLIF layer in their model. But for simplicity, the following experiments all using fixed p_1 and p_2 as described in Algorithm 1 by default.

4   Experiments

We evaluate ARLIF (ConvARLIF2D) with a range of sequential models like SRN and LSTM on (**a**) action recognition and (**b**) object recognition. We implement ARLIF on Keras platform and train it using the backpropagation through time algorithm [25] and our proposed algorithm for the adjustment of f_{thres} dynamically.

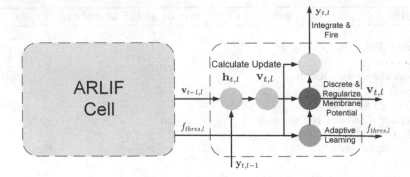

Fig. 2. A diagram of ARLIF cell. The details can be seen in Algorithm 1.

4.1 Action Recognition

As shown in Fig. 4, our network falls into the two-stream paradigm in action recognition where combines optical flow information and RGB image as input. The adoption of the Temporal Conv Layer (especially ConvARLIF2D) is the novelty of this network. Here, **t** is the length of frame sequence, Spatial Conv Layer consists of Conv3D with strides (1, 2, 2), LeakyReLU and Batch Normalization, the target of Temporal Conv Layer is the aggregate of temporal information at each timestep explicitly.

Frame 1   Frame 4   Frame 8   Frame 12   Frame 16

t

Fig. 3. Sampled video clips of UCF-101. (we choose the first **t** frames to generate optical flow and train our network)

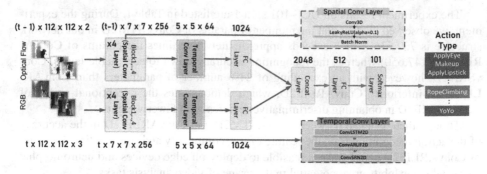

Fig. 4. Our Two-stream Spatial-Temporal Network structure for action recognition. ×4 means there are four Spatial Conv layers in our network, **Conv** is the short form for Convolutional, **FC** for Fully Connected and **Concat** for Concatenate.

In Table 1, we compare our network with different Temporal Conv Layer (ConvSRN2D, ConvARLIF2D and ConvLSTM2D respectively) to the state-of-the-arts works. The input single RGB and optical flow are both resized into resolution of 112×112, note that we sampling video clips at equal temporal spacing as much as possible, if the number of frames in a video is less than $\mathbf{t}, \mathbf{t} \in \{8, 16\}$, we pad the input by repeating the last frame to fill the missing volume. We visualize our sampled video clips in Fig. 3, where it can reflect a relatively complete action when using our sampling tactic.

Moreover, we train our networks on the UCF-101 dataset [22], the algorithm for the computation of optical flow is Brox [2, 15].

Table 1. The comparison of accuracy of SOTA and our two-stream network (with merely the layer of temporal conv changed).

Method		Acc
LRCN [6]		82.92
C3D (1 net) [23]		82.3
C3D (3 nets) [23]		85.2
C3D (3 nets) + iDT [23]		90.4
I3D (input RGB + Flow) [3]		93.4
TSN (input RGB + Flow) [24]		94.0
Ours (Temporal Conv Layer)	$t = 8$	$t = 16$
ConvLSTM2D (input RGB + Flow)	88.88	92.56
ConvLSTM2D (input RGB)	76.17	79.58
ConvSRN2D (input RGB + Flow)	74.93	78.44
ConvSRN2D (input RGB)	65.93	68.20
ConvARLIF2D (input RGB + Flow)	**82.20**	**85.43**
ConvARLIF2D (input RGB)	**74.56**	**76.86**

The experiment results on UCF-101 split 1 are listed in Table 1. During the experiment, we observed the fact that the number of params of ConvLSTM2D in our network structure is 737,536, which exceeds approximately five times the params of ConvARLIF2D (147,650) whereas the recognition accuracy down to acceptable levels. ConvSRN2D, however, with an exceeding of 24% number of parameters than ConvARLIF2D, is inferior to ConvARLIF2D, which demonstrates the exceptional ability of ConvARLIF2D in obtaining discriminative features with fewer weights.

Though there is a gap between ConvLSTM2D and ConvARLIF2D in the accuracy of the action recognition task, the feature of low complexity and computational amount of ConvARLIF2D could make it feasible to deploy on edge devices and neuromorphic chips, which exhibits great potential in the usage of video analysis tasks.

Table 2. Comparison of our work with other SNN models on CIFAR10 [12] ($\mathbf{T} = 10$, **SA** is short for self-adjust).

Model	Training method	Acc
Sengupta et al. [20]	ANN-SNN conversion	91.55
Lee et al. [13]	Spiking BP	90.45
Wu et al. [27]	Surrogate gradient	90.53
ST-Resnet18	BPTT+ SA f_{thres}	**91.72**
ST-Resnet34	BPTT+ SA f_{thres}	90.21

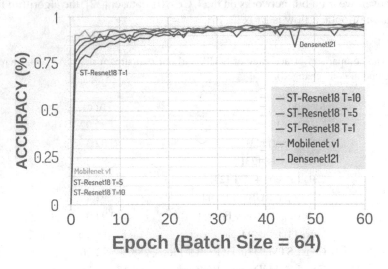

Fig. 5. ST-Resnet18's accuracy on Fashion MNISTT [28] with vary $\mathbf{T} \in \{1, 5, 10\}$. (Both Mobilenet and Densenet are pre-trained on ImageNet.)

4.2 Object Recognition

Here, we choose Fashion MNIST [28] for evaluation given that MNIST is too simple as a benchmark dataset. Fashion MNIST [28] is a dataset that consists of a training set of 60,000 examples and a testing set of 10,000 examples. In our experiment, each 28 × 28 grayscale image with a label annotated, which belongs to 10 classes, i.e. T-shirt, trousers, dress.

To the exploration of SNN with deep architecture to solve complex visual recognition problems as well as verify the effectiveness of ARLIF. Temporal structure is added to Resnet and a spatial-temporal Resnet (ST-Resnet) is built. The differences between ST-Resnet and Resnet are: 1) In order to verify the effect of feature extraction of ARLIF, we replace Conv2D by ConvARLIF2D to make all of the feature extraction layers in our ST-Resnet are the hybrid of ANNs and SNNs. 2) As LN performs well in

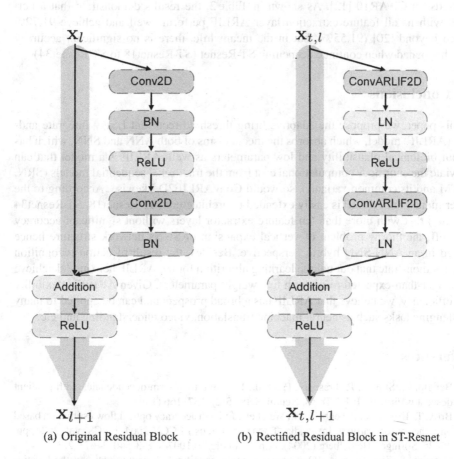

(a) Original Residual Block   (b) Rectified Residual Block in ST-Resnet

Fig. 6. Residual blocks of original Resnet and our ST-Resnet. Unlike original residual block, we extend the rectified residual block into time domain. Therefore, **Layer Normalization** is fit seamlessly after **ConvARLIF2D** and **ReLU** is used in every single step of t.

the paradigms of the recurrent neural network, Batch Normalization (BN) is replaced by Layer Normalization (LN) in ST-Resnet.

The structure of rectified residual block of ST-Resnet is depicted in Fig. 6. Since the input for our ST-Resnet needs to be sequential, then we transform the still images in Fashion MNIST and CIFAR10 into sequential by copy the original data **T** times.

About training settings, we use Adam optimizer with a mini-batch size of 64. The learning rate remains unchanged in two datasets, take 0.0001. Besides, we use categorical cross-entropy as our loss function and dropout mechanism to prevent overfitting while extending [17] to ARLIF to initialize our network parameter.

As we compare our ST-Resnet with ANN's state-of-the-art works on the above two datasets. First, from Fig. 5, we can observe that ST-Resnet18 with **T** $= 10$ achieves the 95.75% on Fashion MNIST, which beyond Densenet (93.45%) and Mobilenet (94.11%). Next, we compare our ST-Resnet architecture with state-of-the-art SNN methods on CIFAR10 [12]. As shown in Table 2, the results demonstrate that a network with its all feature extraction layer ARLIF performs well and achieve 91.72% which beyond [20] (91.55%), but in the meanwhile, there is no significant accuracy drop happened when continue deepening ST-Resnet (ST-Resnet18 to ST-Resnet34).

5 Conclusions

In this paper, we propose the adaptive firing threshold recurrent Leaky Integrate-and-Fire (ARLIF) model, which absorbs the mechanisms of both ANN and SNN, which has potent biological plausibility and low parameters as well. ARLIF is a model that can alleviate the enormous computational cost from the traditional sequential models (SRN, LSTM and its common variants), so would ConvARLIF2D likewise. According to the experiments, our ARLIF is easily extended to architecture (ST-Resnet18, ST-Resnet34 and etc.) that with more than ten feature extractor layers without significant accuracy drop-off, the thorny problem of vertical expansion of SNNs network structure hence solved in an ANN-SNN hybrid perspective. Besides, the result of action recognition could demonstrate that our unique learning algorithm for the ARLIF help model achieve a stronger-than-expected result with few weight parameters. Given ARLIF's flexibility and efficiency, we believe that ARLIF has a broad prospect and can be applied to many challenging tasks such as neural machine translation, video understanding and etc.

References

1. Bengio, Y., Simard, P., Frasconi, P., et al.: Learning long-term dependencies with gradient descent is difficult. IEEE Trans. Neural Netw. **5**(2), 157–166 (1994)
2. Brox, T., Bruhn, A., Papenberg, N., Weickert, J.: High accuracy optical flow estimation based on a theory for warping. In: Pajdla, T., Matas, J. (eds.) ECCV 2004. LNCS, vol. 3024, pp. 25–36. Springer, Heidelberg (2004). https://doi.org/10.1007/978-3-540-24673-2_3
3. Carreira, J., Zisserman, A.: Quo vadis, action recognition? A new model and the kinetics dataset. In: The IEEE Conference on Computer Vision and Pattern Recognition (CVPR), July 2017
4. Cho, K., et al.: Learning phrase representations using RNN encoder-decoder for statistical machine translation. arXiv preprint arXiv:1406.1078 (2014)

5. Chollet, F., et al.: Keras (2015)
6. Donahue, J., et al.: Long-term recurrent convolutional networks for visual recognition and description. In: The IEEE Conference on Computer Vision and Pattern Recognition (CVPR), June 2015
7. FitzHugh, R.: Impulses and physiological states in theoretical models of nerve membrane. Biophys. J. **1**(6), 445–466 (1961)
8. Gerstner, W., Kistler, W.M., Naud, R., Paninski, L.: Neuronal Dynamics: From Single Neurons to Networks and Models of Cognition. Cambridge University Press, Cambridge (2014)
9. Hochreiter, S., Schmidhuber, J.: Long short-term memory. Neural Comput. **9**(8), 1735–1780 (1997)
10. Hodgkin, A.L., Huxley, A.F.: A quantitative description of membrane current and its application to conduction and excitation in nerve. J. Physiol. **117**(4), 500–544 (1952)
11. Izhikevich, E.M.: Simple model of spiking neurons. IEEE Trans. Neural Netw. **14**(6), 1569–1572 (2003)
12. Krizhevsky, A., Hinton, G.: Learning multiple layers of features from tiny images. Technical report, Citeseer (2009)
13. Lee, C., Sarwar, S.S., Roy, K.: Enabling spike-based backpropagation in state-of-the-art deep neural network architectures. arXiv preprint arXiv:1903.06379 (2019)
14. Lee, J.H., Delbruck, T., Pfeiffer, M.: Training deep spiking neural networks using backpropagation. Front. Neurosci. **10**, 508 (2016)
15. Liu, C., et al. Beyond pixels: exploring new representations and applications for motion analysis. Ph.D. thesis, Massachusetts Institute of Technology (2009)
16. Maass, W.: Networks of spiking neurons: the third generation of neural network models. Neural Netw. **10**(9), 1659–1671 (1997)
17. Mishkin, D., Matas, J.: All you need is a good init. arXiv preprint arXiv:1511.06422 (2015)
18. Nagumo, J., Arimoto, S., Yoshizawa, S.: An active pulse transmission line simulating nerve axon. Proc. IRE **50**(10), 2061–2070 (1962)
19. Rumelhart, D.E., Hinton, G.E., Williams, R.J., et al.: Learning representations by back-propagating errors. Cogn. Model. **5**(3), 1 (1988)
20. Sengupta, A., Ye, Y., Wang, R., Liu, C., Roy, K.: Going deeper in spiking neural networks: VGG and residual architectures. Front. Neurosci. **13**, 95 (2019)
21. Shi, X., Chen, Z., Hao, W., Yeung, D.Y., Woo, W.C.: Convolutional LSTM network: a machine learning approach for precipitation nowcasting. In: International Conference on Neural Information Processing Systems (2015)
22. Soomro, K., Zamir, A.R, Shah, M.: UCF101: a dataset of 101 human actions classes from videos in the wild. arXiv preprint arXiv:1212.0402 (2012)
23. Tran, D., Bourdev, L., Fergus, R., Torresani, L., Paluri, M.: Learning spatiotemporal features with 3D convolutional networks. In: The IEEE International Conference on Computer Vision (ICCV), December 2015
24. Wang, L., et al.: Temporal segment networks: towards good practices for deep action recognition. In: Leibe, B., Matas, J., Sebe, N., Welling, M. (eds.) ECCV 2016. LNCS, vol. 9912, pp. 20–36. Springer, Cham (2016). https://doi.org/10.1007/978-3-319-46484-8_2
25. Werbos, P.J.: Backpropagation through time: what it does and how to do it. Proc. IEEE **78**(10), 1550–1560 (1990)
26. Wu, Y., Deng, L., Li, G., Zhu, J., Shi, L.: Spatio-temporal backpropagation for training high-performance spiking neural networks. Front. Neurosci. **12**, 331 (2018)
27. Wu, Y., Deng, L., Li, G., Zhu, J., Xie, Y., Shi, L.: Direct training for spiking neural networks: faster, larger, better. In: Proceedings of the AAAI Conference on Artificial Intelligence, vol. 33, pp. 1311–1318 (2019)
28. Xiao, H., Rasul, K., Vollgraf, R.: Fashion-MNIST: a novel image dataset for benchmarking machine learning algorithms (2017)

Models of Human Behavioral Agents in Bandits, Contextual Bandits and RL

Baihan Lin[1]($\boxtimes$), Guillermo Cecchi[2], Djallel Bouneffouf[2], Jenna Reinen[2], and Irina Rish[3]

[1] Center for Theoretical Neuroscience, Columbia University, New York, USA
baihan.lin@columbia.edu
[2] IBM Thomas J. Watson Research Center, Yorktown Heights, NY, USA
gcecchi@us.ibm.com, {djallel.bouneffouf,jenna.reinen}@ibm.com
[3] Mila - Quebec AI Institute, University of Montreal, Montreal, Canada
irina.rish@mila.quebec

Abstract. Artificial behavioral agents are often evaluated based on their consistent behaviors and performance to take sequential actions in an environment to maximize some notion of cumulative reward. However, human decision making in real life usually involves different strategies and behavioral trajectories that lead to the same empirical outcome. Motivated by clinical literature of a wide range of neurological and psychiatric disorders, we propose here a more general and flexible parametric framework for sequential decision making that involves a two-stream reward processing mechanism. We demonstrated that this framework is flexible and unified enough to incorporate a family of problems spanning multi-armed bandits (MAB), contextual bandits (CB) and reinforcement learning (RL), which decompose the sequential decision making process in different levels. Inspired by the known reward processing abnormalities of many mental disorders, our clinically-inspired agents demonstrated interesting behavioral trajectories and comparable performance on simulated tasks with particular reward distributions, a real-world dataset capturing human decision-making in gambling tasks, and the PacMan game across different reward stationarities in a lifelong learning setting (The codes to reproduce all the experimental results can be accessed at https://github.com/doerlbh/mentalRL.).

Keywords: Reinforcement learning · Contextual bandit · Neuroscience

1 Introduction

In real-life decision making, from deciding where to have lunch to finding an apartment when moving to a new city, and so on, people often face different level of information dependency. In the simplest case, you are given N possible actions ("arms"), each associated with a fixed, unknown and independent reward probability distribution, and the goal is to trade between following a good action chosen

© Springer Nature Singapore Pte Ltd. 2021
Y. Wang (Ed.): HBAI 2020, CCIS 1369, pp. 14–33, 2021.
https://doi.org/10.1007/978-981-16-1288-6_2

previously (exploitation) and obtaining more information about the environment which can possibly lead to better actions in the future (exploration). The *multi-armed bandit (MAB)* (or simply, bandit) typically models this level of exploration-exploitation trade-off [4, 23]. In many scenarios, the best strategy may depend on a context from current environment, such that the goal is to learn the relationship between the context vectors and the rewards, in order to make better prediction which action to choose given the context, modeled as the *contextual bandits (CB)* [2, 24], where the context can be attentive [11, 31] or clustered [28, 33, 34]. In more complex environments, there is an additional dependency between contexts given the action an agent takes, and that is modeled as Markov decision process (MDP) in *reinforcement learning (RL)* problem [43].

To better model and understand human decision making behavior, scientists usually investigate reward processing mechanisms in healthy subjects [37]. However, neurodegenerative and psychiatric disorders, often associated with reward processing disruptions, can provide an additional resource for deeper understanding of human decision making mechanisms. From the perspective of evolutionary psychiatry, various mental disorders, including depression, anxiety, ADHD, addiction and even schizophrenia can be considered as "extreme points" in a continuous spectrum of behaviors and traits developed for various purposes during evolution, and somewhat less extreme versions of those traits can be actually beneficial in specific environments. Thus, modeling decision-making biases and traits associated with various disorders may enrich the existing computational decision-making models, leading to potentially more flexible and better-performing algorithms. In this paper, we extended previous pursuits of human behavioral agents in MAB [10] and RL [29, 30, 32] into CB, built upon the Contextual Thompson Sampling (CTS) [2], a state-of-art approach to CB problem, and unfied all three levels as a parametric family of models, where the reward information is split into two streams, positive and negative.

2   Problem Setting

In this section, we briefly outlined the three problem settings:

Multi-Armed Bandit (MAB). The multi-armed bandit (MAB) problem models a sequential decision-making process, where at each time point a player selects an action from a given finite set of possible actions, attempting to maximize the cumulative reward over time. Optimal solutions have been provided using a stochastic formulation [4, 23], or using an adversarial formulation [3, 5, 9]. Recently, there has been a surge of interest in a Bayesian formulation [12], involving the algorithm known as Thompson sampling [44]. Theoretical analysis in [1] shows that Thompson sampling for Bernoulli bandits is asymptotically optimal.

Contextual Bandit (CB). Following [25], this problem is defined as follows. At each time point (iteration) $t \in \{1, ..., T\}$, an agent is presented with a *context* (*feature vector*) $\mathbf{x}_t \in \mathbf{R}^N$ before choosing an arm $k \in A = \{1, ..., K\}$. We will denote by $X = \{X_1, ..., X_N\}$ the set of features (variables) defining the context. Let $\mathbf{r}_t = (r_t^1, ..., r_t^K)$ denote a reward vector, where $r_t^k \in [0, 1]$ is a reward at time t associated with the arm $k \in A$. Herein, we will primarily focus on the Bernoulli bandit with binary reward, i.e. $r_t^k \in \{0, 1\}$. Let $\pi : X \rightarrow A$ denote a policy. Also, $D_{c,r}$ denotes a joint distribution over $(\mathbf{x}, \mathbf{r})$. We will assume that the expected reward is a linear function of the context, i.e. $E[r_t^k | \mathbf{x}_t] = \mu_k^T \mathbf{x}_t$, where μ_k is an unknown weight vector associated with the arm k.

Reinforcement Learning (RL). Reinforcement learning defines a class of algorithms for solving problems modeled as Markov decision processes (MDP) [43]. An MDP is defined by the tuple (S, A, T, R, γ), where S is a set of possible states, A is a set of actions, T is a transition function defined as $T(s, a, s') = \Pr(s'|s, a)$, where $s, s' \in S$ and $a \in A$, and $R : S \times A \times S \mapsto \mathbb{R}$ is a reward function, γ is a discount factor that decreases the impact of the past reward on current action choice. Typically, the objective is to maximize the discounted long-term reward, assuming an infinite-horizon decision process, i.e. to find a policy function $\pi : S \mapsto A$ which specifies the action to take in a given state, so that the cumulative reward is maximized: $\max_\pi \sum_{t=0}^{\infty} \gamma^t R(s_t, a_t, s_{t+1})$.

3   Background: Contextual Thompson Sampling (CTS)

As pointed out in the introduction, the main methodological contribution of this work is two-fold: (1) fill in the missing piece of split reward processing in the contextual bandit problem, and (2) unify the bandits, contextual bandits, and reinforcement learnings under the same framework of split reward processing mechanism. We first introduce the theoretical model we built upon for the contextual bandit problem: the Contextual Thompson Sampling, due to its known empirical benefits. In the general Thompson Sampling, the reward r_t^i for choosing action i at time t follows a parametric likelihood function $Pr(r_t|\tilde{\mu}_i)$. Following [2], the posterior distribution at time $t + 1$, $Pr(\tilde{\mu}_i|r_t) \propto Pr(r_t|\tilde{\mu}_i)Pr(\tilde{\mu}_i)$ is given by a multivariate Gaussian distribution $\mathcal{N}(\hat{\mu}_i(t+1), v^2 B_i(t+1)^{-1})$, where $B_i(t) = I_d + \sum_{\tau=1}^{t-1} x_\tau x_\tau^\top$, and where d is the context size $\mathbf{x}_i$, $v = R\sqrt{\frac{24}{\epsilon} d \ln(\frac{1}{\gamma})}$ with $R > 0$, $\epsilon \in]0, 1]$, $\gamma \in]0, 1]$ constants, and $\hat{\mu}_i(t) = B_i(t)^{-1}(\sum_{\tau=1}^{t-1} x_\tau r_\tau)$. At every step t, the algorithm generates a d-dimensional sample $\tilde{\mu}_i$ from $\mathcal{N}(\hat{\mu}_i(t), v^2 B_i(t)^{-1})$, selects the arm i that maximizes $x_t^\top \tilde{\mu}_i$, and obtains reward r_t.

4   Two-Stream Split Models in MAB, CB and RL

We now outlined the split models evaluated in our three settings: the MAB case with the Human-Based Thompson Sampling (HBTS) [10], the CB case with the Split Contextual Thompson Sampling (SCTS), and the RL case with the Split Q-Learning [29,32]. All three split agent classes are standardized for their parametric notions (see Table 1 for a complete parametrization and Appendix A for more literature review of these clinically-inspired reward-processing biases).

Split Multi-Armed Bandit Model. The split MAB agent is built upon Human-Based Thompson Sampling (HBTS, Algorithm 1) [10]. The positive and negative streams are each stored in the success and failure counts S_a and F_a.

Algorithm 1 Split MAB: Human-Based Thompson Sampling (HBTS)

1: **Initialize:** $S_{a'} = 1, F_{a'} = 1, \forall a' \in A$.
2: **For** each episode e **do**
3:    Initialize state s
4:    **Repeat** for each step t of the episode e
5:       Sample $\theta_{a'} \sim Beta(S_{a'}, F_{a'}), \forall a' \in A_t$
6:       Take action $a = \arg\max_{a'} \theta_{a'}$, and
7:       Observe r^+ and $r^- \in R_{a'}$
8:       $S_a := \lambda_+ S_a + w_+ r^+$
9:       $F_a := \lambda_- F_a - w_- r^-$
10:    **until** s is the terminal state
11: **End for**

Split Contextual Bandit Model. Similarly, we now extend Contextual Thompson Sampling (CTS) [2] to a more flexible framework, inspired by a wide range of reward-processing biases discussed in Appendix A. The proposed *Split CTS* (Algorithm 2) treats positive and negative rewards in two separate streams. It introduces four hyper-parameters which represent, for both positive and negative streams, the reward processing weights (biases), as well as discount factors for the past rewards: λ_+ and λ_- are the discount factors applied to the previously accumulated positive and negative rewards, respectively, while w_+ and w_- represent the weights on the positive and negative rewards at the current iteration. We assume that at each step, an agent receives both positive and negative rewards, denote r^+ and r^-, respectively (either one of them can be zero, of course). As in HBTS, the two streams are independently updated.

Algorithm 2 Split CB: Split Contextual Thompson Sampling (SCTS)

1: **Initialize:** $B_{a'}^+ = B_{a'}^- = I_d, \hat{\mu}_{a'}^+ = \hat{\mu}_{a'}^- = 0_d, f_{a'}^- = f_{a'}^- = 0_d, \forall a' \in A$.
2: **For** each episode e **do**
3:    Initialize state s
4:    **Repeat** for each step t of the episode e
5:       Receive context x_t
6:       Sample $\tilde{\mu}_{a'}^+ \sim N(\hat{\mu}_{a'}^+, v^2 B_{a'}^{+-1})$ and $\tilde{\mu}_{a'}^- \sim N(\hat{\mu}_{a'}^-, v^2 B_{a'}^{--1}), \forall a' \in A_t$
7:       Take action $a = \arg\max_{a'}(x_t^\top \tilde{\mu}_{a'}^+ + x_t^\top \tilde{\mu}_{a'}^-)$, and
8:       Observe r^+ and $r^- \in R_{a'}$
9:       $B_a^+ := \lambda_+ B_a^+ + x_t x_t^\top, f_a^+ := \lambda_+ f_a^+ + w_+ x_t r^+, \hat{\mu}_a^+ := B_a^{+-1} f_a^+$
10:       $B_a^- := \lambda_- B_a^- + x_t x_t^\top, f_a^- := \lambda_- f_a^- + w_- x_t r^-, \hat{\mu}_a^- := B_a^{--1} f_a^-$
11:    **until** s is the terminal state
12: **End for**

Split Reinforcement Learning Model. The split RL agent is built upon Split Q-Learning (SQL, Algorithm 3) by [29, 32] (and its variant, MaxPain, by

[14]). The processing of the positive and negative streams is handled by the two independently updated Q functions, Q^+ and Q^-.

Algorithm 3 Split RL: Split Q-Learning (SQL)

1: **Initialize:** Q, Q^+, Q^- tables (e.g., to all zeros)
2: **For** each episode e **do**
3:     Initialize state s
4:     **Repeat** for each step t of the episode e
5:         $Q(s,a') := Q^+(s,a') + Q^-(s,a'), \forall a' \in A_t$
6:         Take action $a = \arg\max_{a'} Q(s,a')$, and
7:         Observe $s' \in S$, r^+ and $r^- \in R(s)$, $s \leftarrow s'$
8:         $Q^+(s,a) := \lambda_+ \hat{Q}^+(s,a) + \alpha_t(w_+ r^+ + \gamma \max_{a'} \hat{Q}^+(s',a') - \hat{Q}^+(s,a))$
9:         $Q^-(s,a) := \lambda_- \hat{Q}^-(s,a) + \alpha_t(w_- r^- + \gamma \max_{a'} \hat{Q}^-(s',a') - \hat{Q}^-(s,a))$
10:     **until** s is the terminal state
11: **End for**

Clinically Inspired Reward Processing Biases in Split Models. For each agent, we set the four parameters: λ_+ and λ_- as the weights of the previously accumulated positive and negative rewards, respectively, w_+ and w_- as the weights on the positive and negative rewards at the current iteration. *DISCLAIMER: while we use disorder names for the models, we are not claiming that the models accurately capture all aspects of the corresponding disorders.*

In the following section we describe how specific constraints on the model parameters in the proposed method can generate a range of reward processing biases, and introduce several instances of the split models associated with those biases; the corresponding parameter settings are presented in Table 1. As we demonstrate later, specific biases may be actually beneficial in some settings, and our parameteric approach often outperforms the standard baselines due to increased generality and flexibility of our two-stream, multi-parametric formulation.

Note that the *standard* split approach correspond to setting the four (hyper)parameters used in our model to 1. We also introduce two variants which only learn from one of the two reward streams: negative split models (algorithms that start with N) and positive split models (algorithms that start with P), by setting to zero λ_+ and w_+, or λ_- and w_-, respectively. Next, we introduce the model which incorporates some mild forgetting of the past rewards or losses (0.5 weights) and calibrating the other models with respect to this one; we refer to this model as M for "moderate" forgetting.

We also specified the mental agents differently with the prefix "b-" referring to the MAB version of the split models (as in "bandits'), "cb-" referring to the CB version, and no prefix as the RL version (for its general purposes).

We will now introduced several models inspired by certain reward-processing biases in a range of mental disorders-like behaviors in Table 1.

Recall that PD patients are typically better at learning to avoid negative outcomes than at learning to achieve positive outcomes [17]; one way to model

Table 1. Parameter setting for different types of reward biases in the split models.

	λ_+	w_+	λ_-	w_-
"Addiction" (ADD)	1 ± 0.1	1 ± 0.1	0.5 ± 0.1	1 ± 0.1
"ADHD"	0.2 ± 0.1	1 ± 0.1	0.2 ± 0.1	1 ± 0.1
"Alzheimer's" (AD)	0.1 ± 0.1	1 ± 0.1	0.1 ± 0.1	1 ± 0.1
"Chronic pain" (CP)	0.5 ± 0.1	0.5 ± 0.1	1 ± 0.1	1 ± 0.1
"bvFTD"	0.5 ± 0.1	100 ± 10	0.5 ± 0.1	1 ± 0.1
"Parkinson's" (PD)	0.5 ± 0.1	1 ± 0.1	0.5 ± 0.1	100 ± 10
"moderate" (M)	0.5 ± 0.1	1 ± 0.1	0.5 ± 0.1	1 ± 0.1
Standard (HBTS, SCTS, SQL)	1	1	1	1
Positive (PTS, PCTS, PQL)	1	1	0	0
Negative (NTS, NCTS, NQL)	0	0	1	1

this is to over-emphasize negative rewards, by placing a high weight on them, as compared to the reward processing in healthy individuals. Specifically, we will assume the parameter w_- for PD patients to be much higher than normal w_- (e.g., we use $w_- = 100$ here), while the rest of the parameters will be in the same range for both healthy and PD individuals. Patients with bvFTD are prone to overeating which may represent increased reward representation. To model this impairment in bvFTD patients, the parameter of the model could be modified as follow: $w_+^M \ll w_+$ (e.g., $w_+ = 100$ as shown in Table 1), where w_+ is the parameter of the bvFTD model has, and the rest of these parameters are equal to the normal one. To model apathy in patients with Alzheimer's, including downplaying rewards and losses, we will assume that the parameters λ_+ and λ_- are somewhat smaller than normal, $\lambda_+ < \lambda_+^M$ and $\lambda_- < \lambda_-^M$ (e.g., set to 0.1 in Table 1), which models the tendency to forget both positive and negative rewards. Recall that ADHD may be involve impairments in storing stimulus-response associations. In our ADHD model, the parameters λ_+ and λ_- are smaller than normal, $\lambda_+^M > \lambda_+$ and $\lambda_-^M > \lambda_-$, which models forgetting of both positive and negative rewards. Note that while this model appears similar to Alzheimer's model described above, the forgetting factor will be less pronounced, i.e. the λ_+ and λ_- parameters are larger than those of the Alzheimer's model (e.g., 0.2 instead of 0.1, as shown in Table 1). As mentioned earlier, addiction is associated with inability to properly forget (positive) stimulus-response associations; we model this by setting the weight on previously accumulated positive reward ("memory") higher than normal, $\tau > \lambda_+^M$, e.g. $\lambda_+ = 1$, while $\lambda_+^M = 0.5$. We model the reduced responsiveness to rewards in chronic pain by setting $w_+ < w_+^M$ so there is a decrease in the reward representation, and $\lambda_- > \lambda_-^M$ so the negative rewards are not forgotten (see Table 1).

Of course, the above models should be treated only as first approximations of the reward processing biases in mental disorders, since the actual changes in reward processing are much more complicated, and the parameteric setting must be learned from actual patient data, which is a nontrivial direction for future work. Herein, we simply consider those models as specific variations of our general method, inspired by certain aspects of the corresponding diseases, and focus primarily on the computational aspects of our algorithm, demonstrating that the proposed parametric extension of standard algorithms can learn better than the baselines due to added flexibility.

5   Empirical Evaluation

Empirically, we evaluated the algorithms in four settings: the gambling game of a simple MDP task, a simple MAB task, a real-life Iowa Gambling Task (IGT) [41], and a PacMan game. There is considerable randomness in the reward, and predefined multimodality in the reward distributions of each state-action pairs in all four tasks. We ran split MAB agents in MAB, MDP and IGT tasks, and split CB and RL agents in all four tasks.

5.1   MAB and MDP Tasks with Bimodal Rewards

In this simple MAB example, a player starts from initial state A, choose between two actions: go left to reach state B, or go right to reach state C. Both states B and C reveals a zero rewards. From state B, the player observes a reward from a distribution R_B. From state C, the player observes a reward from a distribution R_C. The reward distributions of states B and C are both multimodal distributions (for instance, the reward r can be drawn from a bi-modal distribution of two normal distributions $N(\mu = 10, \sigma = 5)$ with probability $p = 0.3$ and $N(\mu = -5, \sigma = 1)$ with $p = 0.7$). The left action (go to state B) by default is set to have an expected payout lower than the right action. However, the reward distributions can be spread across both the positive and negative domains. For Split models, the reward is separated into a positive stream (if the revealed reward is positive) and a negative stream (if the revealed reward is negative).

Experiments. To evaluate the robustness of the algorithms, we simulated 100 randomly generated scenarios of bi-modal distributions, where the reward can be drawn from two normal distribution with means as random integers uniformly drawn from -100 to 100, standard deviations as random integers uniformly drawn from 0 to 50, and sampling distribution p uniformly drawn from 0 to 1 (assigning p to one normal distribution and $1 - p$ to the other one). Each scenario was repeated 50 times with standard errors as bounds. In all experiments, the discount factor γ was set to be 0.95. For non-exploration approaches, the exploration is included with ϵ-greedy algorithm with ϵ set to be 0.05. The learning rate was polynomial $\alpha_t(s, a) = 1/n_t(s, a)^{0.8}$, which is better in theory and in practice [15].

Benchmark. We compared the following algorithms: In MAB setting, we have Thompson Sampling (TS) [44], Upper Confidence Bound (UCB) [4], epsilon Greedy (eGreedy) [42], EXP3 [5] (and gEXP3 for the pure greedy version

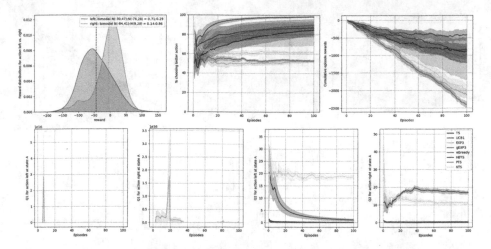

Fig. 1. MAB in MAB task: example where Split MAB performs better than baselines.

of EXP3), Human Based Thompson Sampling (HBTS) [10]. In CB setting, we have Contextual Thompson Sampling (CTS) [2], LinUCB [26], EXP4 [8] and Split Contextual Thompson Sampling (SCTS). In RL setting, we have Q-Learning (QL), Double Q-Learning (DQL) [20], State–action–reward–state–action (SARSA) [38], Standard Split Q-Learning (SQL) [29,32], MaxPain (MP) [14], Positive Q-Learning (PQL) and Negative Q-Learning (NQL).

Evaluation Metric. In order to evaluate the performances of the algorithms, we need a scenario-independent measure which is not dependent on the specific selections of reward distribution parameters and pool of algorithms being considered. The final cumulative rewards might be subject to outliers because they are scenario-specific. The ranking of each algorithms might be subject to selection bias due to different pools of algorithms being considered. The pairwise comparison of the algorithms, however, is independent of the selection of scenario parameters and selection of algorithms. For example, in the 100 randomly generated scenarios, algorithm X beats Y for n times while Y beats X m times. We may compare the robustness of each pairs of algorithms with the proportion $n : m$.

Results. Figure 1 and Fig. 2 are two example scenarios plotting the reward distributions, the percentage of choosing the better action (go right), the cumulative rewards and the changes of two Q-tables (the weights stored in $\tilde{\mu}_a^+$ and $\tilde{\mu}_a^-$) over the number of iterations, drawn with standard errors over multiple runs. Each trial consisted of a synchronous update of all 100 actions. With polynomial learning rates, we see split models (HBTS in bandit agent pool, SCTS in contextual bandit agent pool, and SQL in RL agent pool) converged much more quickly than baselines.

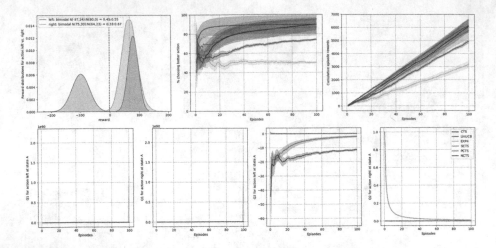

Fig. 2. CB in MAB task: example where SCTS performs better than baselines.

Tables 2 and 4 summarized the pairwise comparisons between the agents with the row labels as the algorithm X and column labels as algorithm Y giving $n : m$ in each cell denoting X beats Y n times and Y beats X m times. For each cell of ith row and jth column, the first number indicates the number of rounds the agent i beats agent j, and the second number the number of rounds the agent j beats agent i. The average wins of each agent is computed as the mean of the win rates against other agents in the pool of agents in the rows. The bold face indicates that the performance of the agent in column j is the best among the agents, or the better one. Among the algorithms, split models never seems to fail catastrophically by maintaining an overall advantages over the other algorithms.

For instance, in the MAB task, among the MAB agent pool, HBTS beats non-split version of TS with a winning rate of 52.65% over 46.72%. In the CB agent pool, LinUCB performed the best with a winning rate of 57.07%. This suggested that upper confidence bound (UCB)-based approach are more suitable for the two-armed MAB task that we proposed, although theoretical analysis in [1] shows that Thompson sampling models for Bernoulli bandits are asymptotically optimal. Further analysis is worth pursuing to explore UCB-based split models. In the RL agent pool, we observe that SARSA algorithm is the most robust among all agents, suggesting a potential benefit of the on-policy learning in the two-armed MAB problem that we proposed. Similarly in the MDP task, the behavior varies. In the MAB agent pool, despite not built with state representation, gEXP, an adversarial bandit algorithm with the epsilon greedy exploration performed the best. We suspected that our non-Gaussian reward distribution might resemble the nonstationary or adversarial setting that EXP3 algorithm is designed for. In the CB agent pool, we observed that LinUCB performed the best, which matched our finding in the similar MAB task above. In the RL agent pool, one of the split models, MP performed the best against all baselines,

Table 2. MAB Task: 100 randomly generated scenarios of Bi-modal rewards

MAB	Baseline					Variants of Split MAB agents		
	TS	UCB1	EXP3	gEXP3	eGreedy	HBTS	PTS	NTS
TS	-	31:49	71:9	73:7	44:36	32:48	46:34	73:7
UCB1	49:31	-	74:6	77:3	55:25	34:46	54:26	74:6
EXP3	9:71	6:74	-	41:39	6:74	10:70	12:68	13:67
gEXP3	7:73	3:77	39:41	-	6:74	11:69	10:70	10:70
eGreedy	36:44	25:55	74:6	74:6	-	28:52	48:32	72:8
HBTS	48:32	46:34	70:10	69:11	52:28	-	59:21	68:12
PTS	34:46	26:54	68:12	70:10	32:48	21:59	-	52:28
NTS	7:73	6:74	67:13	70:10	8:72	12:68	28:52	-
avg wins (%)	46.72	52.65	12.25	10.86	45.08	52.02	38.26	25.00

CB	Baseline			Variants of Split CB Agents		
	CTS	LinUCB	EXP4	SCTS	PCTS	NCTS
CTS	-	19:61	73:7	49:31	48:32	67:13
LinUCB	61:19	-	76:4	71:9	56:24	75:5
EXP4	7:73	4:76	-	2:78	7:73	10:70
SCTS	31:49	9:71	78:2	-	46:34	71:9
PCTS	32:48	24:56	73:7	34:46	-	68:12
NCTS	13:67	5:75	70:10	9:71	12:68	-
avg wins (%)	43.10	57.07	5.05	39.56	38.89	18.35

RL	Baseline			Variants of Split RL agents				
	QL	DQL	SARSA	SQL-alg1	SQL-alg2	MP	PQL	NQL
QL	-	39:41	34:46	43:37	43:37	42:38	59:21	46:34
DQL	41:39	-	38:42	40:40	44:36	44:36	59:21	46:34
SARSA	46:34	42:38	-	44:36	45:35	44:36	51:29	48:32
SQL	37:43	40:40	36:44	-	41:39	38:42	59:21	46:34
SQL2	37:43	36:44	35:45	39:41	-	42:38	55:25	48:32
MP	38:42	36:44	36:44	42:38	38:42	-	52:28	42:38
PQL	21:59	21:59	29:51	21:59	25:55	28:52	-	32:48
NQL	34:46	34:46	32:48	34:46	32:48	38:42	48:32	-
avg wins (%)	38.64	39.39	40.40	37.50	36.87	35.86	22.35	31.82

Table 3. "Mental" Agents in MAB Task: 100 randomly generated scenarios

MAB	b-ADD	b-ADHD	b-AD	b-CP	b-bvFTD	b-PD	b-M	avg wins (%)
TS	39:41	38:42	39:41	41:39	39:41	33:47	30:50	37.37
UCB1	50:30	43:37	54:26	45:35	52:28	38:42	42:38	46.75
EXP3	6:74	12:68	7:73	8:72	7:73	9:71	6:74	7.94
eGreedy	43:37	32:48	36:44	38:42	37:43	34:46	30:50	36.08
HBTS	52:28	40:40	45:35	51:29	47:33	38:42	38:42	44.88
avg wins (%)	42.42	47.47	44.24	43.84	44.04	50.10	51.31	

CB	cb-ADD	cb-ADHD	cb-AD	cb-CP	cb-bvFTD	cb-PD	cb-M	avg wins (%)
CTS	68:12	47:33	72:8	40:40	67:13	68:12	61:19	61.04
LinUCB	75:5	56:24	77:3	53:27	74:6	76:4	72:8	69.70
EXP4	21:59	5:75	18:62	9:71	9:71	10:70	15:65	12.55
SCTS	73:7	39:41	74:6	36:44	70:10	73:7	65:15	62.05
avg wins (%)	20.96	43.69	19.95	45.96	25.25	23.48	27.02	

RL	ADD	ADHD	AD	CP	bvFTD	PD	M	avg wins (%)
QL	65:15	59:21	55:25	64:16	54:26	59:21	56:24	59.45
DQL	62:18	62:18	58:22	62:18	49:31	56:24	50:30	57.58
SARSA	57:23	57:23	59:21	63:17	51:29	59:21	53:27	57.58
SQL	57:23	54:26	48:32	61:19	50:30	52:28	50:30	53.68
avg wins (%)	19.95	22.22	25.25	17.68	29.29	23.74	28.03	

Table 4. MDP Task: 100 randomly generated scenarios of Bi-modal rewards

MAB	Baseline					Variants of Split MAB agents		
	TS	UCB1	EXP3	gEXP3	eGreedy	HBTS	PTS	NTS
TS	-	42:38	38:42	37:43	43:37	40:40	49:31	44:36
UCB1	38:42	-	39:41	29:51	44:36	33:47	42:38	43:37
EXP3	42:38	41:39	-	35:45	39:41	43:37	45:35	46:34
gEXP3	43:37	51:29	45:35	-	42:38	43:37	45:35	47:33
eGreedy	37:43	36:44	41:39	38:42	-	38:42	38:42	36:44
HBTS	40:40	47:33	37:43	37:43	42:38	-	39:41	48:32
PTS	31:49	38:42	35:45	35:45	42:38	41:39	-	37:43
NTS	36:44	37:43	34:46	33:47	44:36	32:48	43:37	-
avg wins (%)	36.99	33.84	36.74	**39.90**	33.33	36.62	32.70	32.70

CB	Baseline			Variants of Split CB Agents		
	CTS	LinUCB	EXP4	SCTS	PCTS	NCTS
CTS	-	6:74	36:44	42:38	30:50	37:43
LinUCB	74:6	-	74:6	74:6	72:8	75:5
EXP4	44:36	6:74	-	45:35	31:49	41:39
SCTS	38:42	6:74	35:45	-	30:50	39:41
PCTS	50:30	8:72	49:31	50:30	-	50:30
NCTS	43:37	5:75	39:41	41:39	30:50	-
avg wins (%)	25.42	**62.12**	28.11	24.92	34.85	26.60

RL	Baseline			Variants of Split RL agents				
	QL	DQL	SARSA	SQL-alg1	SQL-alg2	MP	PQL	NQL
QL	-	62:38	55:45	63:37	54:46	47:53	65:35	90:10
DQL	38:62	-	40:60	48:52	48:52	43:57	55:45	86:14
SARSA	45:55	60:40	-	63:37	51:49	52:48	64:36	88:12
SQL	37:63	52:48	37:63	-	42:58	26:74	55:45	72:28
SQL2	46:54	52:48	49:51	58:42	-	39:61	64:36	72:28
MP	53:47	57:43	48:52	74:26	61:39	-	66:34	82:18
PQL	35:65	45:55	36:64	45:55	36:64	34:66	-	68:32
NQL	10:90	14:86	12:88	28:72	28:72	18:82	32:68	-
avg wins (%)	55.05	45.20	53.41	40.53	47.98	**55.68**	37.75	17.93

Table 5. "Mental" Agents in MDP Task: 100 randomly generated scenarios

MAB	b-ADD	b-ADHD	b-AD	b-CP	b-bvFTD	b-PD	b-M	avg wins (%)
TS	43:37	49:31	45:35	45:35	44:36	39:41	36:44	43.43
UCB1	38:42	48:32	41:39	40:40	39:41	39:41	36:44	40.55
EXP3	38:42	47:33	46:34	41:39	41:39	40:40	36:44	41.70
eGreedy	40:40	44:36	41:39	38:42	41:39	35:45	39:41	40.12
HBTS	40:40	48:32	47:33	43:37	49:31	42:38	39:41	44.44
avg wins (%)	40.61	33.13	36.36	38.99	37.58	41.41	43.23	

CB	cb-ADD	cb-ADHD	cb-AD	cb-CP	cb-bvFTD	cb-PD	cb-M	avg wins (%)
CTS	37:43	41:39	36:44	35:45	35:45	38:42	45:35	38.53
LinUCB	73:7	76:4	73:7	74:6	75:5	74:6	76:4	75.18
EXP4	38:42	38:42	33:47	42:38	41:39	44:36	44:36	40.40
SCTS	36:44	41:39	31:49	39:41	37:43	40:40	43:37	38.53
avg wins (%)	34.34	31.31	37.12	32.83	33.33	31.31	28.28	.

RL	ADD	ADHD	AD	CP	bvFTD	PD	M	avg wins (%)
QL	70:10	44:36	67:13	48:32	58:22	49:31	48:32	55.41
DQL	69:11	42:38	66:14	45:35	56:24	45:35	56:24	54.69
SARSA	75:5	48:32	71:9	53:27	61:19	52:28	54:26	59.74
SQL	68:12	41:39	60:20	38:42	54:26	44:36	43:37	50.22
avg wins (%)	9.60	36.62	14.14	34.34	22.98	32.83	30.05	

MAB

CB

RL

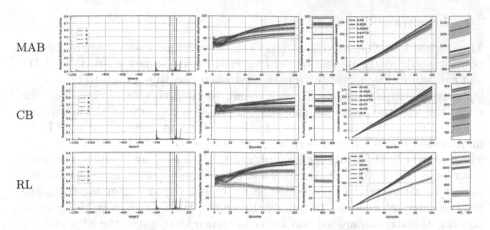

Fig. 3. Learning curves in IGT scheme 1: "Mental" MAB, CB and RL agents.

Table 6. Schemes of Iowa Gambling Task

Decks	Win per card	Loss per card	Expected value	Scheme
A (bad)	+100	Frequent: −150 (p = 0.1), −200 (p = 0.1), −250 (p = 0.1), −300 (p = 0.1), −350 (p = 0.1)	−25	1
B (bad)	+100	Infrequent: −1250 (p = 0.1)	−25	1
C (good)	+50	Frequent: −25 (p = 0.1), −75 (p = 0.1), −50 (p = 0.3)	+25	1
D (good)	+50	Infrequent: −250 (p = 0.1)	+25	1
A (bad)	+100	Frequent: −150 (p = 0.1), −200 (p = 0.1), −250 (p = 0.1), −300 (p = 0.1), −350 (p = 0.1)	−25	2
B (bad)	+100	Infrequent: −1250 (p = 0.1)	−25	2
C (good)	+50	Infrequent: −50 (p = 0.5)	+25	2
D (good)	+50	Infrequent: −250 (p = 0.1)	+25	2

suggesting a benefit in the split mechanism in the MDP environments that we generated.

To explore the variants of split models representing different mental disorders, we also performed the same experiments on the 7 disease models proposed above. Tables 3 and 5 summarized their pairwise comparisons with the standard ones, where the average wins are computed averaged against three standard baseline models. Overall, PD ("Parkinson's"), CP ("chronic pain"), ADHD and M ("moderate") performed relatively well. In the MAB setting, the optimal reward bias are PD and M for the split MAB models, ADHD and CP for the split CB models, and bvFTD and M for the split RL models. In the MDP setting, the optimal reward bias are PD and M for the split MAB models, ADHD and bvFTD for the split CB models, and ADHD and CP for the split RL models.

5.2   Iowa Gambling Task

The original Iowa Gambling Task (IGT) studies decision making where the participant needs to choose one out of four card decks (named A, B, C, and D), and can win or lose money with each card when choosing a deck to draw from [7], over around 100 actions. In each round, the participants receives feedback about the win (the money he/she wins), the loss (the money he/she loses), and the combined gain (win minus lose). In the MDP setup, from initial state I, the player select one of the four deck to go to state A, B, C, or D, and reveals positive reward r^+ (the win), negative reward r^- (the loss) and combined reward $r = r^+ + r^-$ simultaneously. Decks A and B by default is set to have an expected payout (-25) lower than the better decks, C and D ($+25$). For baselines, the combined reward r is used to update the agents. For split models, the positive and negative streams are fed and learned independently given the r^+ and r^-.

There are two major payoff schemes in IGT. In the traditional payoff scheme, the net outcome of every 10 cards from the bad decks (i.e., decks A and B) is -250, and $+250$ in the case of the good decks (i.e., decks C and D). There are two decks with frequent losses (decks A and C), and two decks with infrequent losses (decks B and D). All decks have consistent wins (A and B to have $+100$, while C and D to have $+50$) and variable losses (summarized in Table 6, where scheme 1 [18] has a more variable losses for deck C than scheme 2 [22]). We performed the each scheme for 200 times over 500 actions.

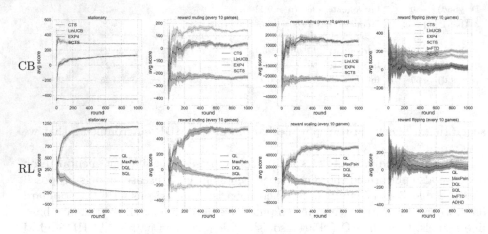

Fig. 4. Average final scores in Pacman with different stationarities: Columns as (a) stationary; (b) stochastic reward muting by every 10 rounds; (c) stochastic reward scaling by every 10 rounds; (d) stochastic reward flipping by every 10 rounds.

Results. Among the variants of Split models and baselines, the split contextual bandit (SCTS) performs best in scheme 1 with an averaged final cumulative rewards of 1200.76 over 500 draws of cards, significantly better than the MAB baseline TS (991.26), CB baseline LinUCB (1165.23) and RL baseline QL (1086.33). Mental variants of SCTS, such as CP ("chronic pain", 1136.38), also performed quite well. This is consistent to the clinical implication of chronic pain patients which tend to forget about positive reward information (as modeled by a smaller λ_+) and lack of drive to pursue rewards (as modeled by a smaller w_+). In scheme 2, eGreedy performs best with the final score of 1198.32, followed by CP (1155.84) and SCTS (1150.22). These examples suggest that the proposed framework has the flexibility to map out different behavior trajectories in real-life decision making (such as IGT). Figure 3 demonstrated the short-term (in 100 actions) and long-term behaviors of different mental agents, which matches clinical discoveries. For instance, ADD ("addiction") quickly learns about the actual values of each decks (as reflected by the short-term curve) but in the long-term sticks with the decks with a larger wins (despite also with even larger losses). At around 20 actions, ADD performs better than baselines in learning about the decks with the better gains. In all three agent pools (MAB agents, CB agents, RL agents), we observed interesting trajectories revealed by the short-term dynamics (Fig. 3), suggesting a promising next step to map from behavioral trajectories to clinically relevant reward processing bias of the human subjects.

5.3 PacMan Game Across Various Stationarities

We demonstrate the merits of the proposed algorithm using the classic game of PacMan. The goal of the agent is to eat all the dots in the maze, known as Pac-Dots, as soon as possible while simultaneously avoiding collision with ghosts, which roam the maze trying to kill PacMan. The rules for the environment (adopted from Berkeley AI PacMan[1]) are as follows. There are two types of negative rewards: on collision with a ghost, PacMan loses the game and gets a negative reward of −500; and at each time frame, there is a constant time-penalty of −1 for every step taken. There are three types of positive rewards. On eating a Pac-Dot, the agent obtains a reward of +10. On successfully eating all the Pac-Dots, the agent wins the game and obtains a reward of +500. The game also has two special dots called Power Pellets in the corners of the maze, which on consumption, give PacMan the temporary ability of "eating" ghosts. During this phase, the ghosts are in a "scared" state for 40 frames and move at half their speed. On eating a "scared" ghost, the agent gets a reward of +200, the ghost returns to the center box and returns to its normal "unscared" state. As a more realistic scenarios as real-world agents, we define the agents to receive their rewards in positive and negative streams separately. Traditional agents sum the two streams as a regular reward, while Split agents use two streams separately.

We applied several types of stationarities to PacMan as in [27]. In order to simulate a lifelong learning setting, we assume that the environmental settings

---

[1] http://ai.berkeley.edu/project_overview.html.

arrive in batches (or stages) of episodes, and the specific rule of the game (i.e., reward distributions) may change across batches, while remaining stationary within each batch. The change is defined by a stochastic process of the game setting that an event A is defined for the positive stream and an event B is defined for the negative stream, independent of each other ($A \perp B$). The stochastic process is resampled every 10 rounds (i.e. a batch size of 10).

Stochastic Reward Muting. To simulate the changes of turning on or off of a certain reward stream, we define the event A as turning off the positive reward stream (i.e. all the positive rewards are set to be zero) and the event B as turning off the negative reward stream (i.e. all the penalties are set to be zero). $\mathbb{P}(A) = \mathbb{P}(B) = 0.5$ in the experiments.

Stochastic Reward Scaling. To simulate the changes of scaling up a certain reward stream, we define the event A as scaling up the positive reward stream by 100 (i.e. all the positive rewards are multiplied by 100) and the event B as scaling up the negative reward stream (i.e. all the penalties are multiplied by 100). $\mathbb{P}(A) = \mathbb{P}(B) = 0.5$ in the experiments.

Stochastic Reward Flipping. To simulate the changes of flipping certain reward stream, we define the event A as flipping the positive reward stream (i.e. all the positive rewards are multiplied by -1 and considered penalties) and the event B as flipping the negative reward stream (i.e. all the penalties are multiplied by -1 and considered positive rewards). We set $\mathbb{P}(A) = \mathbb{P}(B) = 0.5$.

We ran the proposed agents across these different stationarities for 200 episodes over multiple runs and plotted their average final scores with standard errors.

Results. As in Fig. 4, in all four scenarios, the split models demonstrated competitive performance against their baselines. In the CB agent pools, where the state-less agents were not designed for such a complicated gaming environment, we still observe a converging learning behaviors from these agents. LinUCB as a CB baseline, performed better than the SCTS, which suggested a potentially better theoretical model to integrate split mechanism for this game environment. However, it is worth noting that in the reward flipping scenario, several mental agents are even more advantageous than the standard split models as in Fig. 4(d), which matches clinical discoveries and the theory of evolutionary psychiatry. For instance, ADHD-like fast-switching attention seems to be especially beneficial in this very non-stationary setting of flipping reward streams. Even in a full stationary setting, the behaviors of these mental agents can have interesting clinical implications. For instance, the video of a CP ("chronic pain") agent playing Pac-Man shows a clear avoidance behavior to penalties by staying at a corner very distant from the ghosts and a comparatively lack of interest to reward pursuit by not eating nearby Pac-Dots, matching the clinical characters of chronic pain patients. From the video, we observe that the agent ignored all the rewards in front of it and spent its life hiding from the ghosts, trying to elongate its life span at all costs, even if that implies a constant time penalty to a very negative final score (The videos of the mental agents playing PacMan after training here[2]).

6   Conclusions

This research proposes a novel parametric family of algorithms for multi-armed bandits, contextual bandits and RL problems, extending the classical algorithms to model a wide range of potential reward processing biases. Our approach draws an inspiration from extensive literature on decision-making behavior in neurological and psychiatric disorders stemming from disturbances of the reward processing system, and demonstrates high flexibility of our multi-parameter model which allows to tune the weights on incoming two-stream rewards and memories about the prior reward history. Our preliminary results support multiple prior observations about reward processing biases in a range of mental disorders, thus indicating the potential of the proposed model and its future extensions to capture reward-processing aspects across various neurological and psychiatric conditions.

The contribution of this research is two-fold: from the machine learning perspective, we propose a simple yet powerful and more adaptive approach to MAB, CB and RL problems; from the neuroscience perspective, this work is the first attempt at a general, unifying model of reward processing and its disruptions across a wide population including both healthy subjects and those with mental disorders, which has a potential to become a useful computational tool for neuroscientists and psychiatrists studying such disorders. Among the directions for future work, we plan to investigate the optimal parameters in a series of computer games evaluated on different criteria, for example, longest survival time vs. highest final score. Further work includes exploring the multi-agent interactions given different reward processing bias. These discoveries can help build more interpretable real-world humanoid decision making systems. On the neuroscience side, the next steps would include further tuning and extending the proposed model to better capture observations in modern literature, as well as testing the model on both healthy subjects and patients with mental conditions.

A   Further Motivation from Neuroscience

In the following section, we provide further discussion with a literature review on the neuroscience and clinical studies related to the reward processing systems.

Cellular Computation of Reward and Reward Violation. Decades of evidence has linked dopamine function to reinforcement learning via neurons in the midbrain and its connections in the basal ganglia, limbic regions, and cortex. Firing rates of dopamine neurons computationally represent reward magnitude, expectancy, and violations (prediction error) and other value-based signals [39].

---

[2] https://github.com/doerlbh/mentalRL/tree/master/video

This allows an animal to update and maintain value expectations associated with particular states and actions. When functioning properly, this helps an animal develop a policy to maximize outcomes by approaching/choosing cues with higher expected value and avoiding cues associated with loss or punishment. The mechanism is conceptually similar to reinforcement learning widely used in computing and robotics [43], suggesting mechanistic overlap in humans and AI. Evidence of Q-learning and actor-critic models have been observed in spiking activity in midbrain dopamine neurons in primates [6] and in the human striatum using the BOLD signal [36].

Positive vs. Negative Learning Signals. Phasic dopamine signaling represents bidirectional (positive and negative) coding for prediction error signals [19], but underlying mechanisms show differentiation for reward relative to punishment learning [40]. Though representation of cellular-level aversive error signaling has been debated [13], it is widely thought that rewarding, salient information is represented by phasic dopamine signals, whereas reward omission or punishment signals are represented by dips or pauses in baseline dopamine firing [39]. These mechanisms have downstream effects on motivation, approach behavior, and action selection. Reward signaling in a direct pathway links striatum to cortex via dopamine neurons that disinhibit the thalamus via the internal segment of the globus pallidus and facilitate action and approach behavior. Alternatively, aversive signals may have an opposite effect in the indirect pathway mediated by D2 neurons inhibiting thalamic function and ultimately action, as well [16]. Manipulating these circuits through pharmacological measures or disease has demonstrated computationally-predictable effects that bias learning from positive or negative prediction error in humans [17], and contribute to our understanding of perceptible differences in human decision making when differentially motivated by loss or gain [45].

Clinical Implications. Highlighting the importance of using computational models to understand predict disease outcomes, many symptoms of neurological and psychiatric disease are related to biases in learning from positive and negative feedback [35]. Studies in humans have shown that when reward signaling in the direct pathway is over-expressed, this may enhance the value associated with a state and incur pathological reward-seeking behavior, like gambling or substance use. Conversely, when aversive error signals are enhanced, this results in dampening of reward experience and increased motor inhibition, causing symptoms that decrease motivation, such as apathy, social withdrawal, fatigue, and depression. Further, it has been proposed that exposure to a particular distribution of experiences during critical periods of development can biologically predispose an individual to learn from positive or negative outcomes, making them more or less susceptible to risk for brain-based illnesses [21]. These points distinctly highlight the need for a greater understanding of how intelligent systems differentially learn from rewards or punishments, and how experience sampling may impact reinforcement learning during influential training periods.

References

1. Agrawal, S., Goyal, N.: Analysis of Thompson Sampling for the multi-armed bandit problem. In: COLT 2012 - The 25th Annual Conference on Learning Theory, Edinburgh, Scotland, 25–27 June 2012, pp. 39.1–39.26 (2012). http://www.jmlr.org/proceedings/papers/v23/agrawal12/agrawal12.pdf
2. Agrawal, S., Goyal, N.: Thompson sampling for contextual bandits with linear payoffs. In: ICML, no. 3, pp. 127–135 (2013)
3. Auer, P., Cesa-Bianchi, N.: On-line learning with malicious noise and the closure algorithm. Ann. Math. Artif. Intell. **23**(1–2), 83–99 (1998)
4. Auer, P., Cesa-Bianchi, N., Fischer, P.: Finite-time analysis of the multiarmed bandit problem. Mach. Learn. **47**(2–3), 235–256 (2002)
5. Auer, P., Cesa-Bianchi, N., Freund, Y., Schapire, R.E.: The nonstochastic multi-armed bandit problem. SIAM J. Comput. **32**(1), 48–77 (2002)
6. Bayer, H.M., Glimcher, P.W.: Midbrain dopamine neurons encode a quantitative reward prediction error signal. Neuron **47**(1), 129–141 (2005). https://doi.org/10.1016/j.neuron.2005.05.020.   http://www.ncbi.nlm.nih.gov/pubmed/15996553. http://www.pubmedcentral.nih.gov/articlerender.fcgi?artid=PMC1564381. http://www.linkinghub.elsevier.com/retrieve/pii/S0896627305004678
7. Bechara, A., Damasio, A.R., Damasio, H., Anderson, S.W.: Insensitivity to future consequences following damage to human prefrontal cortex. Cognition **50**(1–3), 7–15 (1994)
8. Beygelzimer, A., Langford, J., Li, L., Reyzin, L., Schapire, R.: Contextual bandit algorithms with supervised learning guarantees. In: Proceedings of the Fourteenth International Conference on Artificial Intelligence and Statistics, pp. 19–26 (2011)
9. Bouneffouf, D., Féraud, R.: Multi-armed bandit problem with known trend. Neurocomputing **205**, 16–21 (2016). https://doi.org/10.1016/j.neucom.2016.02.052
10. Bouneffouf, D., Rish, I., Cecchi, G.A.: Bandit models of human behavior: reward processing in mental disorders. In: Everitt, T., Goertzel, B., Potapov, A. (eds.) AGI 2017. LNCS (LNAI), vol. 10414, pp. 237–248. Springer, Cham (2017). https://doi.org/10.1007/978-3-319-63703-7_22
11. Bouneffouf, D., Rish, I., Cecchi, G.A., Féraud, R.: Context attentive bandits: contextual bandit with restricted context. In: Proceedings of the 26th International Joint Conference on Artificial Intelligence, pp. 1468–1475 (2017)
12. Chapelle, O., Li, L.: An empirical evaluation of Thompson sampling. In: Advances in Neural Information Processing Systems, pp. 2249–2257 (2011)
13. Dayan, P., Niv, Y.: Reinforcement learning: the good, the bad and the ugly. Curr. Opin. Neurobiol. **18**(2), 185–196 (2008)
14. Elfwing, S., Seymour, B.: Parallel reward and punishment control in humans and robots: Safe reinforcement learning using the MaxPain algorithm. In: 2017 Joint IEEE International Conference on Development and Learning and Epigenetic Robotics (ICDL-EpiRob), pp. 140–147. IEEE (2017)
15. Even-Dar, E., Mansour, Y.: Learning rates for q-learning. J. Mach. Learn. Res. **5**, 1–25 (2003)
16. Frank, M.J., O'Reilly, R.C.: A mechanistic account of striatal dopamine function in human cognition: psychopharmacological studies with cabergoline and haloperidol. Behav. Neurosci. **120**(3), 497–517 (2006). https://doi.org/10.1037/0735-7044.120.3.497
17. Frank, M.J., Seeberger, L.C., O'reilly, R.C.: By carrot or by stick: cognitive reinforcement learning in parkinsonism. Science **306**(5703), 1940–1943 (2004)

18. Fridberg, D.J., et al.: Cognitive mechanisms underlying risky decision-making in chronic cannabis users. J. Math. Psychol. **54**(1), 28–38 (2010)
19. Hart, A.S., Rutledge, R.B., Glimcher, P.W., Phillips, P.E.M.: Phasic dopamine release in the rat nucleus accumbens symmetrically encodes a reward prediction error term. J. Neurosci. **34**(3), 698–704 (2014). https://doi.org/10.1523/JNEUROSCI.2489-13.2014. http://citeseerx.ist.psu.edu/viewdoc/download?doi=10.1.1.645.2368&rep=rep1&type=pdf
20. Hasselt, H.V.: Double q-learning. In: Advances in Neural Information Processing Systems, pp. 2613–2621 (2010)
21. Holmes, A.J., Patrick, L.M.: The myth of optimality in clinical neuroscience. Trends Cogn. Sci. **22**(3), 241–257 (2018). https://doi.org/10.1016/j.tics.2017.12.006. http://linkinghub.elsevier.com/retrieve/pii/S1364661317302681
22. Horstmann, A., Villringer, A., Neumann, J.: Iowa gambling task: there is more to consider than long-term outcome. Using a linear equation model to disentangle the impact of outcome and frequency of gains and losses. Front. Neurosci. **6**, 61 (2012)
23. Lai, T.L., Robbins, H.: Asymptotically efficient adaptive allocation rules. Adv. Appl. Math. **6**(1), 4–22 (1985). http://www.cs.utexas.edu/~shivaram
24. Langford, J., Zhang, T.: The Epoch-Greedy algorithm for contextual multi-armed bandits (2007)
25. Langford, J., Zhang, T.: The Epoch-Greedy algorithm for multi-armed bandits with side information. In: Advances in Neural Information Processing Systems, pp. 817–824 (2008)
26. Li, L., Chu, W., Langford, J., Wang, X.: Unbiased offline evaluation of contextual-bandit-based news article recommendation algorithms. In: King, I., Nejdl, W., Li, H. (eds.) WSDM, pp. 297–306. ACM (2011). http://dblp.uni-trier.de/db/conf/wsdm/wsdm2011.html#LiCLW11
27. Lin, B.: Diabolical games: reinforcement learning environments for lifelong learning (2020)
28. Lin, B.: Online semi-supervised learning in contextual bandits with episodic reward. arXiv preprint arXiv:2009.08457 (2020)
29. Lin, B., Bouneffouf, D., Cecchi, G.: Split q learning: reinforcement learning with two-stream rewards. In: Proceedings of the 28th International Joint Conference on Artificial Intelligence, pp. 6448–6449. AAAI Press (2019)
30. Lin, B., Bouneffouf, D., Cecchi, G.: Online learning in iterated prisoner's dilemma to mimic human behavior. arXiv preprint arXiv:2006.06580 (2020)
31. Lin, B., Bouneffouf, D., Cecchi, G.A., Rish, I.: Contextual bandit with adaptive feature extraction. In: 2018 IEEE International Conference on Data Mining Workshops (ICDMW), pp. 937–944. IEEE (2018)
32. Lin, B., Bouneffouf, D., Reinen, J., Rish, I., Cecchi, G.: A story of two streams: reinforcement learning models from human behavior and neuropsychiatry. In: Proceedings of the Nineteenth International Conference on Autonomous Agents and Multi-Agent Systems, AAMAS 2020, pp. 744–752. International Foundation for Autonomous Agents and Multiagent Systems, May 2020
33. Lin, B., Zhang, X.: Speaker diarization as a fully online learning problem in MiniVox. arXiv preprint arXiv:2006.04376 (2020)
34. Lin, B., Zhang, X.: VoiceID on the fly: a speaker recognition system that learns from scratch. In: INTERSPEECH (2020)
35. Maia, T.V., Frank, M.J.: From reinforcement learning models to psychiatric and neurological disorders. Nat. Neurosci. **14**(2), 154–162 (2011). https://doi.org/10.1038/nn.2723

36. O'Doherty, J., Dayan, P., Schultz, J., Deichmann, R., Friston, K., Dolan, R.J.: Dissociable roles of ventral and dorsal striatum in instrumental. Science **304**, 452–454 (2004). https://doi.org/10.1126/science.1094285. http://www.sciencemag.org/content/304/5669/452.full.html. http://www.sciencemag.org/content/suppl/2004/04/13/304.5669.452.DC1.html. http://www.sciencemag.org/content/304/5669/452.full.html#related-urls. http://www.sciencemag.org/cgi/collection/neuroscience
37. Perry, D.C., Kramer, J.H.: Reward processing in neurodegenerative disease. Neurocase **21**(1), 120–133 (2015)
38. Rummery, G.A., Niranjan, M.: On-line Q-learning using connectionist systems, vol. 37. University of Cambridge, Department of Engineering Cambridge, England (1994)
39. Schultz, W., Dayan, P., Montague, P.R.: A neural substrate of prediction and reward. Science **275**(5306), 1593–1599 (1997). https://doi.org/10.1126/science.275.5306.1593. http://www.sciencemag.org/cgi/doi/10.1126/science.275.5306.1593
40. Seymour, B., Singer, T., Dolan, R.: The neurobiology of punishment. Nat. Rev. Neurosci. **8**(4), 300–311 (2007). https://doi.org/10.1038/nrn2119. http://www.nature.com/articles/nrn2119
41. Steingroever, H., et al.: Data from 617 healthy participants performing the iowa gambling task: a "Many Labs" collaboration. J. Open Psychol. Data **3**(1), 340–353 (2015)
42. Sutton, R.S., Barto, A.G.: Introduction to Reinforcement Learning, 1st edn. MIT Press, Cambridge (1998)
43. Sutton, R.S., Barto, A.G., et al.: Introduction to Reinforcement Learning, vol. 135. MIT press Cambridge (1998)
44. Thompson, W.: On the likelihood that one unknown probability exceeds another in view of the evidence of two samples. Biometrika **25**, 285–294 (1933)
45. Tversky, A., Kahneman, D.: The framing of decisions and the psychology of choice. Science **211**(4481), 453–458 (1981). https://fenix.tecnico.ulisboa.pt/downloadFile/3779576281111/Theframingofdecisionsandthepsychologyofchoice.pdf

Machines Develop Consciousness Through Autonomous Programming for General Purposes (APFGP)

Juyang Weng[1,2](✉)

[1] Department of Computer Science, Cognitive Science Program,
Neuroscience Program, Michigan State University, East Lansing, MI 48824, USA
weng@msu.edu
[2] GENISAMA LLC, Okemos, MI 48864, USA

Abstract. Consider a question, "Can machines be conscious?" The subject "consciousness" is vague and challenging. Although there has been a rich collection of literature on consciousness, computational modeling of consciousness that is both holistic in scope and detailed in simulatable computation is lacking. Based on recent advances on a new capability—Autonomous Programming For General Purposes (APFGP)—this work presents APFGP as a clearer, deeper and more practical characterization of consciousness, for natural (biological) and artificial (machine) systems. All animals have APFGP but traditional AI systems do not. This work reports a new kind of AI systems—conscious machines. Instead of arguing what static tasks a conscious machine should be able to do, this work suggests that APFGP is a computationally clearer and necessary criterion for us to dynamically judge whether a system can become maturely conscious through lifelong development, even if it (e.g., a fruit fly) does not have a full array of primate like capabilities such as vision, audition, and natural language understanding. The results here involve a series of new concepts and experimental studies for vision, audition, and natural languages with new developmental capabilities that are not present in many published systems, e.g., IBM Deep Blue, IBM Watson, AlphaGo, AlphaFold and other traditional AI systems and intelligent robots.

Keywords: Consciousness · Brain · AI · Natural intelligence · Autonomous development · Vision · Audition · Natural language understanding

1 Introduction

We can trace the origin of modern concept of consciousness to John Locke's "Essay Concerning Human Understanding", published in 1690, in which he defined consciousness as "the perception of what passes in a man's own mind".

Merriam-Webster On-line Dictionary defined consciousness as 1. a: the quality or state of being aware especially of something within oneself; b: the state

Y. Wang (Ed.): HBAI 2020, CCIS 1369, pp. 34–55, 2021.
https://doi.org/10.1007/978-981-16-1288-6_3

or fact of being conscious of an external object, state, or fact; c: awareness; 2: the state of being characterized by sensation, emotion, volition, and thought: mind; 3: the totality of conscious states of an individual; 4: the normal state of conscious life; 5: the upper level of mental life of which the person is aware as contrasted with unconscious processes.

Christof Koch [6] wrote: "Consciousness is everything you experience. It is the tune stuck in your head, the sweetness of chocolate mousse, the throbbing pain of a toothache, the fierce love for your child and the bitter knowledge that eventually all feelings will end."

As we can see, the term "consciousness" has been very *vague* and *superficial*, without a computational basis that has been mathematically proven to bear the claim of "totality" (Merriam-Webster) and "everything" (Koch), at least in principle. This paper intends to clarify this *vagueness* and ground this *superficialness* on a deep foundation. This computational basis is a well-established theory called Universal Turing Machines.

A Dialogue of *AMD Newsletters* has a topic: "will social robots need to be consciously aware?", Yasuko Kitano, Conelius Weber & Stefan Wermter, Justin Hart & Brain Scassellati, Axel Cleereman, Juyang Weng, and Guy Hoffman & Moran Cerf made a total of six commentaries. The Dialogue coordinator Jenet Wiles wrote: "Weng [21] takes a different position from the other commentaries, starting from the assertion that all aspects of awareness are tightly interrelated and each cannot function without the others. He calls attention to his brain scale models ... Integrative systems are needed in modeling, but we should be sceptical of approaches that exclude progress on understanding the biological sub-systems of different neural regions." The title "Consciousness for a social robot is not piecemeal" in Weng [21] does not mean to "exclude progress" on piecemeal studies of "subsystems". But rather, it means that we need a holistic approach in order not to get lost in the maze of this extremely rich subject.

This work further explains why. As we will see from the theory of emergent Universal Turing Machine here, "subsystems of different neural regions" are like a block of computer memory of a particular Universal Turing Machine. When one studies each sub-system of consciousness without a holistic theory about consciousness, he is like one of the blind men in Fig. 1. Many disciplines like biology, neuroscience, psychology, electrical engineering, computer science, mathematics, and physics are related to consciousness. Yes, we often say physics is everything. In my humble personal view, each such traditional discipline is like a blind man when it studies a biological brain in general and its consciousness in particular. If the reader has learned the theory of Universal Turing Machines, he can understand why there are many kinds of Universal Turing Machines and better appreciate that each brain, ranging from fruit flies to humans, is a different Universal Turing Machine. No two brains should be exactly the same!

Why is each discipline like a blind man? The term "consciousness" has been used in very different contexts. In particular, the term involves extremely complex physical entities, such as brain, body, environment, life and biology. For example, how does a cattle or a human in Fig. 2 learn consciousness so that

Fig. 1. When we study only a sub-system of consciousness of the brain without a holistic understanding, each of us is like a blind man touching an elephant. Furthermore, among biology, neuroscience, psychology, electrical engineering, computer science, mathematics, and physics each discipline is like a blind man.

it navigates autonomously through the hustle and bustle of streets to reach its home daily? Can an artificial machine learn to do the same and much more? The theory of emergent Universal Turing Machine as a computational basis can explain all such complexity and richness in a principled way.

Therefore as a science of consciousness, we need a concise, but highly precise description of a minimal set of computational mechanisms that have a potential to give rise to natural consciousness and verifiable artificial consciousness. Such a set is not meant to explain every minor detail of all biological systems. This is because any model of biology is inevitably an approximation. However, I argue that we must take a holistic approach. Even though such a holistic approach is still an approximation, it is more insightful than piecemeal approaches.

This minimal holistic set has a potential to make consciousness clearer and deeply understood. Hopefully, the set not only accounts for a wide variety of natural consciousness, but also guides developments of artificial consciousness. By artificial consciousness, I mean a robot that displays a repertoire of sensorimotor behaviors that resemble what we call "consciousness", like that from lower to higher animals.

The remainder of this paper is organized as follows. Section 2 overviews the theory of Turing Machines. Section 3 introduces the theory of Universal Turing Machines. Section 4 discusses eight (8) necessary conditions as GENISAMA that seem to be necessary for realizing consciousness. Section 5 presents the new characterization of consciousness—the APFGP capability that are made possible by GENISAMA Universal Turing Machines. Section 6 describes Development Networks that have a potential to give rise to consciousness through lifetime development. Section 7 outlines motivation which includes emotion. Section 8 summaries properties of DN. Section 9 discusses how a DN learns consciousness. Some early experimental results are reported in Sect. 10. Section 11 provides concluding remarks.

Fig. 2. A cattle (solid ellipse) and a human (dashed ellipse) navigate on a busy street of New Delhi, India. They are conducting conscious learning, as defined in Definition 2.

2 Turing Machines

We assume natural and artificial consciousness all arises from computations of information. Before we talk about what we mean by computation, let us look at a well-known but extremely simple model of computing.

Turing Machines, originally proposed by Alan Turing [18] in 1936, were not meant to explain consciousness at all. However, as we will surprisingly see below, we need the assistance of Turing Machines to understand how consciousness arises from computations by a machine, both natural and artificial.

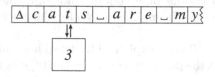

Fig. 3. An example of Turing Machine. Each cell of the tape bears only a symbol. The controller has a current state (3 in the figure) at each integer time.

A Turing Machine (TM) [3,10], illustrated in Fig. 3, consists of an infinite tape, a read-write head, and a controller. The controller consists of a sequence of moves where each move is a 5-word sentence of the following form:

$$(q, \gamma) \rightarrow (q', \gamma', d) \tag{1}$$

meaning that if the current state is q and the current input that the head senses is γ on the tape, then the machine enters to next state q', writes γ' onto the tape, and its head moves in direction d (left, right, or stay) but no more than one cell away. The Turing Machine starts from the initial state q_0 and input on the tape. When the state is halt h, what on the tape is the output computed by the TM from the input.

Intuitively speaking, let us consider each symbol in the above 5-word expression as a "word". Then all such 5-word expressions are "sentences". Thus, a human-handcrafted "program" is a sequence of such 5-word sentences the TM must follow in computation. Obviously, although such sentences are not a natural language, they are more precise than a natural language.

After we have tried a variety of small programs, such as (1) checking whether a sequence satisfies a predefined property (e.g., it contains an odd number of symbol b), (2) doing arithmetic computations (e.g., additions, subtractions, multiplications, and divisions); (3) enabling a program to call another program, and so on, we came up with a thesis: A Turing Machine can do any number of computations that a paper-and-pencil procedure allows a human to do by hand. This is called the Church-Turing thesis [3, 10].

Weng 2015 [20] proposed that the 5-word vector in Eq. (1) can be conceptually simplified by combining the right side as a new space of state/action, so that the control of any Turing machine can be modelled by a finite automaton (FA) by expanding the state on the left side to the new space.

The remaining problem then that Alan Turing faced was that such a program is for a *special purpose*, and such a machine is called a special-purpose computer. The revolution discussed in the next section broke this restriction.

3   Universal Turing Machines

How can we make the above machine of general purposes? Turing found that we do not need to change the above definition. All we need is to augment the meaning of the input on the tape!

His bright idea is that the tape contains not only the input *data* for the machine to process, but also the input *program* for the machine to emulate using the input data!

In his 1936 paper [18], Turing explained in detail how this emulation is done. His main idea is to treat the program section on the tape as a sequence of 5-word moves. This new machine has a new program, called a compiler that compiles any valid program and emulates the input program on the input data. This new kind of Turing Machines is called Universal Turing Machines (UTM). We called it *universal* because the program on the tape is open-ended, supplied by any users for any purposes. This great ideas of universal computers gave rise to today's thriving computer industry.

However, Universal Turing Machines do not explain consciousness. They are still not conscious as we know it. The important rule of Universal Turing Machines in helping us understand consciousness is not known until this paper.

Furthermore, traditionally consciousness is a subject primarily of philosophy. This challenging subject has been largely off-limit to AI other than many recent piecemeal discussions.

To see the link between Turing Machines and consciousness, we must break a series of restrictions in Turing Machines, as explained in the next section, so that a new kind of super machines can do AGPFG like brains.

4 Eight Requirements for Consciousness

The eight requirements below were not well known as necessary for consciousness. At least the APFGP capability in the title requires all of them. However, they are insufficient for giving rise to APFGP without the full Developmental Networks (DN) to be discussed in the next section.

To facilitate memorization, let us summarize the eight requirements in eight words: Grounded, Emergent, Natural, Incremental, Skulled, Attentive, Motivated, and Abstractive, or acronym GENISAMA. Let us explain each of them below.

Grounded: Grounded means sensors and effectors of a learner must directly grounded in the physical world in which the learner lives or operates. IBM Deep Blue, IBM Watson, and AlphaGo are not grounded. Instead, it is humans who synthesize symbols from the physical world, and thus shield them off from the rich physical game environments, including their opponents.

Emergent: The signals in the sensors, effectors and all representations inside the "skull" of the learner must emerge automatically through interactions between the learner and the physical world by way of sensors, effectors, and genome (aka developmental program). Because genome is meant to fit the physical world through the entire life, not only for only a specific task during the life. For example, fruit flies must do foraging, fighting and mating. Thus, task-specific handcrafting of representation in sensors, effectors, and inside the "skull" is inconsistent to consciousness. The emergence requirement ruled out task-specific and handcrafted representations, such as weights duplication in convolution used by deep learning [5, 7–9, 13, 15, 26, 27]. Likewise, an artificial genetic algorithm without lifetime learning/development does not have anything to emerge since each individual does not learn/develop in life.

Natural: The learner must use natural sensory and natural motor signals, instead of human hand-synthesized features from sensors or hand-synthesized class labels for effectors, because such symbols and labels are not natural without a human in the loop. For robots, natural signals are those directly available from a sensor (e.g., RGB pixel values from a camera) and raw signals for an effector/actuator. IBM Deep Blue, IBM Watson and AlphaGo all used handcrafted symbols for the board configurations and symbolic labels for game actions. Such symbols are not natural, not directly from cameras and not directly for robot arms.

Incremental: Because the current action from the learner will affect the next input to the learner (e.g., turn left will allow you to see left view), learning must take place incrementally in time. IBM Deep Blue, IBM Watson and AlphaGo appear to have used a batch learning method: all game configurations are available as a batch for the learner to learn. The learner is not aware how it has improved from early mistakes in the lifetime.

Skulled: The skull closes the brain of the learner so that any teacher interactions with the internal brain representation (e.g., twisting internal parameters) are not permitted. For example, Gary Kasparov [16] "accused the Deep Blue team of cheating. The allegation was that a grandmaster, presumably a top rival, had been behind the move." If this allegation is true, such tempering with Deep Blue during a game violated the skull-closed rule. Likewise, how can the brain be ware of what a neurosurgeon did inside its skull?

Attentive: The learner must learn how to attend to various entities in its environment—the body and extra-body environment. The entities include location (where to attend), type (what to attend) and scale to attend (e.g., body, face, or nose), as well as abstract concepts that the learner learned in life (e.g., am I doing the right thing?). IBM Deep Blue, IBM Watson and AlphaGo did not seem to think "what am I doing?".

Motivated: The beautiful logic that a Universal Turing Machine posses to emulate any valid program does not give rise to consciousness as we know it. By motivation, we mean that the learner must learn motivation based on its intrinsic motives, such as pain avoidance, pleasure seeking, uncertainty awareness, and sensitivity to novelty. A system that is designed to do facial recognition does not have a motive to do things other than facial recognition. IBM Deep Blue, IBM Watson and AlphaGo did not feel real pleasure when they won a game.

Abstractive: Although a shallow definition of consciousness means awareness, full awareness requires a general capability to abstract higher concepts from concrete examples. By higher concepts here I mean those concepts that a normal individual of a species is expected to be able to abstract. Consider movie "Rain Man": If a kiss by a lady on the lip is sensed only as "wet", there is a lack of abstraction. A baby cannot abstract love from the first kiss, but a normal human adult is expected to be able to. Thus, abstraction is a learning process.

With the above eight requirements, we are ready to discuss GENISAMA Universal Turing Machines as a characterization of consciousness.

5   GENISAMA Super Universal Turing Machines: APFGP

This section describes how a Developmental Network (DN) is capable of learning any GENISAMA Universal Turing Machine, or GENISAMA UTM for short. Such a GENISAMA UTM is further capable of APFGP, which the unique capability that motivated me to propose here as an alternative characterization of consciousness.

First, we need recognize that there are different degrees of consciousness. A baby, a first grader in a primary school, a freshman in a college, and a professor all has different awareness in terms of knowledge. In other words, consciousness is related to the environment and the age. However, the APFGP capability would allow a baby to be a professor of any discipline.

Second, a dog of 10 years old has a different degree of consciousness than a normal human child of the same age. Namely, consciousness is related to how much computational resources (e.g., the size of the brain) as well as the genome (i.e., developmental programs of each species). Thus, APFGP is bounded by the computational resources and the genome.

Third, if we propose APFGP as a characterization of consciousness, where does a conscious learner's input programs from? A UTM takes a program from the tape along with its data to apply to. However, a conscious machine must not only do the same. It should be able to run a UTM, but it should also learn various programs from its environments. That is, the learned programs are from the physical environments, including school teaching.

We consider five entities W, Z, Y, X, X' at times $t, t = 0, 1, 2, ...$, as illustrated in the following Table 1. We use discrete times indexed by non-negative numbers so as to facilitate understanding how consciousness arises in natural and artificial devices through discrete times sampled from real time.

Table 1. Unfolding time for APFGP in DN

Time	0	1	2	3	4	5	6	7	...	t
Actable world W	$W(0)$	$W(1)$	$W(2)$	$W(3)$	$W(4)$	$W(5)$	$W(6)$	$W(7)$	...	$W(t)$
Motor Z	$Z(0)$	$Z(1)$	$Z(2)$	$Z(3)$	$Z(4)$	$Z(5)$	$Z(6)$	$Z(7)$	...	$Z(t)$
Skulled brain Y	$Y(0)$	$Y(1)$	$Y(2)$	$Y(3)$	$Y(4)$	$Y(5)$	$Y(6)$	$Y(7)$	...	$Y(t)$
Sensor X	$X(0)$	$X(1)$	$X(2)$	$X(3)$	$X(4)$	$X(5)$	$X(6)$	$X(7)$	...	$X(t)$
Sensible world W'	$W'(0)$	$W'(1)$	$W'(2)$	$W'(3)$	$W'(4)$	$W'(5)$	$W'(6)$	$W'(7)$	...	$W'(t)$

The first row in the table gives the sample times, indexed by non-negative integers.

The second row denote the actable world W, such as the body which acts on W, such as a hand-tool or two shoes.

The third row is the motor Z, which has muscles to drive effectors, such as arms, legs, and mouth to speak.

The fourth row in the skull-closed brain Y. The computation inside the brain Y must be fully autonomous, without intervention from any external teachers, in a task nonspecific way [28].

The fifth row is the sensor X, such as cameras, microphones, and touch sensors (e.g., skin).

The last row is the sensible world, such as surfaces of objects that reflects light received by cameras.

The actable world W is typically not exactly the same as the sensible world W', because where sensors sense from and where effectors act on can be different.

Next, we discuss the rules about how a DN denoted as $N = (X, Y, Z)$ works in W and W'.

Extend the tape of the Turing Machine to record the images from sensors, instead of symbol σ. Let X be the original emergent version of input, e.g., a vector that contains values of all pixels.

Extend the output from the Turing Machine (q', γ', d) to be the muscle images from motor Z, instead of symbols. Thus, the GENISAMA Turing Machine directly acts on the physical world.

Unfolding Time: We treat X and Z as external because they can be "supervised" by the physical environment as well as "self-supervised" by the network itself. We add the internal area Y to be hidden—cannot be directly supervised by external teachers. Furthermore, we should unfold the time t and allow the network to have three areas X, Y, and Z that learns incrementally through time $t = 0, 1, 2, ...$:

$$\begin{bmatrix} Z(0) \\ Y(0) \\ X(0) \end{bmatrix} \rightarrow \begin{bmatrix} Z(1) \\ Y(1) \\ X(1) \end{bmatrix} \rightarrow \begin{bmatrix} Z(2) \\ Y(2) \\ X(2) \end{bmatrix} \rightarrow ... \tag{2}$$

where $\rightarrow$ means neurons on the left adaptively links to the neurons on the right.

Note, all neurons in every column t use only the values of the column $t - 1$ to its immediate left, but use nothing from other columns. This is true for all columns t, with integers $t \geq 1$. Otherwise, iterations are required. Namely, by unfolding time in the above expression, the highly recurrent operations in recurrent DN become not recurrent in time-unfolded DN. In fact, DN runs in real time.

Now, we are ready to see how a natural or artificial machine learns consciousness in principle:

The motor area Z starting from $Z(0)$, represents many muscles signals in a developing body, from an embryo all the way to an adult. The larger the developing body, the more muscle neurons are dynamically grown where cell deaths and cell grows both take place. Muscle cells at time t take inputs from the Y area and the Z area at the $t-1$ column, acting on the environment and also learning from the physical environment mostly through self-supervision—trials and practices.

Likewise, the sensory area X, starting from $X(0)$, also develops within a developing body, also from an embryo all the way to adult. What is different between the motor area Z and the sensory area X is that the latter develops receptors that sense the environment instead of neurons that drive muscles.

Concurrently, the brain Y, starting from $Y(0)$, also dynamically develops, from an embryo all the way to an adult. Each Y neuron at time t gets multiple inputs from all three areas, X, Y and Z, at the $t-1$ column. Competition among neurons allows only few Y neurons to win. These winner Y neurons at the time t column directly link to firing neurons in the muscle area Z at the $t+1$ column.

As time goes by, the learner looks more and more rule-like, since a GENISAMA Universal Turing Machine emerges as proven mathematically in [20]. In the brain this machine autonomously makes an increasingly sophisticated, highly integrated program. In the eyes of humans, this learner becomes increasingly conscious. The next section discusses what network this process results.

6   Developmental Networks for Learning Consciousness

A Developmental Network (DN) is meant for consciousness because it is a holistic model for a biological brain, also fully implementable on an artificial machine.

6.1   DN-1

The following section presents Developmental Network 1 (DN-1).

The hidden Y area corresponds to the entire "brain". In the following, we assume the brain has a single area Y but it will enable many subareas to emerge.

The response vector $\mathbf{y}$ the hidden Y area of DN is then used by Z and X areas to predict the next $\mathbf{z}$ and $\mathbf{x}$ respectively in discrete time $t = 1, 2, , 3, ...$:

$$\begin{bmatrix} \mathbf{z}(t-1) \\ \mathbf{y}(t-1) \\ \mathbf{x}(t-1) \end{bmatrix} \rightarrow \mathbf{y}(t) \rightarrow \begin{bmatrix} \mathbf{z}(t+1) \\ \mathbf{y}(t+1) \\ \mathbf{x}(t+1) \end{bmatrix} \tag{3}$$

where $\rightarrow$ denotes the update on the left side using the left side as input. The first $\rightarrow$ above is highly nonlinear because of the top-1 competition so that only one Y neuron fires (i.e., exactly one component in binary $\mathbf{y}$ is 1). The second $\rightarrow$ consists of simply links from the single firing Y neurons to all firing neurons on the right side.

The expression in Eq. (3) is extremely rich as illustrated in Fig. 4 as a schematic diagram of the DN that realizes Eq. 3.

Self-wiring within a Developmental Network (DN) as the control of GENISAMA TM, based on statistics of activities through "lifetime", without any central controller, Master Map, handcrafted features, and convolution.

The above vector formalization is simple but very powerful in practice. The pattern in Z can represent the binary pattern of any abstract concept—context, state, muscles, action, intent, object type, object group, object relation. However, as far as DN is concerned, they mean the same—a firing pattern of the Z area.

Equation (3) indicates that each neuron in the hidden area Y of the network has six fields in general: Sensory Receptive Field (SRF), Sensory Effective Field (SEF), Motor Receptive Field (MRF), Motoric Effective Field (MEF), and Lateral Receptive Field (LRF) and Lateral Effective Field (LEF). S: Sensory; M: motoric; L: lateral; R: receptive; E: effective; F: field. But simulated neurons in X do not have Sensory Receptive Field (SRF) and Sensory Effective Field (SEF) because they only effect Y and those in Z do not have Motor Receptive Field (MRF) and Motoric Effective Field (MEF) because they only receive from Y. Figure 4(b) shows the resulting self-wired architecture of DN with Occipital, Temporal, Parietal, and Frontal lobes. Regulated by a general-purpose Developmental Program (DP), the DN self-wires by "living" in the physical world. The X and Z areas are supervised by body and the physical world which includes teachers.

Through the synaptic maintenance, some Y neurons gradually lost their early connections (dashed lines) with X (Z) areas and become "later" (early) Y areas. In the (later) Parietal and Temporal lobes, some neurons further gradually lost

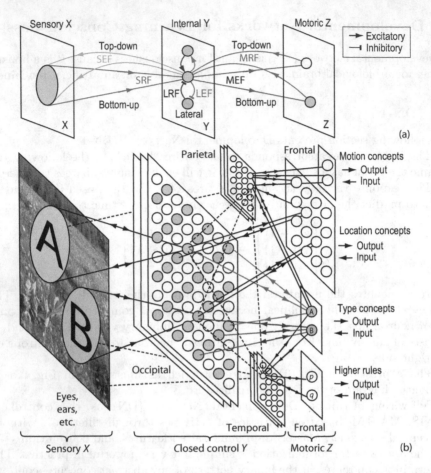

Fig. 4. A conscious learning brain Y is theoretically modeled by an emergent DN as the two-way bridge of the sensory bank X and the motor bank Z. All the connections shown are learned, grown, updated and trimmed automatically by DN.

their connections with the (early) Occipital area and become rule-like neurons. These self-wired connections give rise to a complex dynamic network, with shallow and deep connections instead of a deep cascade of areas. Object location and motion are non-declarative concepts and object type and language sequence are declarative concepts. Concepts and rules are abstract with the desired specificities and invariances. DN does not have any static Brodmann areas.

To explain how DN-1 learns any Turing Machine, $\mathbf{y}$ to $\mathbf{y}$ connections are not needed, because in a Turing Machine, actions and states at each time are symbolic, which can be explicitly represented by vectors in the motor area Z. This gives us the *external form* of DN transition below:

$$\begin{bmatrix} \mathbf{z}(t-1) \\ \mathbf{x}(t-1) \end{bmatrix} \rightarrow \mathbf{y}(t) \rightarrow \begin{bmatrix} \mathbf{z}(t+1) \\ \mathbf{x}(t+1) \end{bmatrix} \tag{4}$$

Definition 1 (External form). *By external form in Eq. (4), we mean that the hidden area $Y(t)$ does not taken hidden area $Y(t-1)$ as input for $t = 1, 2, 3, ...$, namely, all states/actions must be external in Z—no lateral Y to Y connections, compared with the general form in Eq. (3).*

The external form Eq. (4) is sufficient to prove that a DN can learn any Turing Machine one-transition at a time without any errors as long as there are a sufficient number of hidden neurons [20].

Like the transition function of a Turing Machine, each prediction of $\mathbf{z}(t+1)$ in Eq. (4) is called a *transition*. but now in real-valued vector, without any symbols. The same $\mathbf{y}(t)$ can also be used to predict the binary (or real-valued) $\mathbf{x}(t+1) \in X$ in Eq. (4). The quality of prediction of $(\mathbf{z}(t+1), \mathbf{x}(t+1))$ depends on how state Z abstracts the external world sensed by X. The more mature the DN is in its "lifetime" learning, the better its predictions.

The brain or DN takes input from vector $(\mathbf{z}, \mathbf{x})$, not just sensory $\mathbf{x}$ but also motor $\mathbf{z}$, to produce an internal response vector $\mathbf{y}$ which represents the best match of $(\mathbf{z}, \mathbf{x})$ with one of many internally stored patterns of $(\mathbf{z}, \mathbf{x})$:

The winner-take-all learning rule, which is highly nonlinear and simulates parallel lateral inhibition in the internal (hidden) area Y is sufficient to prove in [20] that a DN that has sufficient hidden neurons learns any Turing Machine perfectly, immediately, and error-free.

The n neurons in Y give a response vector $\mathbf{y} = (y_1, y_2, ...y_n)$ of n neurons in which only the best-matched neuron fires at value 1 and all other neurons do not fire giving value 0:

$$y_j = \begin{cases} 1 & \text{if } j = \underset{1 \leq i \leq n}{\operatorname{argmax}} \{f(\mathbf{t}_i, \mathbf{z}, \mathbf{b}_i, \mathbf{x})\} \\ 0 & \text{otherwise} \end{cases} \qquad j = 1, 2, ...n, \qquad (5)$$

where f is a function that measures the similarity between the top-down weight vector $\mathbf{t}_i$ and the top-down input vector $\mathbf{z}$ as well as the similarity between the bottom-up weight vector $\mathbf{b}_i$ and the bottom-up input vector $\mathbf{x}$. The value of similarity is the inner product of their length-normalized versions [20]. Corresponding to FA, both the top-down weight and the bottom-up weight must match well for f to give a high value as inner product.

Namely, unified numerical processing-and-prediction in DN amounts to any abstract concepts above. In symbolic representations, it is a human to handcraft every abstract concept as a symbol; but DN does not have a human in the "skull". it simply learns, processes, and generates vectors. In the eyes of a human outside the "skull", the DN gets smarter and smarter.

In DN-1, each of multiple Y sub-areas has a static set of neurons so that the competition within each sub-area is based on a top-k principle within each sub-area. Namely, inhibition among neurons within each area is implicitly modeled by top-k competition.

A DN-1 of internal form Eq. (3) does allow Y-to-Y connections, but each Y sub-area has a fixed number of neurons which compete based on a sub-area top-k competition within the sub-area. The external form of DN-1 in Eq. 4 has only one hidden area Y, but it is sufficient to learn any Turing Machines since a Turing Machine does not have any hidden representations (i.e., no hidden area Y).

See Weng [22] for more mathematical details about how DN-1 conducts APFGP and Weng [25] for a more detailed explanation of APFGP meant for cognitive scientists.

6.2   DN-2

Developmental Network 2 (DN-2) [30] is different from DN-1 primarily in the following sense.

In DN-2, there is no static assignment of neurons to any regions, so that regions in DN-2 automatically emerges, along their scales, cascade, and nesting. A direct advantage of DN-2 is that a human programmer is not in the loop of deciding the distribution of neurons within the hidden Y sub-area, relieving human from this highly complex and intractable task. However, the primary advantage of DN-2 is to enable DN-2 to fully automatically generate hidden neurons that represent a time span longer than a single time frame without going external area Z. In other words, a DN-2 can automatically learn to think without being externally supervised through its motor area Z what to think about.

The computational explanation of DN-2 is out of the scope of this paper since APFGP is sufficient to be explained by the external form of DN-1. The reader is referred to [29] for DN-2.

7   Motivation

Motivation is very rich. It has two major aspects (a) and (b) in the current DN model. All reinforcement-learning methods other than DN, as far as we know, are for symbolic methods (e.g., Q-learning [12,17]) and are in aspect (a) exclusively. DN uses concepts (e.g., important events) instead of the rigid time-discount in Q-learning to avoid the failure of far goals.

(a) Pain avoidance and pleasure seeking to speed up learning important events. Signals from pain (aversive) sensors release a special kind of neural transmitters (e.g., serotonin [1]) that diffuse into all neurons that suppress Z firing neurons but speed up the learning rates of the firing Y neurons. Signals from sweet (appetitive) sensors release a special kind of neural transmitters (e.g., dopamine [4]) that diffuse into all neurons that excite Z firing neurons but also speed up the learning rates of the firing Y neurons. Higher pains (e.g., loss of loved ones and jealousy) and higher pleasure (e.g., praises and respects) develop at later ages from lower pains and pleasures, respectively.

(b) Synaptic maintenance—grow and trim the spines of synapses [2,19]—to segment object/event and motivate curiosity. Each synapse incrementally estimates the average error β between the pre-synaptic signal and the synaptic conductance (weight), represented by a kind of neural transmitter (e.g., acetylcholine [33]). Each neuron estimates the average deviation $\bar{\beta}$ as the average across all its synapses. The ratio $\beta/\bar{\beta}$ is the novelty represented by a kind of neural transmitters (e.g., norepinephrine, [33]) at each synapse. The synaptogenic factor $f(\beta, \bar{\beta})$ at each synaptic spine and full synapse enables the spine to grow if the ratio is low (1.0 as default) and to shrink if the ratio is high (1.5 as default).

8   Optimal Properties Proven for DN

If a DN can learn quickly like other normal animals, we may have to call it retarded with only a limited consciousness compared to other animals of the same age. We do not want a DN to get stuck into a local minimum, as many nonlinear artificial systems have suffered.

Weng 2015 [20] has proved: (1) The control of a TM is a Finite Automaton (FA). Thus, the emergent FA can learn a emergent UTM for APFGP. (2) The DN is always optimal in the sense of maximum likelihood conditioned on the number of neurons and the learning experience. When there are neurons in the hidden brain to be initialized, the learning is further error-free. This implies that the DN has solved the century-old problem of local minima. The DN framework is mathematically rigorous, not hand-wavy. In particular, the theory of Universal Turing Machines has proved that a Universal Turing Machine of a finite-length tape can learn any tasks, provided that the tape length is sufficiently long, but finite [11]. Note, rules of any purpose are learned from the external physical environment. For more detail, read [20].

In summary, every DN is optimal in the sense of maximum likelihood, proven mathematically in [20]. Put intuitively, all DN are optimal, given the same learning environment, the same learning experience, and the same number of neurons in the "brain". There might be many possible network solutions some of which got stuck into local minima in their search for a good network. However, each DN is the most likely one, without got into local minima. This is because although a DN starts with random weights, all random weights result in the same network.

However, this does not mean that the learning environment is the best possible one or the number of neurons is best possible one for many lifetime tasks. Search for a better educational environment will be human challenge for their future children, both natural and artificial kinds.

9   Conscious Learning Examples

A formal training in Universal Turing Machines seems necessary in order to understand the above highly mathematical material here, such as Table 1 and Eq. (2). A self-teaching process of automata theories could be insufficient. The following presents examples for an analytical reader who has had a formal training in Universal Turing Machines.

Suppose each time frame in Table 1 represents 20 ms, namely the real time is sampled at $1000\,\text{ms}/20\,\text{ms} = 50\,\text{Hz}$. Thus, the frames in Table 1 and Eq. (2) run very fast in real time, as a real physical learner interacts with its physical environment via its sensors and effectors. Let us consider the following two assumptions.

Assumption 1 (Supervised). *At each time t, a teacher supervises $\mathbf{z}(t)$ of the learner so that $\mathbf{z}(t)$ predicts correct state/actions for a Universal Turing Machine, for all times $t = 0, 1, 2, \ldots.$*

This assumption is relatively easier to understand but not very practical since it is difficult for any teacher to always supervise correctly in real time at 50 Hz.

Assumption 2 (Unsupervised). *At each time t, the learner self-generates $\mathbf{z}(t)$ so that $\mathbf{z}(t)$ approximates state/actions for a Universal Turing Machine, for all times $t = 0, 1, 2, \ldots.$*

This assumption is more practical but, like a child, requires more practices, through trials and errors, to improve its approximation of states/actions. The motivational system plays an important rule, such as pain avoidance and pleasure seeking explained in Sect. 7. This is a process called *scaffolding* [32] where early-learned simple skills assist the learning of later more complex skills.

What is *scaffolding* and why is it powerful? In visual learning, the early learned skills of recognizing a person's face facilitates later learning of recognizing his body. In auditory learning, the early-learned skill of recognizing phonemes facilitates latter learning of words. In language learning, the early learned skills of recognizing words like "have" and "time" facilitates latter learning of phrases like "have time". The learning of simple skills like English during early life facilitates later learning of algebra and calculus in later school life. Such a learning process of algebra and calculus may be through classroom teaching during which sensory inputs (visual, auditory and language) about the skills for algebra and calculus are translated into skills of conducting vision-guided, audition-assisted, language-directed writing procedures of algebra and calculus. This leads to our definition of conscious learning.

Definition 2 (Conscious learning). *The conscious learning by a biological or artificial machine is that the learner is conscious throughout its lifetime learning—it bootstraps its consciousness, from defaultly conscious, to increasingly conscious, to maturely conscious.*

The term "defaultly conscious" is species specific. For lower animals, inborn behaviors that are reflexive can be called defaultly conscious.

As we can see from the above discussion, *scaffolding* not only facilitates learning skills from simple to complex, but is also essential for a machine to bootstrap its consciousness—being conscious during learning, so that it consciously applies early learned conscious skills to learning later more complex conscious skills.

In practice, a real learning system interacts with its environment, which contains different teachers at different ages. The mother, the father, schoolteachers, colleagues, and physical facts are all teachers. This process of interactions amounts to a lifelong process of *scaffolding*, making Assumptions 1 and 2 true at different times, for different sensory modalities, on different motor modalities.

Regardless what environment a learner has, the acquisition of skills, from simple to complex, throughout a lifetime requires that the skull-closed brain to be fully automatic inside the skull, off-limit to manual intervention by any human teacher based on the test set. In [23,24], Weng pointed out that (1) in symbolic AI, a programmer handcrafts a set of symbols and (2) in connectionist AI, many neural networks require handpicking features in the hidden areas. Weng argued that both (1) and (2) require the human programmer to know the test set and, therefore, amount to PSUTS.

Weng [20] has proven mathematically that an external form of DN-1 under Assumption 1 learns any Turing Machine (which includes all Universal Turing Machines) free of any error, as long as it has a sufficient but finite number of hidden neurons.

10   Early Conscious Learning Experiments

We have conducted early experiments that learned consciousness in vision, audition and language understanding, respectively. These experiments are early ones since we hope many more experiments will take place around the world empowered by the theory of consciousness here. We claim conscious vision, conscious audition, and conscious language understanding because this is the first work, as far as we know, that is for general-purpose vision, audition, and understanding of natural languages, respectively. It is important to note that according to the definition of consciousness by the Merriam-Webster On-line Dictionary (definition b above), the state or fact of being conscious of an external object, state, or fact is consciousness. In these early experiments, we did not intend to demonstrate other aspects of consciousness in Merriam-Webster.

In terms of novelty of the experimental work outlined here, there has been no work in the computer vision area that used general-purpose vision as an emergent Turing Machine. The same is true for audition and natural language processing areas. It is worth noting the subject of language acquisition includes, but is more than, the subject of language understanding. In contrast, if a traditional computer vision system that is handcrafted to detect human faces, to recognize a particular human face, or to classify a particular set of other patterns (e.g., finger prints), we hope that Merriam-Webster On-line Dictionary did not intend to treat such special-purpose system as conscious even in terms of definition b.

Collectively, these three experiments seem to be also the first time where the three sensing modalities use a single general-purpose learning engine in space-time. Hopefully, when such systems are mature enough in the future after extensive "living" and "learning" in the real physical world, such machines will have a rich degree of animal-like consciousness in the eyes of human observers.

It is worth noting that at this early stage, there are no other experimental systems about consciousness and therefore there are no other experimental general-purpose methods to compare the performance with.

What above comparing with special-purpose systems? DN and its predecessor Cresceptron are the only two artificial systems we are aware of that do not suffer from the controversy of PSUTS (Post Selection Using Test Sets) [23, 24]. In other words, if the PSUTS practice is banned, DN is the only system that is not only free of PSUTS but also gives the best performance by far [23, 24] for every given amount of computational resource and every given incremental lifetime learning experience.

Vision from a "Lifelong" Retina Sequence: How does a DN become visually conscious demonstrated by its motor behaviors? Let it learn by artificially "living" in the real world!

Figure 5 provides an overview of the extensiveness of the training, regular training, and blindfolded testing sessions. The inputs to the DN were from the same mobile phone that performs computation. They include the current image from the monocular camera, the current desirable direction from the Google Map API and the Google Directions API. If the teacher imposes the state in Z, this is treated as the supervised state. Otherwise, the DN outputs its predicted state from Z. The DN learned to attend critical visual information in the current image (e.g., scene type, road features, landmarks, and obstacles) depending on the context of desired direction and the context state. Each state from DN includes heading direction or stop, the location of the attention, and the type of object to be detected (which detects a landmark), and the scale of attention (global or local), all represented as binary patterns. None is a symbol.

Below, we discuss two more sensory modalities, audition and natural languages.

Audition from a "Lifelong" Cochlear Sequence: How does a DN become auditory conscious demonstrated by its motor behaviors? Let it learn by artificially "living" in the real world!

For the audition modality, each input image to X is the pattern that simulates the output from an array of hair cells in the cochlea. We model the cochlea in the following way. The cells in the base of the cochlea correspond to filters with a high pass band. The cells in the top correspond to filters with a low pass band. At the same height, cells have different phase shifts. Potentially, such a cochlear model could deal with music and other natural sound, more general than the popular Mel Frequency Cepstral Coefficients (MFCCs) that are mainly for human speech processing. The performance will be reported elsewhere due to the limited space.

Take /u:/ as an example shown in Fig. 6. The state of concept 2 keeps as silence when inputs are silence frames. It becomes a "free" state when phoneme frames are coming in, and changes to /u:/ state when first silence frame shows up at the end. At the same time, the states of concept 1 count temporally dense stages.

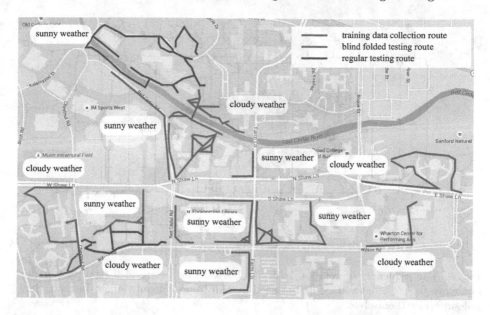

Fig. 5. Training, regular testing, and blind-folded testing sessions conducted on campus of Michigan State University (MSU), under different times of day and different natural lighting conditions (e.g., there are extensive shadows in images). Disjoint testing sessions were conducted along paths that the machine has not learned. This is the first time for visual awareness to be learned by GENISAMA Turing Machines.

Natural Languages from a "Lifelong" Word Sequence: How does a DN become language conscious demonstrated by its motor behaviors? Let it learn by artificially "living" in the real world! Here, we assume grounded words are emergent patterns, not symbols.

As far as we know, this seems to be the first work that deals with language acquisition in a bilingual environment, largely because the DN learns directly from emergent patterns, both in word input and in action input (supervision), instead of static symbols.

The input to X is a 12-bit binary pattern, each represents a word, which potentially can represent 2^{12} words using binary patterns. The system was taught 1,862 English and French sentences from [14], using 2,338 unique words (case sensitive). As an example of the sentences: English: "Christine used to wait for me every evening at the exit." French: "Christine m'attendait tours les soirs à la sortie."

The Z area was taught two concepts: language type (English, French, and language neutral, e.g., a number or name) represented by 3 neurons (top-1 firing), and the language-independent meanings as meaning states, as shown in Fig. 7. The latter is represented by 18 neurons (18-bit binary pattern), always top 5 neurons firing, capable of representing $C(18,5) = 8,568$ possible combinations as states, but only 6,638 actual meanings were recorded. Therefore, the Z area

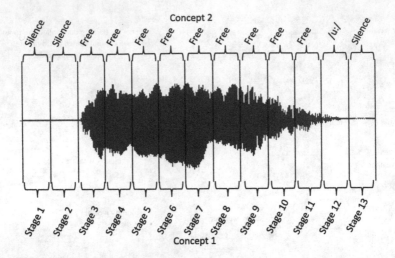

Fig. 6. The sequences of concept 1 (dense, bottom) and concept 2 (sparse, top) for phoneme /u:/. The latest DNs do not need human to provide any labels. Instead, they self-supervise themselves.

has $3 + 18 = 21$ neurons, potentially capable of representing a huge number 2^{21} binary patterns if all possible binary patterns are allowed.

However, the DN actually observed only $8,333$ Z patterns (both concepts combined) from the training experience, and $10,202$ distinct (Z, X) patterns—FA transitions. Consider a traditional symbolic FA using a symbolic transition table, which has $6,638 \times 3 = 19,914$ rows and $2,338$ columns. This amounts to $19,914 \times 2,338 = 46,558,932$ table entries.

But only $10,202/46,558,932 \approx 0.022\%$ of the entries were detected by the hidden neurons, representing that only 0.02% of the FA transition table was observed and accommodated by the DN. Namely, the DN has a potential to deal with n-tuples of words with a very large n but bounded by DN size, because most un-observed n-tuples are never represented. The FA transition table is extremely large, but never generated.

Without adding noise to the input X, the recognition error is zero, provided that there is a sufficient number of Y neurons. We added Gaussian noise into the bits of X. Let α represent the relative power of the signal in the noisy signal. When α is 60%, the state recognition rate of DN is around 98%. When α is 90%, the DN has reached 0% error rate, again thanks to the power of DN internal interpolation that converts a huge discrete (symbolic) problem into a considerably smaller continuous (numeric) problem.

Again, as the only difference from the above two modalities is the patterns in the X area and the Z area, the same DN learns the word inputs and the supervised states.

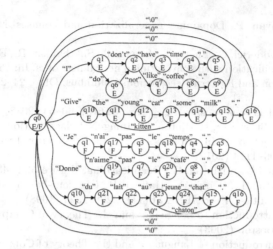

Fig. 7. The finite automaton for the English and French versions of some sentences. The DN learned a much larger finite automaton. Cross-language meanings of partial- and full-sentences are represented by the same state of meaning context q_i, $i = 0, 1, 2, ..., 24$. See, e.g., q_1, q_3, q_4, and q_5. But the language specific context is represented by another concept: language type. The last letter is the return character that indicates the end of a sentence.

11   Conclusions

We hope that the new APFGP characterization is now much clearer than existing other characterizations for notoriously vague term "consciousness" as we discussed in the first section. Hopefully, it would give rise to animal-like artificial consciousness so future AI receive a long-overdue credulity. It might be also useful as a computational model for unifying natural consciousness and artificial consciousness, due to its holistic nature backed by the new capability APFGP of GENISAMA Universal Turing Machines. Much exciting practical work on learning consciousness remains to be done in the future.

Acknowledgements. The author likes to thank Zejia Zheng, Xiang Wu and Juan Castro-Garcia for conducting the experiments, vision, audition, and natural language acquisition, respectively, outlined here with more details reported in [31].

References

1. Daw, N.D., Kakade, S., Dayan, P.: Opponent interactions between serotonin and dopamine. Neural Netw. **15**(4–6), 603–616 (2002)
2. Guo, Q., Wu, X., Weng, J.: Cross-domain and within-domain synaptic maintenance for autonomous development of visual areas. In: Proceedings of the Fifth Joint IEEE International Conference on Development and Learning and on Epigenetic Robotics, Providence, RI, 13–16 August 2015, pp. +1–6 (2015)
3. Hopcroft, J.E., Motwani, R., Ullman, J.D.: Introduction to Automata Theory, Languages, and Computation. Addison-Wesley, Boston (2006)

4. Kakade, S., Dayan, P.: Dopamine: generalization and bonuses. Neural Netw. **15**, 549–559 (2002)
5. Karpathy, A., Toderici, G., Shetty, S., Leung, T., Sukthankar, R., Fei-Fei, L.: Large-scale video classification with convolutional neural networks. In: Proceedings of the Computer Vision and Pattern Recognition, Columbus, Ohio, 24–27 June 2014, pp. +1–8 (2014)
6. Koch, C.: What is consciousness? Sci. Am. **318**(6), 60–64 (2018)
7. Krizhevsky, A., Sutskever, I., Hinton, G.: ImageNet classification with deep convolutional neural networks. In: Advances in Neural Information Processing Systems, vol. 25, pp. 1106–1114 (2012)
8. LeCun, Y., Bengio, L., Hinton, G.: Deep learning. Nature **521**, 436–444 (2015)
9. LeCun, Y., Bottou, L., Bengio, Y., Haffner, P.: Gradient-based learning applied to document recognition. Proc. IEEE **86**(11), 2278–2324 (1998)
10. Martin, J.C.: Introduction to Languages and the Theory of Computation, 3rd edn. McGraw Hill, Boston (2003)
11. Martin, J.C.: Introduction to Languages and the Theory of Computation, 4th edn. McGraw Hill, New York (2011)
12. Mnih, V., et al.: Human-level control through deep reinforcement learning. Nature **518**, 529–533 (2015)
13. Riesenhuber, M., Poggio, T.: Hierarchical models of object recognition in cortex. Nat. Neurosci. **2**(11), 1019–1025 (1999)
14. Scriven, R., Amiot-Cadey, G.: Collins: Collins French grammar. HarperCollins, Glasgow (2011)
15. Serre, T., Wolf, L., Bileschi, S., Riesenhuber, M., Poggio, T.: Robust object recognition with cortex-like mechanisms. IEEE Trans. Pattern Anal. Mach. Intell. **29**(3), 411–426 (2007)
16. Silver, A.: Deep blue's cheating move. Chess News, 19 February 2015. https://en.chessbase.com/post/deep-blue-s-cheating-move
17. Sutton, R.S., Barto, A.: Reinforcement Learning. MIT Press, Cambridge (1998)
18. Turing, A.M.: On computable numbers with an application to the Entscheidungsproblem. Proc. Lond. Math. Soc. **s2-42**, 230–265 (1936). A correction, ibid., **43**, 544–546
19. Wang, Y., Wu, X., Weng, J.: Synapse maintenance in the where-what network. In: Proceedings of the International Joint Conference on Neural Networks, San Jose, CA, 31 July–5 August 2011, pp. 2823–2829 (2011)
20. Weng, J.: Brain as an emergent finite automaton: a theory and three theorems. Int. J. Intell. Sci. **5**(2), 112–131 (2015)
21. Weng, J.: Consciousness for a social robot is not piecemeal. IEEE CIS Auton. Ment. Dev. Newslett. **12**(1), 10–11 (2015)
22. Weng, J.: Autonomous programming for general purposes: theory. Int. J. Huamnoid Robot. **17**(14), 1–36 (2020)
23. Weng, J.: Did Turing Awards go to fraud? YouTube Video, 4 June 2020. 1:04 hours. https://youtu.be/Rz6CFlKrx2k
24. Weng, J.: Life is science (36): Did Turing Awards go to fraud? Facebook blog, 8 March 2020. www.facebook.com/juyang.weng/posts/10158319020739783
25. Weng, J.: A unified hierarchy for AI and natural intelligence through auto-programming for general purposes. J. Cogn. Sci. **21**, 53–102 (2020)
26. Weng, J., Ahuja, N., Huang, T.S.: Cresceptron: a self-organizing neural network which grows adaptively. In: Proceedings of the International Joint Conference on Neural Networks, Baltimore, Maryland, vol. 1, pp. 576–581, June 1992

27. Weng, J., Ahuja, N., Huang, T.S.: Learning recognition and segmentation using the cresceptron. Int. J. Comput. Vis. **25**(2), 109–143 (1997). https://doi.org/10.1023/A:1007967800668
28. Weng, J., et al.: Autonomous mental development by robots and animals. Science **291**(5504), 599–600 (2001)
29. Weng, J., Zheng, Z., Wu, X.: Developmental network two, its optimality, and emergent turing machines. U.S. Provisional Patent Application Serial Number: 62/624,898, 1 February 2018
30. Weng, J., Zheng, Z., Wu, X., Zhu, S.: Developmental network 2 (DN-2) and auto-programming operating systems (AOS). Patent document in preparation to be submitted to USPTO (2017). The data and in-house performance are being used in the AIML Contest 2017
31. Weng, J., Zheng, Z., Wu, X., Castro-Garcia, J.: Auto-programming for general purposes: theory and experiments. In: Proceedings of the International Joint Conference on Neural Networks, Glasgow, UK, 19–24 July 2020, pp. 1–8 (2020)
32. Woodin, M.A., Ganguly, K., Poo, M.M.: Coincident pre- and postsynaptic activity modifies GABAergic synapses by postsynaptic changes in CL-transporter activity. Neuron **39**, 807–820 (2003)
33. Yu, A.J., Dayan, P.: Uncertainty, neuromodulation, and attention. Neuron **46**, 681–692 (2005)

Incorporating Task-Related Information in Dimensionality Reduction of Neural Population Using Autoencoders

Qi Lian[1,2], Yunzhu Liu[3,4], Yu Zhao[1,2], and Yu Qi[2,5,6(✉)]

[1] Qiushi Academy for Advanced Studies, Zhejiang University, Hangzhou, China
[2] College of Computer Science and Technology, Zhejiang University, Hangzhou, China
qiyu@zju.edu.cn
[3] Information Technology Research Center, China Electronics Standardization Institute, Beijing, China
[4] China National Information Technology Standardization Technical Committee Secretariat, Beijing, China
[5] Frontiers Science Center for Brain and Brain-Machine Integration, Zhejiang University, Hangzhou, China
[6] Zhejiang Lab, Hangzhou, China

Abstract. Dimensionality reduction plays an important role in neural signal analysis. Most dimensionality reduction methods can effectively describe the majority of the variance of the data, such as principal component analysis (PCA) and locally linear embedding (LLE). However, they may not be able to capture useful information given a specific task, since these approaches are unsupervised. This study proposes an autoencoder-based approach that incorporates task-related information as strong guidance to the dimensionality reduction process, such that the low dimensional representations can better reflect information directly related to the task. Experimental results show that the proposed method is capable of finding task-related features of the neural population effectively.

Keywords: Neural population activity · Supervised dimensionality reduction · Long short-term memory network · Autoencoder

1 Introduction

In recent years, neural activities recorded from the primate cortex by implanted arrays of microelectrodes have gradually become a common tool for neural mechanism analysis [18,39]. Based on the extracted neural signals, several brain-machine interface (BMI) applications have been successfully applied. For example, algorithms that convert neural activity of a human with tetraplegia into the desired prosthetic actuator movements [14,15]. However, it remains a question about what insights can we gain from the recordings of a population of neurons

© Springer Nature Singapore Pte Ltd. 2021
Y. Wang (Ed.): HBAI 2020, CCIS 1369, pp. 56–71, 2021.
https://doi.org/10.1007/978-981-16-1288-6_4

[32,33]. It is reported that population analyses are necessary for situations in which the neural mechanisms involve coordination of responses across neurons, where some mechanisms exist only at the level of the population and not at the level of single neurons [8]. Many studies of neural systems are shifting from single-neuron to population-level analyses.

The dimensionality reduction methods are traditionally defined as methods that map the high-dimensional data to low-dimensional data, which discover and extract features of interest into the shared latent variables [41]. Nowadays, dimensionality reduction plays an important role in the shifting process of neural signal analysis [8,10,31]. On the one hand, the recorded neural signal of a channel corresponds to an underlying neuron ensemble, the response of a particular neuron may obscure the information of other neurons within the ensemble. On the other hand, activities of nearby neurons tend to be dependent on each other, and they may be recorded by nearby channels [29]. Therefore, fewer channels are needed for the explanation of the recorded neural signals, and it is a common practice to select channels before subsequent analysis. Rather than inspecting each neuron separately, dimensionality reduction methods can analyze neural population recordings as a whole [8].

Several classical dimensionality reduction methods including linear and non-linear dimensionality reduction methods have been adopted to analyze neural signals. Principle component analysis (PCA) [19] is a linear dimensionality reduction method that projects the high-dimensional neural data into a new coordinate system, where the input data can be expressed with fewer variables and most of the variance of the data set can be captured. Non-linear dimensionality reduction methods have also been applied, such as the locally linear embedding method (LLE) [36] and Isomap [40]. LLE exploits local symmetries of linear reconstructions of the original dataset, it learns manifolds close to the dataset and project input data onto them. Isomap first determines the adjacency of the points on the manifold, and then the geodesic distances between all pairs of points are calculated on the manifold. Finally, the multidimensional scaling method is applied to obtain the embedding of data. The dimensionality reduction methods were employed using the population response signals alone in most existing studies [1,7,9,38]. In a real-world scenario, each data point in the high-dimensional firing rate space has a corresponding label comprised of one or more dependent variables, such as the subject's behavior, the subject's mental state, and so on. Neglecting the task-related information may cause the dimensionality reduction methods to fail to capture representative information of a specific task [24,30]. However, classical dimensionality reduction methods are unsupervised methods without effective ways to incorporate supervised task-related information.

Recent advances in deep artificial neural networks provide new techniques for nonlinear dimensionality reduction. The nonlinearity in neural networks enables non-linear multivariate data compression and visualization [5,13]. The autoencoder (AE) is firstly introduced in the 1980s, which plays an important role in unsupervised learning [37]. It is a simple yet effective unsupervised method to compress information of the input data. By reconstructing outputs from inputs using the criterion of the minimum possible amount of Euclidean distance, it learns a transformation that transforms inputs into a latent representation space [5]. Improvements of autoencoder including the denoising autoencoder (DAE) [42] and the variational autoencoder (VAE) [21] enhance the ability to learn effective representations from data. DAE aims to reconstruct clean data from noisy inputs. It can learn representations that are robust to the noise by adding Gaussian noises to samples or masking variables of samples randomly. The stacked denoising autoencoder explores a greedy strategy for building deep neural networks consist of several layers of denoising autoencoder [43]. The stacked layers are trained sequentially and a fine-tuning process is adopted to calibrate the whole neural network. VAE is proposed to learn better feature representation which can generate samples from the decoder. Instead of learning the encodings directly, it uses a variational Bayesian approach to optimize an approximation to the intractable posterior, which produces more stable and robust results. The strong feature extraction ability of the AEs can be employed for the dimensionality reduction of the neural population signals.

With the introduction of the task-related information, the objective of dimensionality reduction for the neural population can now be defined as to project the data while differences in the dependent variables are preserved as many as possible. In the extreme, we can seek to 'demix' the effects of the different dependent variables, such that each latent variable captures the characteristic of a single dependent variable [8]. The AEs are powerful non-linear unsupervised models that can learn effective low-dimensional representation for neural population signals. They are also flexible models that can easily incorporate supervised task-related information into the learning process. Further, given that the neural population activities are time-series data that are recorded sequentially. We can learn even better low-dimensional representation by treating it as another type of task-related information, which is incorporated through the architecture design of our model. Specifically, the long short-term memory (LSTM) model [16] which is a type of recurrent neural network (RNN) [27] is adopted to incorporate the information.

In this paper, we investigate supervised dimensionality reduction techniques for the neural population. The learned low-dimensional representation can better capture features of interest directly related to the task. The contributions of this paper are two-fold. Firstly, we propose a supervised dimensionality reduction architecture which is suitable for different kinds of autoencoders. The architecture incorporates task-related information into the learning process of low-dimensional representation through an artificial neural network module, which is termed as 'regressor'. The autoencoder takes multi-channel neural recordings from the primary motor cortex as input and reconstructs them. In the meantime, the regressor predicts the task-related information from the learned low-dimensional latent representations. Secondly, we propose a supervised architecture that considers the time-series nature of neural population activities. A sequential encoder and a sequential decoder based on LSTM are employed to transform the input data into the latent space and reconstruct the input data from the latent space, respectively. The task-related information is also employed through a regressor in this architecture. Experiments are carried out with different kinds of autoencoders under different settings. The results show that our proposed method learns a more effective task-related low-dimensional representation of the neural population.

2   Method

In this section, we first introduce the dataset we used in this paper. Then we give the background knowledge of various autoencoders and the LSTM. Finally, we introduce our proposed supervised autoencoder-based dimensionality reduction method for the neural population.

2.1   Dataset

A dataset that contains multi-channel spike firing signals with synchronous kinematic information is adopted to evaluate the performances of the supervised and unsupervised dimensionality reduction methods [44]. The dataset is recorded from a male macaque monkey that performs a radial-4 center-out task in a 2-D horizontal plane. For each trial, a target ball appears on the screen in front of the monkey, and the monkey is requested to move a cursor to the target with the joystick. Once the monkey hits the target ball within 2 s and holds for 300 ms, rewards will be given. The neural signal is recorded by a 96-microelectrode Utah array which is implanted in the monkey's arm area of the primary motor cortex contralateral to the arm used in the experiments. A total of 96 channels of neural signals are recorded with Cerebus multichannel system at a sample rate of 30 kHz. The raw signals are filtered by a high-pass Butterworth filter and the detected spikes are sorted with Offline Sorter software to produce binned spike rates. The trajectory of the joystick is recorded synchronously with neural signals by a micro-controller system at a sample rate of 1 kHz. We downsample the trajectory to correspond to the bins of spike rates. A channel selection method and a data selection method are further employed such that 8 subsets of spike data are obtained. The details of the dataset are shown in Table 1.

2.2   Prerequisites

Autoencoder and Its Variations. Consider a data set of samples $\{\mathbf{x}_n\}$ where $n = 1, \cdots, N$, and $\mathbf{x}_n$ is a Euclidean variable with dimensionality D. A fully connected layer of the neural network can be defined as

$$y = \phi(Wx + b), \tag{1}$$

where W and b denote trainable weights and bias, and ϕ denotes a non-linearity function. A basic autoencoder consists of an encoder and a decoder. The encoder

Table 1. The details of the dataset.

Subset	#Neuron	#Trials	#Up	#Down	#Left	#Right
1	61	74	17	19	17	21
2	63	81	19	21	18	23
3	61	70	17	14	19	20
4	56	64	20	11	19	14
5	49	83	25	19	22	17
6	56	75	21	14	21	19
7	61	85	17	23	20	25
8	61	79	14	23	17	25

The #Neuron denotes the number of neurons and the #Trials denotes the number of total trials. The #Up, #Down, #Left, #Right denote the number of trials with up, down, left, and right directions, respectively.

is comprised of several fully connected layers and the layers are usually stacked one by one with reducing dimensionality. We can denote the encoded latent feature as $\mathbf{z}$, which is a Euclidean variable with dimensionality M. Then the encoder $E(\mathbf{x})$ can be defined as

$$E(\mathbf{x}) = \mathbf{z} = \phi_L(W^L \phi_{L-1}(W^{L-1}\phi_{L-1}(\cdots W^1 \phi_1(\mathbf{x}) + b^1 \cdots) + b^{L-1}) + b^L), \quad (2)$$

where L denotes the number of stacked fully connected layers. Similarly, the decoder $D(\mathbf{z})$ can be defined as

$$D(\mathbf{z}) = \tilde{\mathbf{x}} = \phi_L(W^L \phi_{L-1}(W^{L-1}\phi_{L-1}(\cdots W^1 \phi_1(\mathbf{z}) + b^1 \cdots) + b^{L-1}) + b^L), \quad (3)$$

where $\tilde{\mathbf{x}}$ denotes the reconstruction of $\mathbf{x}$. The loss function of the autoencoder is usually defined as the mean squared error between the input $\mathbf{x}$ and the reconstruction $\tilde{\mathbf{x}}$, which can be defined as

$$\mathcal{L}_{reconstruction} = \frac{1}{N}\sum_{i=1}^{N}(\mathbf{x}_n - \tilde{\mathbf{x}}_n)^2, \quad (4)$$

where $\mathbf{x}_n$ and $\tilde{\mathbf{x}}_n$ denote the nth sample and its reconstruction, respectively. In [5], the stacked fully connected layers of the encoder and decoder are trained layer-wise using a greedy strategy. However, as the proposed of more advanced techniques such as the Relu non-linearity function [28], the second-order optimizer Adam [20], and the batch normalization layer [17], the layer-wise training strategy is no longer needed. In this paper, we directly optimize the entire neural network for all autoencoder-based models.

The denoising autoencoder is proposed to make the learned representations robust to partial corruption of the input pattern [43]. It first corrupts the initial input $\mathbf{x}$ to get a partially destroyed version $\hat{\mathbf{x}}$ through a stochastic mapping.

The stochastic mapping process is usually defined as a randomly masking process, where a fixed number of features are chosen at random and their values are forced to 0. Another common corruption choice is to add Gaussian noise to each feature separately. In this paper, the stochastic mapping process that randomly masks features is selected as the default corruption choice.

The variational autoencoder introduces a stochastic variational inference that can deal with intractable posterior distributions [21]. Let us define the probabilistic encoder as $q_\varphi(\mathbf{z}|\mathbf{x})$ and the posterior of the generative model as $p_\theta(\mathbf{x}, \mathbf{z})$. The prior over the latent variables can be defined to be a centered isotropic multivariate Gaussian $p_\theta(\mathbf{z}) = \mathcal{N}(\mathbf{z}; \mathbf{0}, \mathbf{I})$. We can then define $p_\theta(\mathbf{x}|\mathbf{z})$ to be a multivariate Gaussian whose distribution parameters are estimated from $\mathbf{z}$ with an artificial neural network with multiple fully connected layers. Assume that the true posterior follows an approximate Gaussian with diagonal covariance, which is defined as

$$log q_\varphi(\mathbf{z}|\mathbf{x}^i) = log\mathcal{N}(\mathbf{z}; \boldsymbol{\mu}^i, \boldsymbol{\sigma}^{2(i)}\mathbf{I}), \tag{5}$$

where the mean and standard deviation are outputs of the encoding artificial neural network. Using the reparameterization trick, the estimator for the model and data point $\mathbf{x}^i$ is defined as

$$\mathcal{L}(\boldsymbol{\theta}, \boldsymbol{\varphi}; \mathbf{x}^i) \simeq \frac{1}{2}\sum_{j=1}^{J}(1+log((\sigma_j^{(i)})^2)-(\mu_j^{(i)})^2-(\sigma_j^{(i)})^2)+\frac{1}{L}\sum_{l=1}^{L}log p_\theta(\mathbf{x}^i|\mathbf{z}^{i,l}), \tag{6}$$

where $\mathbf{z}^{i,l} = \boldsymbol{\mu}^i + \boldsymbol{\sigma}^i \odot \epsilon^l$ and $\epsilon^l \sim \mathcal{N}(0, \mathbf{I})$, and $\odot$ denotes element-wise product. The entire network can then be optimized with a standard back-propagation method [23].

Long Short-Term Memory. The LSTM is an improvement of vanilla RNN that aims to mitigate the gradient vanishing problem [6]. The input sequence is denoted as $\mathbf{x} = (x_1, \cdots, x_T)$, the hidden vector sequence is denoted as $\mathbf{h} = (h_1, \cdots, h_T)$, and the output vector sequence is denoted as $\mathbf{y} = (y_1, \cdots, y_T)$. The update rule of the hidden vector sequence of the vanilla RNN can be defined as

$$h_t = \tanh(W_{xh}x_t + W_{hh}h_{t-1} + b_h), \tag{7}$$

where tanh denotes the hyperbolic tangent function, W_{xh} and W_{hh} are learnable weights and b_h is learnable bias. The output at timestamp t can be defined as

$$y_t = W_{hy}h_t + b_y, \tag{8}$$

where W_{hy} is the learnable weights and b_y is the learnable bias.

The LSTM architecture used in this paper is defined as

$$
\begin{aligned}
i_t &= \tanh(W_{xi}x_t + W_{hi}h_{t-1} + b_i), \\
j_t &= \text{sigm}(W_{xj}x_t + W_{hj}h_{t-1} + b_j), \\
f_t &= \text{sigm}(W_{xf}x_t + W_{hf}h_{t-1} + b_f), \\
o_t &= \tanh(W_{xo}x_t + W_{ho}h_{t-1} + b_o), \\
c_t &= c_{t-1} \odot f_t + i_t \odot j_t, \\
h_t &= \tanh(c_t) \odot o_t,
\end{aligned}
\tag{9}
$$

where sigm denotes the sigmoid function, the W_* variables are learnable weights and the b_* variables are learnable biases.

2.3 Supervised Autoencoders-Based Dimensionality Reduction for Neural Population

The architecture of our proposed supervised autoencoders for neural signal dimensionality reduction is shown in Fig. 1. Binned and smoothed neural firings are served as raw inputs. The supervised autoencoder module is divided into three parts including the encoder, the latent representation, and the decoder. The encoder first transforms the raw inputs into their latent representations through the encoder. Two separate forks stem from the latent representation. The first one is the unsupervised decoder which reconstructs the inputs from the latent representations. The second one is a supervised regressor which incorporates the task-specific information (kinematic information). The supervised regressor is implemented as an artificial neural network that takes the latent representation as input and predicts corresponding task-related information. The artificial neural network can be built by stacking several fully connected layers. The distance between the predicted movements and the kinematic information is measured by the mean squared error function.

The architecture of our proposed supervised autoencoder based on LSTM that considers the time sequence characteristic of the neural population is shown in Fig. 2. In Fig. 1, the encoder and the decoder are built as artificial neural networks that consist of fully connected layers. Now the encoder and the decoder are built as multi-layer LSTM networks. At each timestamp, the LSTM encoder takes current spikes and the previous hidden state as input and generates current hidden state and output. The output is considered as the latent representation, and two forks stem from the latent representation including the unsupervised LSTM decoder and the supervised regressor. The unsupervised LSTM decoder takes the latent representation as input and reconstructs the input spikes. The supervised regressor is the same as the one shown in Fig. 1, which takes the latent representation as input and predicts task-related information. Note that, we reconstruct the input spikes and predict task-related information at each timestamp.

The loss of our proposed model consists of two parts including the unsupervised reconstruction loss and the supervised regression loss. The unsupervised

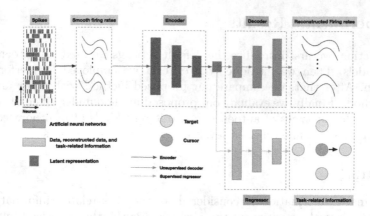

Fig. 1. The architecture of our supervised Autoencoders for dimensionality reduction. Binned and smoothed neural firings are served as raw inputs. The supervised autoencoder module can be divided into three parts including the encoder, the latent representations, and the decoder. The supervised encoder first transforms the raw inputs into their latent representations. Then two separate forks stem from the latent representation including the unsupervised decoder and the supervised regressor.

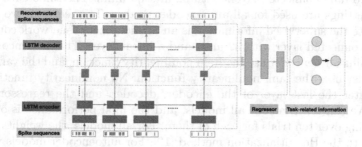

Fig. 2. The architecture of our proposed supervised autoencoder based on LSTM. This model considers the time sequence characteristic of the neural population. At each timestamp, the LSTM encoder takes current spikes and the previous hidden state as input and generates current hidden state and output. The LSTM decoder reconstructs the input spikes and the regressor predicts the task-relation information.

reconstruction loss computes the mean square error between the input spikes and the reconstructed spikes, which is denoted as $\mathcal{L}_{reconstruction}$. The supervised regression loss computes the mean square error between the predicted task-related information and the ground truth recorded simultaneously with the spikes, which can be denoted as $\mathcal{L}_{regression}$. We have also added an L2-regularization to the network to prevent overfitting, and its loss can be denoted as $\mathcal{L}_{regularization}$. Thus, the overall loss of our model can be defined as

$$\mathcal{L} = \mathcal{L}_{reconstruction} + \lambda_1 * \mathcal{L}_{regression} + \lambda_2 * \mathcal{L}_{regularization}, \qquad (10)$$

where λ_1 and λ_2 are coefficients that trade off different losses. The entire network can be optimized using the standard back-propagation method.

3 Experimental Results

In this section, we first introduce the default settings we used for autoencoder-based models. Then we introduce the criteria we employed for performance evaluation. After that, we compare our proposed method with other unsupervised methods. Finally, we evaluate our proposed method under different settings including different types of autoencoders, different kinds of incorporated task-related information, and different levels of added noises to inputs.

3.1 Settings

The kinematic information is considered as the task-related information by default, which is the position of the joystick. Firstly, the recorded neural signals and kinematic information are smoothed with a window size set to 5. Then we standardize and scale the smoothed spikes to the range $[0, 1]$. The parameters λ_1 and λ_2 are set to 1 and $1e-4$, respectively. The encoder we used in this paper is an artificial neural network consists of two fully connected layers with 64 and 32 units. The decoder we used in this paper is an artificial neural network consists of two fully connected layers with 32 and 64 units. The same encoder and decoder settings are used for all autoencoder models. The regressor we used to incorporate the supervised information is an artificial neural network consists of one fully connected layer with 32 units and a linear layer. The autoencoder and the denoising autoencoder use the Relu nonlinearity function, and the variational autoencoder uses the tanh nonlinearity function. No nonlinearity functions are applied after the last layer of the encoder, decoder, and the regressor for all models. We run ten trials for all models, and the final performance is obtained by averaging over ten trials for each of them. For all models, the weights are initialized with the He initialization method [12]. For autoencoder models without LSTM, the batch size is set to 64, the learning rate is set to $1e-3$, and we run 200 epochs for each trial. The Adam optimizer is adopted for optimization.

For the autoencoder model based on LSTM, we mean-center the recorded neural signals and the kinematic information. The batch size is set to the number of trials of the subset, which means we optimize the network using the whole data of a subset at each step. We train the whole network for 5000 steps. The LSTM encoder is a two-layer LSTM network with 64 and 32 units. The LSTM decoder is a two-layer LSTM network with 32 and 64 units. The regressor is an artificial neural network consists of one fully connected layer with 32 units and a linear layer. The learning rate is set to $5e-3$, and we decay the learning rate with a ratio set to 0.95 for every 500 steps. The Rmsprop is adopted for optimization [4]. The layer normalization is applied in our LSTM encoder and LSTM decoder [3]. Hereafter, the supervised versions of AE, DAE, and VAE are denoted as SAE, SDAE, and SVAE. Without loss of generality and to avoid introducing assumptions upon the dataset, the supervised autoencoder based on LSTM uses vanilla AE as building blocks and we denote it as LSTM-SAE.

3.2   Criterion

Two criteria are employed for performance comparison. The first one is the intra-class distance, the inter-class distance, and their ratio. The intra-class distance is defined as

$$d(\Omega_i)^2 = \frac{1}{N_i N_i} \sum_{k=1}^{N_i} \sum_{l=1}^{N_i} \|\mathbf{x}_k^i - \mathbf{x}_l^i\|_2^2, \tag{11}$$

where Ω_i denotes the ith class, $\mathbf{x}_k^i$ denotes the kth samples of the ith class, and N_i denotes the number of samples of the ith class. The inter-class distance is defined as

$$d(\Omega_i, \Omega_j) = \frac{1}{N_i N_j} \sum_{k=1}^{N_i} \sum_{l=1}^{N_j} \|\mathbf{x}_k^i - \mathbf{x}_l^j\|_2^2, \tag{12}$$

and the ratio is defined as

$$\mathcal{R} = \frac{1}{2(C-1)} \frac{\sum d(\Omega_i, \Omega_j)}{\sum d(\Omega_i)^2}, \tag{13}$$

where C denotes the number of classes. The second criterion is the silhouette score [34], which is a measure of how similar an object is to its own cluster compared to other clusters. Its value ranges from -1 to 1, where a high value indicates that the object is well matched to its own cluster and poorly matched to neighboring clusters.

Table 2. Performance comparison with existing methods.

Method	$d(\Omega_i)^2$	$d(\Omega_i, \Omega_j)$	$\mathcal{R}$	Silhouette score
PCA	4.1199	8.8835	0.3700	0.1362
LLE	2.5551	8.5650	0.7292	0.3231
Isomap	3.2198	11.0912	0.6513	0.3129
LDA	3.2950	11.3075	0.5748	0.3799
NCA	3.2897	10.5672	0.5380	0.3879
KDA	**1.4771**	9.3935	**1.0720**	0.5128
AE	3.6004 ± 0.1268	9.5917 ± 0.2535	0.4626 ± 0.0149	0.2323 ± 0.0122
DAE	3.5703 ± 0.0757	8.8452 ± 0.1283	0.4277 ± 0.0104	0.1964 ± 0.0142
VAE	3.9912 ± 0.0528	9.0624 ± 0.0989	0.3873 ± 0.0088	0.1492 ± 0.0089
SAE	2.5356 ± 0.1340	11.3700 ± 0.3324	0.7983 ± 0.0683	0.5197 ± 0.0403
SDAE	2.5473 ± 0.0872	9.9521 ± 0.3430	0.6767 ± 0.0286	0.4653 ± 0.0218
SVAE	2.7154 ± 0.0558	11.6781 ± 0.1991	0.7281 ± 0.0049	0.5486 ± 0.0047
LSTM-SAE	2.3423 ± 0.1148	$\mathbf{13.7175 \pm 0.3547}$	1.0279 ± 0.0313	$\mathbf{0.6458 \pm 0.0115}$

AE, DAE, and VAE denote autoencoder, denoising autoencoder, and variational autoencoder, respectively. SAE, SDAE, SVAE denote supervised autoencoder, supervised denoising autoencoder, and supervised variational autoencoder, respectively. LSTM-SAE denotes the supervised autoencoder based on LSTM.

3.3 Comparison with Existing Methods

Several classical unsupervised and supervised methods are employed for comparison with our proposed supervised autoencoder methods. The unsupervised methods include PCA [19], LLE [36], and Isomap [40]. The number of neighbors is setting to 5 for LLE and Isomap. The supervised methods include LDA [26], NCA [35], and KDA [11]. The employed KDA uses the 'RBF' kernel and the corresponding parameter gamma is setting to 5. Note that, the discrete direction information is adopted as the task-related information for the classical supervised methods. The targeted dimensionality reduction methods for neuronal population data including dPCA [22], TDR [25] mTDR [2] are not considered in this paper because of the limited number of experimental task variables of the adopted dataset. We have also included the unsupervised autoencoder and its variations for comparison. The corruption ratios of the DAE and SDAE are set to 0.1. The dimensionality of the latent representation is set to 2. The learned features are scaled to the range [0, 1] before we compute the distances, ratio, and silhouette of the trials.

The results are shown in Table 2. As we can see, our proposed LSTM-SAE obtains the best performance of the inter-class distance and the Silhouette score. The KDA obtains the best performance of the intra-class distance and the best ratio. Our LSTM-SAE obtains an intra-class distance of 2.3423 and an inter-class distance of 13.7175, which leads to a ratio of 1.0279 that is comparable to the best ratio of 1.0720 obtained by KDA. Our LSTM-SAE also obtains the best Silhouette score of 0.6458. The better intra-class distance and ratio obtained by KDA is mainly due to the fact that KDA only considers the direction information and neglects the trace information. The consequences are two-fold, on the one hand, KDA can maps samples into a more compact region of the low-dimensional space, which results in better intra-class distance and ratio. On the other hand, KDA may fail to separate points from different directions in the low-dimensional space, given limited direction information and powerful kernel. The statement is confirmed by the visualization we will discuss later. KDA obtains the best performance among the baseline methods and outperforms unsupervised autoencoders. The supervised autoencoders (SAE, SDAE, and SVAE) obtain comparable performances with KDA. The supervised autoencoders beat their corresponding unsupervised versions by big margins. The results show that the incorporation of supervised information is crucial for the learning of discriminative low-dimensional representations.

The visualizations of the learned representations of different methods are shown in Fig. 3. The eighth subset of the dataset is selected for visualization. We use different colors for different classes, which represent different directions. The red lines plot trials with direction 'up', the green lines plot trials with direction 'down', the blue lines plot trials with direction 'left', and the yellow lines plot trials with direction 'right'. The numbers of trials with different directions are shown in Table 1, each trial is visualized as a single line. As we can see in Fig. 3, compares with other existing methods, KDA obtains better latent representations with better cohesion within each class and separation between classes.

Autoencoders without supervised information including AE, DAE, and VAE fail to learn discriminative latent representations. However, autoencoders that take advantage of supervised information including SAE, SDAE, and SVAE learn better latent representations, as we can see from the improved performances in Table 2 and the discriminative latent representations in Fig. 3. As shown by our proposed LSTM-SAE, considering the time-series nature of the neural population and incorporating it into the architecture design can further improve the performance. As we have mentioned earlier, KDA maps samples into a more compact region with disordered lines of different directions, and some directions can be indistinguishable.

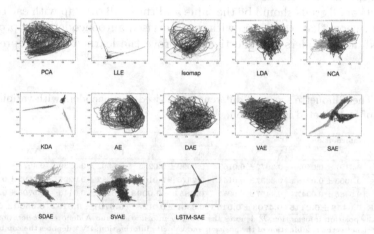

Fig. 3. The visualizations of the latent representations of different methods. We visualize classical unsupervised methods including PCA, LLE, and Isomap, and supervised methods including LDA, NCA, and KDA. Unsupervised autoencoders including AE, DAE, and VAE are also visualized. Our proposed methods including SAE, SDAE, SVAE, and LSTM-SAE are visualized in the second and the third row. The red lines plot trials with direction 'up', the green lines plot trials with direction 'down', the blue lines plot trials with direction 'left', and the yellow lines plot trials with direction 'right'. (Color figure online)

3.4 Model Evaluation Under Different Settings

In this section, we evaluate our proposed supervised autoencoder-based methods under different settings. Firstly, we evaluate our proposed methods with different types of autoencoders. Then we evaluate our proposed methods with different kinds of task-related information. After that, we evaluate the performances with different levels of noise adding to the inputs.

We first evaluate the performances of our proposed methods with different types of autoencoders. The results are shown in Table 2, and their corresponding visualizations are shown in Fig. 3. Compared with AE, SAE improves the ratio from 0.4626 to 0.7983 and the silhouette score from 0.2323 to 0.5197. Compared with DAE, SDAE improves the ratio from 0.4277 to 0.6767 and the silhouette score from 0.1964 to 0.4653. Compared with VAE, SVAE improves the ratio from 0.3873 to 0.7281 and the silhouette score from 0.1492 to 0.5486. As shown in Fig. 3, unsupervised autoencoders fail to learn discriminative latent representations of different directions. On the opposite, our proposed supervised autoencoders successfully learn discriminative latent representations for most of the trials. LSTM-SAE learns near-optimal latent representations, given that the start points of all trials should be the same and thus will overlap with each other. The results show that, compared with unsupervised autoencoders, our proposed supervised autoencoders can effectively improve the learned latent representations.

Table 3. The Silhouette scores of different supervised autoencoders with various combinations of task-related information.

Method	Information				
	P	V	A	PV	PVA
SAE	0.5197 ± 0.0403	0.3972 ± 0.0163	0.3090 ± 0.0233	0.5302 ± 0.0239	0.4675 ± 0.0195
SDAE	0.4653 ± 0.0218	0.3237 ± 0.0151	0.2576 ± 0.0165	0.4082 ± 0.0227	0.3695 ± 0.0194
SVAE	0.5486 ± 0.0047	0.4457 ± 0.0055	$\mathbf{0.3851 \pm 0.0098}$	0.6125 ± 0.0116	0.5795 ± 0.0089
LSTM-SAE	$\mathbf{0.6458 \pm 0.0115}$	$\mathbf{0.4703 \pm 0.0165}$	0.3361 ± 0.0127	$\mathbf{0.6701 \pm 0.0192}$	$\mathbf{0.6500 \pm 0.0059}$

P denotes the position information, V denotes the velocity information, and A denotes acceleration information. PV denotes the combination of the position and velocity information. PVA denotes the combination of the position, velocity, and acceleration information.

Next, we evaluate the performances of our proposed methods with different kinds of task-related information. Three kinds of task-related information are considered in this paper including the position, velocity, and acceleration. Five sets of experiments are carried out with different combinations of them. The Silhouette scores are shown in Table 3. As we can see, the most informative task-related information is the position, since all supervised models obtain their best performance given solely the position information. Comparison with position information available solely, the addition of velocity information on the basis of position information improves the performances of SAE, SVAE and LSTM-SAE, and hurts the performance of SDAE. Comparison with position information available solely, the addition of velocity and acceleration information hurts the performances of SAE and SDAE, but slightly improves the performance of SVAE and LSTM-SAE. As the results showed, LSTM-SAE obtains best performances in most cases, and SVAE utilizes the additional information most effectively.

Table 4. The Silhouette scores of different supervised autoencoders with various noise levels.

Method	Noise level				
	0.00	0.05	0.1	0.15	0.2
SAE	0.5197 ± 0.0403	0.4691 ± 0.0178	0.3939 ± 0.0230	0.3378 ± 0.0245	0.3039 ± 0.0156
SDAE	0.5176 ± 0.0234	0.5102 ± 0.0292	0.4663 ± 0.0187	0.4265 ± 0.0198	0.3933 ± 0.0240
SVAE	0.5486 ± 0.0047	0.4759 ± 0.0072	0.4032 ± 0.0080	0.3394 ± 0.0053	0.2836 ± 0.0052
LSTM-SAE	**0.6458 ± 0.0115**	**0.6358 ± 0.0207**	**0.6374 ± 0.0206**	**0.6158 ± 0.0181**	**0.5748 ± 0.0135**

Finally, we evaluate the performances of our proposed supervised autoencoders with different levels of added noises. The noises we added to the samples are identical to the corruption process we applied for the denoising autoencoder. Different corruption ratios are considered including 0.05, 0.1, 0.15 and 0.2. The noises are added in the testing stage after training completed. The performances are shown in Table 4. As we can see, as the level of noise increases, the performances of all models decrease. Compared with SAE and SVAE, SDAE is more robust to noise, which is a reasonable result because the training process of DAE has already considered robustness to noises. It is a surprise that our proposed LSTM-SAE also represents robustness to noises. We conjecture that the robustness may come from the time-series nature of the neural population, which implies that LSTM-SAE has successfully learned the dynamical time structure of the neural population.

4 Conclusions

In this paper, we address the problem of information loss using unsupervised dimensionality reduction methods on neural population signals. We design a supervised architecture base on autoencoder which incorporates task-related information as strong guidance to the dimensionality reduction process, thus the low dimensional representations can better capture information that is directly related to the task. We also consider the time-series nature of the neural population and incorporate it using an LSTM based autoencoder. Our experimental results show that the proposed architecture captures information related to the task effectively.

Acknowledgments. This work was partly supported by the grants from National Key R&D Program of China (2018YFA0701400), National Natural Science Foundation of China (No. 61673340), Zhejiang Provincial Natural Science Foundation of China (LZ17F030001), Fundamental Research Funds for the Central Universities (2020FZZX001-05), and the Zhejiang Lab (2019KE0AD01).

References

1. Afshar, A., Santhanam, G., Byron, M.Y., Ryu, S.I., Sahani, M., Shenoy, K.V.: Single-trial neural correlates of arm movement preparation. Neuron **71**(3), 555–564 (2011)

2. Aoi, M., Pillow, J.W.: Model-based targeted dimensionality reduction for neuronal population data. In: Advances in Neural Information Processing Systems, pp. 6690–6699 (2018)
3. Ba, J.L., Kiros, J.R., Hinton, G.E.: Layer normalization. arXiv preprint arXiv:1607.06450 (2016)
4. Bengio, Y., CA, M.: RMSProp and equilibrated adaptive learning rates for non-convex optimization. Corr abs/1502.04390 (2015)
5. Bengio, Y., Lamblin, P., Popovici, D., Larochelle, H.: Greedy layer-wise training of deep networks. In: Advances in Neural Information Processing Systems, pp. 153–160 (2007)
6. Bengio, Y., Simard, P., Frasconi, P.: Learning long-term dependencies with gradient descent is difficult. IEEE Trans. Neural Netw. **5**(2), 157–166 (1994)
7. Briggman, K.L., Abarbanel, H.D., Kristan, W.B.: Optical imaging of neuronal populations during decision-making. Science **307**(5711), 896–901 (2005)
8. Cunningham, J.P., Byron, M.Y.: Dimensionality reduction for large-scale neural recordings. Nature Neurosci. **17**(11), 1500–1509 (2014)
9. Durstewitz, D., Vittoz, N.M., Floresco, S.B., Seamans, J.K.: Abrupt transitions between prefrontal neural ensemble states accompany behavioral transitions during rule learning. Neuron **66**(3), 438–448 (2010)
10. Gibson, S., Judy, J.W., Markovic, D.: Technology-aware algorithm design for neural spike detection, feature extraction, and dimensionality reduction. IEEE Trans. Neural Syst. Rehabil. Eng. **18**(5), 469–478 (2010)
11. Hand, D.J.: Kernel Discriminant Analysis, p. 264. Wiley, New York (1982)
12. He, K., Zhang, X., Ren, S., Sun, J.: Deep residual learning for image recognition. In: Proceedings of the IEEE Conference on Computer Vision and Pattern Recognition, pp. 770–778 (2016)
13. Hinton, G.E., Salakhutdinov, R.R.: Reducing the dimensionality of data with neural networks. Science **313**(5786), 504–507 (2006)
14. Hochberg, L.R., et al.: Reach and grasp by people with tetraplegia using a neurally controlled robotic arm. Nature **485**(7398), 372–375 (2012)
15. Hochberg, L.R., et al.: Neuronal ensemble control of prosthetic devices by a human with tetraplegia. Nature **442**(7099), 164–171 (2006)
16. Hochreiter, S., Schmidhuber, J.: Long short-term memory. Neural Comput. **9**(8), 1735–1780 (1997)
17. Ioffe, S., Szegedy, C.: Batch normalization: accelerating deep network training by reducing internal covariate shift. arXiv preprint arXiv:1502.03167 (2015)
18. Jackson, A., Mavoori, J., Fetz, E.E.: Long-term motor cortex plasticity induced by an electronic neural implant. Nature **444**(7115), 56–60 (2006)
19. Jolliffe, I.T., Cadima, J.: Principal component analysis: a review and recent developments. Philos. Trans. R. Soc. A Math. Phys. Eng. Sci. **374**(2065), 20150202 (2016)
20. Kingma, D.P., Ba, J.: Adam: a method for stochastic optimization. arXiv preprint arXiv:1412.6980 (2014)
21. Kingma, D.P., Welling, M.: Auto-encoding variational bayes. arXiv preprint arXiv:1312.6114 (2013)
22. Kobak, D., et al.: Demixed principal component analysis of neural population data. Elife **5**, e10989 (2016)
23. LeCun, Y., et al.: Handwritten digit recognition with a back-propagation network. In: Advances in Neural Information Processing Systems, pp. 396–404 (1990)
24. Lian, Q., Qi, Y., Pan, G., Wang, Y.: Learning graph in graph convolutional neural networks for robust seizure prediction. J. Neural Eng. **17**, 035004 (2020)

25. Mante, V., Sussillo, D., Shenoy, K.V., Newsome, W.T.: Context-dependent computation by recurrent dynamics in prefrontal cortex. Nature **503**(7474), 78–84 (2013)
26. McLachlan, G.J.: Discriminant Analysis and Statistical Pattern Recognition, vol. 544. Wiley, New York (2004)
27. Mikolov, T., Karafiát, M., Burget, L., Černocky, J., Khudanpur, S.: Recurrent neural network based language model. In: Eleventh Annual Conference of the International Speech Communication Association, pp. 1045–1048 (2010)
28. Nair, V., Hinton, G.E.: Rectified linear units improve restricted Boltzmann machines. In: ICML (2010)
29. Nordhausen, C.T., Maynard, E.M., Normann, R.A.: Single unit recording capabilities of a 100 microelectrode array. Brain Res. **726**(1–2), 129–140 (1996)
30. Pan, G., et al.: Rapid decoding of hand gestures in electrocorticography using recurrent neural networks. Front. Neurosci. **12**, 555 (2018)
31. Pang, R., Lansdell, B.J., Fairhall, A.L.: Dimensionality reduction in neuroscience. Current Biol. **26**(14), R656–R660 (2016)
32. Panzeri, S., Macke, J.H., Gross, J., Kayser, C.: Neural population coding: combining insights from microscopic and mass signals. Trends Cogn. Sci. **19**(3), 162–172 (2015)
33. Qi, Y., Liu, B., Wang, Y., Pan, G.: Dynamic ensemble modeling approach to nonstationary neural decoding in brain-computer interfaces. In: Advances in Neural Information Processing Systems, pp. 6089–6098 (2019)
34. Rousseeuw, P.J.: Silhouettes: a graphical aid to the interpretation and validation of cluster analysis. J. Comput. Appl. Math. **20**, 53–65 (1987)
35. Roweis, S., Hinton, G., Salakhutdinov, R.: Neighbourhood component analysis. Adv. Neural Inf. Process. Syst. (NIPS) **17**, 513–520 (2004)
36. Roweis, S.T., Saul, L.K.: Nonlinear dimensionality reduction by locally linear embedding. Science **290**(5500), 2323–2326 (2000)
37. Rumelhart, D.E., Hinton, G.E., Williams, R.J.: Learning internal representations by error propagation. California Univ., San Diego, La Jolla, Inst. for Cognitive Science, Technical report (1985)
38. Seidemann, E., Meilijson, I., Abeles, M., Bergman, H., Vaadia, E.: Simultaneously recorded single units in the frontal cortex go through sequences of discrete and stable states in monkeys performing a delayed localization task. J. Neurosci. **16**(2), 752–768 (1996)
39. Suner, S., Fellows, M.R., Vargas-Irwin, C., Nakata, G.K., Donoghue, J.P.: Reliability of signals from a chronically implanted, silicon-based electrode array in non-human primate primary motor cortex. IEEE Trans. Neural Syst. Rehabil. Eng. **13**(4), 524–541 (2005)
40. Tenenbaum, J.B., De Silva, V., Langford, J.C.: A global geometric framework for nonlinear dimensionality reduction. Science **290**(5500), 2319–2323 (2000)
41. Van Der Maaten, L., Postma, E., Van den Herik, J.: Dimensionality reduction: a comparative. J. Mach. Learn. Res. **10**(66–71), 13 (2009)
42. Vincent, P., Larochelle, H., Bengio, Y., Manzagol, P.A.: Extracting and composing robust features with denoising autoencoders. In: Proceedings of the 25th International Conference on Machine Learning, pp. 1096–1103 (2008)
43. Vincent, P., Larochelle, H., Lajoie, I., Bengio, Y., Manzagol, P.A., Bottou, L.: Stacked denoising autoencoders: learning useful representations in a deep network with a local denoising criterion. J. Mach. Learn. Res. **11**(12), 3371–3408 (2010)
44. Zhou, L., et al.: Decoding motor cortical activities of monkey: a dataset. In: 2014 International Joint Conference on Neural Networks (IJCNN), pp. 3865–3870. IEEE (2014)

Effective and Efficient ROI-wise Visual Encoding Using an End-to-End CNN Regression Model and Selective Optimization

Kai Qiao, Chi Zhang, Jian Chen, Linyuan Wang, Li Tong, and Bin Yan[✉]

Henan Key Laboratory of Imaging and Intelligence Processing, PLA Strategy Support Force Information Engineering University, Zhengzhou 450001, China

Abstract. In neuroscience, visual encoding based on functional magnetic resonance imaging (fMRI) has been attracting much attention, especially with the recent development of deep learning. Visual encoding model is aimed at predicting subjects' brain activity in response to presented image stimuli . Current visual encoding models firstly extract image features through a pre-trained convolutional neural network (CNN) model, and secondly learn to linearly map the extracted CNN features to each voxel. However, it is hard for the two-step manner of visual encoding model to guarantee the extracted features are linearly well-matched with fMRI voxels, which reduces final encoding performance. Analogizing the development of the computer vision domain, we introduced the end-to-end manner into the visual encoding domain. In this study, we designed an end-to-end convolution regression model (ETECRM) and selective optimization based on the region of interest (ROI)-wise manner to accomplish more effective and efficient visual encoding. The model can automatically learn to extract better-matched features for encoding performance based on the end-to-end manner. The model can directly encode an entire visual ROI containing enormous voxels for encoding efficiency based on the ROI-wise manner, where the selective optimization was used to avoid the interference of some ineffective voxels in the same ROI. Experimental results demonstrated that ETECRM obtained improved encoding performance and efficiency than previous two-step models. Comparative analysis implied that the end-to-end manner and large volume of fMRI data are potential for the visual encoding domain.

Keywords: Visual encoding · End-to-end manner · Convolutional neural network (CNN) · Selective optimization

1 Introduction

In the neuroscience domain, researchers have been exploring how visual perception from the external visual stimuli to neuron activity is formed in the human vision system. Functional magnetic resonance imaging (fMRI) can effectively reflect neuron activity, hence, visual encoding models [1, 2] that predict the corresponding fMRI voxels in response to external visual stimuli, have attracted much too attention in these years. Meanwhile,

© Springer Nature Singapore Pte Ltd. 2021
Y. Wang (Ed.): HBAI 2020, CCIS 1369, pp. 72–86, 2021.
https://doi.org/10.1007/978-981-16-1288-6_5

other modalities such as EEG, functional near-infrared spectroscopy (fNIRS), and so on, also were employed to model the visual perception [3–5]. In this study, we mainly focus on visual encoding models based on fMRI because of the high spatial resolution.

In the human vision system, the mapping from external visual stimuli to neuron activity is usually deemed highly nonlinear. To simulate the nonlinear mapping, linearizing encoding manner [2] is used widely. The linearizing encoding manner is mainly composed of one nonlinear mapping from image stimuli to image features, and one linear mapping from image features to voxels of visual areas. Some simple linear regression models with regularization are commonly used to realize the linear mapping, hence, how to construct an effective nonlinear mapping, namely feature transformation [6] is important for a linearizing encoding model.

In the computer vision domain, how to construct a better nonlinear feature transformation is also the most critical part whether for image classification or object detection or other tasks [7, 8]. Therefore, visual encoding and computer vision domains can share a lot in terms of feature transformation. Hence, visual encoding models are designed mainly based on existing feature transformation in the computer vision domain. In the early period of the computer vision domain, many methods mainly depended on the hand-crafted feature transformation [9], such as Gabor wavelet pyramid (GWP), histogram of oriented gradient (HOG), local binary patterns (LBP), scale-invariant feature transform (SIFT) and so on. Kay et al. employed GWP features to construct the famous encoding model [10], and obtained major improvement for encoding primary visual cortices. For high-level visual cortices, visual encoding models are usually based on hand-marked image labels [11], because high-level semantic features are hard to design manually. Since the big breakthrough [12] made by deep network and big data [13], deep networks with hierarchical feature transformation have driven the enormous advance in the computer vision domain [14, 15]. In contrast, deep networks can automatically learn or mine more effective features from big data towards a specific task, especially for those tasks that require high-level semantic features. Shortly afterwards, the hierarchical and powerful feature transformation was introduced into the visual encoding domain [16], obtaining better encoding performance and deeper understanding of the human vision system once again [17–20]. Recently, some new network architectures were used to construct visual encoding models, such as ResNet [21], recurrent neural network [22], variational autoencoder [23], and Capsule Network [24].

From the above review, the two domains have been crossing and learning from each other. Researchers have been pursuing a kind of nonlinear feature transformation well-matched with the human vision system. Therefore, choosing effective features is important and directly influences subsequent encoding performance. At present, some hand-crafted and learned features have been validated and accepted, for example, Gabor features are similar to the visual representation of primary visual cortices, and hierarchical pre-trained convolutional neural network (CNN) architecture better accords with hierarchical visual representation in the human vision system. Although these methods have obtained fine results, there is still far from accurately predicting human neuron activity [20, 25], which suggests that these features still are limitedly matched with neuron activity, hence, the performance of visual encoding is unsatisfactory. Besides, our previous work [26] proposed a visual encoding method based on transfer learning and the improvement owing to the nonlinear regression mapping indicated the extracted features based on pre-trained deep models are not well matched with neuron activity.

However, it is hard to determine what kind of feature transformation is the best for visual encoding, because there is only little prior information about neuron activity at hand. The prior information usually confines that the primary and high-level visual cortices are responsible for low-level features (edges, corners, and so on) and semantic features (object shape, category, and so on), respectively. Hence, a very natural question emerges for visual encoding domain: *with the development from hand-crafted features to deep learning features, from the computer vision to visual encoding domain, what is the next breakthrough for visual encoding?*

In conclusion, current encoding paradigm can be defined as one two-step manner of encoding including firstly choosing well-matched feature transformation with fMRI voxels, and secondly encoding each voxel through linear regression models. Essentially, it is hard for this kind of two-step manner to find well-matched features for the sake of a good encoding performance, because it is hard to obtain the knowledge about encoded voxels before constructing the next step of linear mapping. In the computer vision domain, except the CNN architecture, the other deep learning elements including the end-to-end manner and big data also contribute to significantly improving the performance compared with the two-step manner of feature engineering method (e.g. combining hand-crafted features and classifiers for the classical image classification task). These elements together drive enormous advances in many computer vision tasks. The employed CNN feature extractor is learned from some kind of computer vision task instead of the visual encoding task. Hence, the extracted features are hard to be matched with beforehand unknown voxels of visual areas. That is to say, mismatching data and task [10, 27] make it inappropriate to directly transfer the fixed CNN feature extractor into the visual encoding domain. According to the above analysis, we think of replacing the two-step visual encoding manner with the end-to-end manner. In this way, the encoding model can automatically learn better-matched features and linear weights (linear regression mapping) from fMRI data for visual encoding.

Previous methods constructed visual encoding models using the voxel-wise manner [2]. In this way, an individual linear regression model needs to be trained for each voxel. Eventually, thousands of regression models are constructed for several visual regions of interest (ROIs) containing thousands of voxels. In order to improve the encoding efficiency, we assume that voxels from one visual ROI can be characterized by a kind of specific features and propose a new ROI-wise encoding model that encodes entire voxels in each visual ROI once.

However, not all voxels in one visual ROI can be effectively or easily encoded, which can be seen from encoding results of previous work. The phenomenon may be caused by two aspects of problems. On one hand, the employed features are not suitable for those voxels; on the other hand, those voxels with much low signal-noise ratio (SNR) rarely reflect the neuron activity of presented stimuli, thus cannot be effectively encoded. The first problem can be solved by learning better-matched features through the end-to-end manner. The second problem indicated that there exist ineffective voxels in each visual ROI and these voxels will influence the optimization of effective voxels during the ROI-wise and end-to-end encoding. That is to say, although the end-to-end method is a well-established method, direct employment of this method for visual encoding is difficult. Hence, the end-to-end encoding manner needs a kind of selective optimization, during which those effective voxels are focused and ineffective voxels are ignored. In this study, we propose a series of operations for the selective optimization to construct an encoding model in an end-to-end manner.

The contributions of this study are as follows: 1) we analysed current drawbacks of visual encoding in terms of the development of the computer vision and visual encoding domain; 2) we introduced the end-to-end manner to learn better-matched features, improving encoding performance of low-level visual cortices; and 3) we proposed a series of selective optimization operations to realize ROI-wise encoding in the end-to-end manner.

2 Materials and Methods

2.1 Experimental Data

The dataset used in this study was provided from the previous studies [10]. The dataset included visual image stimuli and corresponding voxels in V1, V2, V3, V4, and LO visual areas for two subjects. In total, the dataset is composed of 1750 training and 120 testing samples for each subject. In detail, each subject went through five sessions and each session included 5 training runs and 2 testing runs, respectively. In each training run, 70 different images were presented two times. In each testing run, 12 different images were presented 13 times. In total, 1750 (5 sessions × 5 runs × 70) images and 120 (5 sessions × 2 runs × 12) images were presented to each subject for the training and testing set. The detailed information could refer to the previous studies [10]. The dataset is open source and can be found in http://crcns.org/data-sets/vc/vim-1.

2.2 Method Overview

Generally, two computation models are required for the two-step manner of visual encoding. As shown in Fig. 1a, the first model is used to map input stimulus space to feature space (S2F model: feature transformation), and the second model is used to map feature space to voxel space (F2V model: regression). Usually, the parameters of S2F model are fixed and do not need to be retrained, and only linear weights of F2V regression model need to be trained. The famous GWP model based on Gabor features can be seen in Fig. 1b. The two-step manner of visual encoding models based on CNN features only replaces the Gabor features with CNN features, and similarly, the parameters of CNN models used to extract image features are fixed.

Convolutional neural networks (CNNs) with powerful feature representation have been widely used in the computer vision domain. In this study, we proposed a convolutional regression model and train it in the end-to-end manner (ETECRM) to improve the two-step manner of visual encoding. As shown in Fig. 1c, ETECRM also can be divided into two parts, and the front convolutional operations belong to S2F part and the last linear fully connected (FC) layer represents F2V part. Most importantly, ETECRM is trained in an end-to-end manner. The end-to-end learning manner is from the deep learning domain, during which all of the parameters are trained jointly. For visual encoding,

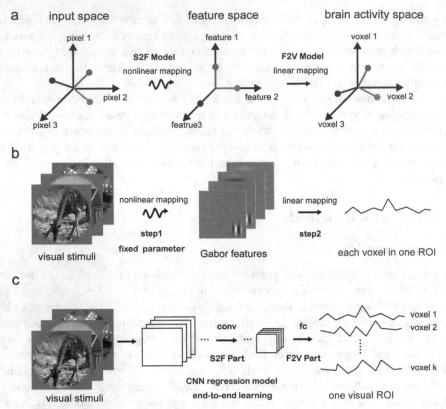

Fig. 1. The proposed method based on end-to-end learning and ROI-wise encoding. a. Three spaces and two mappings are included in the linearizing encoding manner. b. The two-step manner of visual encoding model including a nonlinear feature transformation with fixed parameters and a linear regression mapping with weights learning. c. The convolution regression model for ROI-wise encoding in an end-to-end learning manner.

it means that the proposed model can directly learn the mapping from stimulus space to voxel space (S2V model), that is to say, the parameters of S2F part and F2V part in the convolution regression model are learned together from fMRI data samples. In this way, the S2F part can approach better-matched feature transformation with training samples thus obtain better encoding performance.

Different from general linear regression models with regularization, F2V part or FC layer employed self-adapting regression weights to render voxels can pay more attention to those features well related to themselves. Besides, an ROI-wise encoding manner is used to replace the traditional voxel-wise encoding, which can be seen from Fig. 1c. About the loss, we employed the Pearson correlation (PC) instead of mean square error (MSE) between the observed and predicted voxel responses. To avoid the interference of those ineffective voxels during ROI-wise encoding, the weighted correlation loss and noise regularization are used to accomplish the selective optimization. In conclusion, ETECRM is trained in the end-to-end manner and map stimuli to entire voxels of visual

ROI once, which realize an effective and efficient visual encoding model. Next, we introduce the proposed model's details including loss function for the selective optimization, corresponding control models, and the evaluation.

2.3 CNN Feature Transformation and Self-adapting Regression

In ETECRM, the F2V part mainly composed of several convolutional layers is used to extract features of input images. Through the stack of convolution layers with stride 2 and Rectified Linear Unit (ReLU) activation function, defined feature transformation F_{w_c} in the Eq. (1) can transform one image stimulus s_i into the last layer of convolution features f_i. w_c represents the weights of all convolutional layers in the S2F part. Each layer of weights includes convolutional kernel parameters and corresponding intercepts. The dimensionality of convolutional kernel parameters is $c_1 \times c_2 \times s \times s$, where the kernel number c_1 is 128, the kernel size s is 3×3 or 5×5 (see Table 1) and previous features' channel c_2 is 128, except that the initial grey image has 1 colour channel. The dimensionality of intercepts is the same as the kernel number c_1. F_{w_c} represents schematically the mapping F with the parameters w_c extracting image features to be fed to the final linear regression layer. As shown in Eq. (2), predicted voxels v' in a specific visual ROI can be obtained based on a linear regression model. In this study, we assume that bigger weight values in the matrix w_{fc} indicate that corresponding features are more important than those features whose corresponding weight values are smaller. Hence, we replace w_{fc} with w_{fc}^2. The dimensionality of w_{fc} is $n_1 \times n_2$, where n_1 and n_2 represent the number of predicted voxels v' and the size of the last image features $c_1 \times s \times s$, respectively, where s changes with the number of convolutional layers d with stride 2 and is $128/2^d$. The corresponding intercept b has the same dimensionality as the number of voxels in a specific visual ROI. In this way, weight learning can dynamically adjust the learning rate of weights according to the current status, which contributes to selective optimization. Equation (3) gives the computation of gradient through the backpropagation with the chain rule, hence, the learning rate of weights becomes self-adapting μw_{fc} compared to previously fixed learning rate μ during optimization.

Table 1 Network configuration. The "conv" represents the convolutional layer with the kernels "3×3" or "5×5", and "fc" is the fully connected layer and used as the regression mapping from features to predicted voxels.

ROI	V1	V2	V3	V4	LO
S2F part	$3 \times$ conv (3×3)	$3 \times$ conv (3×3)	$3 \times$ conv (5×5)	$4 \times$ conv (5×5)	$4 \times$ conv (5×5)
F2V part	$1 \times$ fc	$1 \times$ fc	$1 \times$ fc	$1 \times$ fc	$1 \times$ fc

$$f_i = F_{w_c}(s_i) \tag{1}$$

$$v' = w_{fc}f_i + b \rightarrow v' = w_{fc}^2 f_i + b \tag{2}$$

$$\Delta w_{fc} = -\mu w_{fc} \Delta v' \tag{3}$$

2.4 Weighted Correlation Loss and Noise Regularization

In the linear regression mapping, the predicted v' and true v represent entire voxels in a specific ROI (V1, V2, V3, V4, or LO). Hence, to relieve the influence of those ineffective voxels during optimizing effective voxels in the ROI-wise encoding, we add gauss noise n_g with zero mean and one variance multiplying by the super-parameter φ on each of predicted voxels v' to restrain those ineffective voxels in the Eq. (4). The added noise can make those ineffective voxels harder to optimize from the perspective of SNR. The hyperparameter φ is used to control the rate of the added noise. To update weights of S2F and F2V parts of ETECRM in an end-to-end manner, we use PC values to measure the encoding performance, instead of MSE. Equation (5) presents the computation of correlation of K_{th} voxels in a specific visual ROI. Note that, in the experiment, v_k is a matrix whose dimensionality is $m \times n$, and n_g has the same dimensionality. n is the number of voxels in a specific ROI, and m is the batch size. Each predicted voxel k in one ROI has a PC value defined as cor_k.

$$v' = v' + \varphi \cdot n_g \tag{4}$$

$$cor_k = cor\left(v_k, v'_k\right) = \frac{Cov\left(v_k, v'_k\right)}{\sqrt{Var(v_k) \cdot Var\left(v'_k\right)}} \tag{5}$$

Instead of computing the mean value of PC values for all voxels in an entire ROI as the loss function, we think of introducing the weighted PC loss defined as L to further make the optimization pay attention to those effective voxels. However, whether the K_{th} voxel is important is unknown before optimization, hence the corresponding weight value η_k is hard to determine in Eq. (6). In this study, we employed the current iteration of cor_k to determine its weight. The cor_k is a value that ranges from -1 to 1, and the absolute value of cor_k indicates the importance of the k th voxels. In this way, we use the cor_k^2 as the weight in Eq. (7), which can realize dynamic adjustment during the optimization. If one voxel has a higher encoding correlation, its learning rate of optimized weights can be bigger, and vice versa. Besides, a kind of noise regularization is added to prevent the predicted voxels v' from becoming bigger to make the added gauss noise n_g ineffective. The super-parameter γ is used to balance the fidelity and regularization. Equation (8) gives the final loss function, and the super-parameter γ is used to adjust the proportion of the regular term and fidelity term. In the end-to-end learning, all parameters (w_c and w_{fc}) in ETECRM are updated at the same time. We solve the problem through gradient descent to minimize the loss function based on the open-source of deep learning framework PyTorch.

$$L = -\frac{\sum_k \eta_k cor_k}{n} + \gamma \left| \frac{\sum_k v'_k}{n} \right| \tag{6}$$

$$\eta_k = cor_k^2 \tag{7}$$

$$L = -\frac{\sum_k \eta_k cor_k}{n} + \gamma \left| \frac{\sum_k v'_k}{n} \right| = -\frac{\sum_k cor_k^3}{n} + \gamma \left| \frac{\sum_k v'_k}{n} \right| \tag{8}$$

2.5 Control Models and Evaluations of Encoding Performance

In the experiment, we selected two two-step manner of control encoding models to validate ETECRM. The two methods are the GWP-based model [10] (GWPM) and CNN features-based model (CNNM) [15], respectively. GWPM extracted Gabor wavelet features and CNNM uses the pre-trained AlexNet [9] to extract CNN features for input images. The two methods both use the sparse linear regression [28] to map the extracted features to voxel responses. For CNNM, we totally constructed 8 encoding models for each layer of AlexNet and choose the model with the best encoding performance as the control model.

To evaluate the encoding performance, we used the Pearson correlation (PC) value between the true and the predicted voxel responses for all 120 images in the testing set. Hence, we can obtain a PC value of GWPM, CNNM, and ETECRM for each voxel in all visual regions. In order to evaluate the encoding performance of each visual region for different methods, we Firstly made a scatter diagram of voxels for each visual ROI in Figs. 3a and 4a, and we presented the corresponding number of voxels when PC value's distance between the two methods locates at specific abscissa intervals in Figs. 3b and 4b. Secondly, for each visual ROI, the voxels are sorted in descending order according to the PC values to demonstrate the relationship between the PC value and the number of effective encoding voxels for GWPM, CNNM, and ETECRM. To evaluate the encoding efficiency, we presented the training time for different methods in the Experiment Details.

3 Result

3.1 Experiment Details

Table 1 presents the details of the network configuration and Table 2 presents the corresponding encoding performance for the two subjects. Since lower-level and higher-level visual ROIs have smaller and bigger receptive fields, respectively, the S2F part employs a smaller convolutional kernel (3×3) for V1 and V2, and bigger convolutional kernel (5×5) for V3, V4, and LO to extract image features. The F2V part includes one FC layer for linear regression. The hyperparameters φ and γ are given in Table 2. During the end-to-end training, we employ the PyTorch deep network framework, set batch size as 64, and use Adam optimization with learning rate 0.001 to update togetherly the parameters of the S2F and F2V parts through gradient descent. On the Ubuntu 16.04 system with one NVIDIA Titan Xp graphics card, about 20 epochs are required to obtain stable results, which lasts about 3 min for encoding one visual ROI. After training, the proposed method can achieve real-time predicting for one visual region, which is efficient. The two-step model additionally still needs about 40 min for one visual ROI using one layer of CNN features, excluding the feature extraction of all image stimuli. In this way, the ROI-wise manner has much higher efficiency than the two-step manner. After all, the proposed method can encode one visual ROI once, which makes the training and testing efficient. Hence, the following section focus on the comparison of encoding performance between the proposed method and control methods.

Table 2. Encoding performance. "Mean PC" represents the mean Person correlation of entire voxels in a specific visual ROI, and "Top-300 mean PC" represents the mean Person correlation of top 300 better-encoded voxels in a specific visual ROI.

Subject	–	V1	V2	V3	V4	LO
Subject 1	φ	1.0	1.0	1.0	1.0	1.0
	γ	1e−3	1e−3	1e−4	1e−5	1e−5
	Mean PC	0.257	0.189	0.110	0.085	0.046
	Top-300 mean PC	0.650	0.612	0.429	0.312	0.131
Subject 2	φ	0.1	0.1	0.1	0.1	0.1
	γ	1e−4	1e−4	1e−5	1e−5	1e−5
	Mean PC	0.162	0.129	0.067	0.043	0.029
	Top-300 mean PC	0.491	0.442	0.248	0.052	0.031

The mean PC value of entire voxels and selected voxels (Top-k, k = 300) in each visual ROI are given in Table 2. The detailed comparison with control models can be seen in the below subsection. Meanwhile, we can see that many voxels are not successfully encoded, in terms of the big difference between mean and Top-300 mean correlation, which validates the necessity of selective optimization in ROI-wise encoding.

3.2 Selective Optimization

A series of optimization strategies including self-adapting regression weights, weighted correlation loss, and noise regularization are used in ETECRM, to selectively optimize those effective voxels and suppress those ineffective voxels. Figure 3 presents the distribution of PC values of V1 (1294 voxels in total) on the training set and testing set, respectively. We can see that the sparse distribution of PC values, and voxels have higher or lower PC values. By restraining those ineffective voxels and paying more attention to those important voxels, the model can automatically learn effective features in an end-to-end manner and obtain better encoding performance. The sparse distribution validates the selective optimization of the proposed method during the ROI-wise encoding (Fig. 2).

3.3 Comparison with Two-Step Manner of Visual Encoding

Firstly, we make a comparison with GWPM in Fig. 3. It can be seen that ETECRM was extremely better than GWPM and about 90% of voxels for all ROIs can be better encoded by our model. It can be seen that ETECRM almost exceeds all voxels, especially in V4 and LO, and only a few voxels can be better explained by the GWPM. The results demonstrate a significant advantage of end-to-end learning than hand-crafted Gabor features.

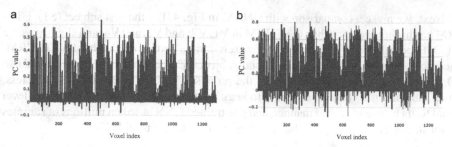

Fig. 2. The distribution of PC value of each voxel in V1 on a. the training set and b. the testing set during optimization, respectively.

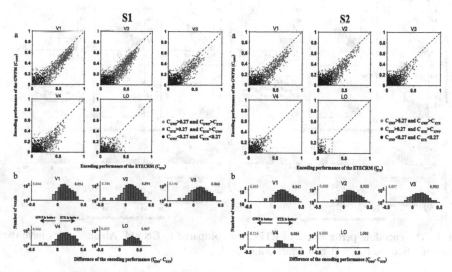

Fig. 3. The encoding performance of ETECRM compared to GWPM. a. Each subfigure presents a comparison of the two models in a specific visual ROI. In each subfigure, the ordinate and abscissa of each dot represent the PC values of GWPM and ETECRM respectively. The green dashed lines represent the threshold (0.27, p < 0.001) for significant PC value, hence, the black dots correspond to those voxels that cannot be effectively encoded (under 0.27) by either of GEPM and ETECRM. The red dots correspond to those voxels that can be better encoded by ETECRM than GWPM and vice versa for the cyan dots. b. Distribution of the encoding performance between ETECRM and GWPM. The ordinate and abscissa of each subfigure represent the number of voxels and the PC value's distance between the two methods, respectively. Those pillars compute the number of the voxels whose PC value's distance between the two methods locates at specific abscissa intervals. The red and cyan pillars indicate better encoding performance for ETECRM and GWPM, respectively. The number for each side represents the fraction of voxels whose encoding performance is higher than that of the other model. (Color figure online)

Next, we make a comparison with CNNM in Fig. 4. For the first subject (S1), ETE-CRM has higher accuracy than the CNNM in V1, V2, and V3, and V4, and slightly worse in LO. Especially for V1, about 80% of voxels can be better encoded by the ETECRM. The encoding performance on the second subject (S2) behaved similarly. From V1 to LO, we can see that the advantages of the proposed ETECRM become less and less, which indicates that it becomes harder to learn the feature representation of higher-level visual ROIs in an end-to-end manner, and pre-trained CNN based on millions of samples demonstrates the advantage in the encoding of high-level visual ROIs.

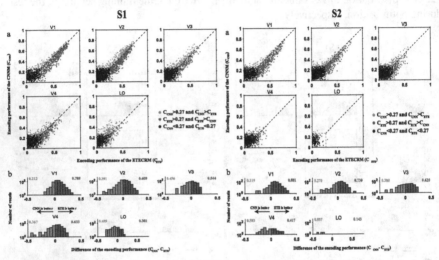

Fig. 4. The encoding performance of ETECRM compared to CNNM. All subfigures have the same definitions as Fig. 3. (Color figure online)

3.4 Model Comparison by Sorting Voxels in PC Values

Besides, we took out the voxels that were significantly predicted (PC > 0.27) [10] by GWPM, CNNM, and ETECRM, and sorted them in descending order according to the PC values in Fig. 5. For the first subject (S1), ETECRM (red line) and CNNM (blue line) showed better encoding performance than GWPM (cyan line). Hence, we mainly focus on the comparison with CNNM. For V1, V2, and V4, the red line is above the blue line, which indicated that the encoding performance of ETECRM is better. For V3, the red line roughly exceeds the blue line, and slightly better performance was obtained by ETECRM. For LO, ETECRM behaves worse than CNNM. The encoding performance on the second subject (S2) is similar. In conclusion, ETECRM performs better in V1, V2, and V3; slightly better in V4; worse in LO than CNNM, which behaves gradually descending advantage from low-level to high-level visual cortices. We speculate that relatively more data is required for encoding high-level visual ROIs that are responsible for high-level visual representation, and current fewer data suppresses the function of the end-to-end manner, hence, reduce the encoding performance.

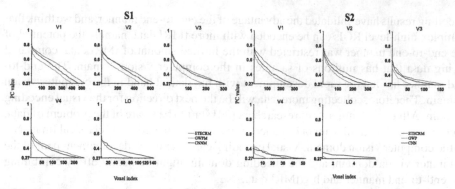

Fig. 5. Encoding performance of ETECRM compared to GWPM and CNNM. Effectively predicted voxels are sorted in descending order according to PC values. ETECRM, GWPM, and CNNM are represented by the red, cyan, and blue lines, respectively. (Color figure online)

4 Discussion

4.1 The Step-by-Step and End-to-End Methods

The step-by-step method is a common way to solve a complex problem by decomposing it into several simple sub-steps. In the traditional computer vision domain, it is also a widely adopted manner. For example, several steps such as preprocessing, feature extraction and selection, and classifier design are included to solve the image recognition task. The step-by-step method makes the sub-problems or sub-steps simple, controllable, and easier to solve, compared to the overall problem. However, its disadvantages are equally obvious: the optimal solutions of sub-problems do not necessarily mean the global optima of the initial problem. On the contrary, deep learning with a powerful nonlinear ability provides a useful tool to emphasize the end-to-end learning instead of artificially dividing steps or sub-problems, it is completely handed over to neural networks to directly learn the mapping from the original input and the expected output. Compared to the step-by-step strategy, the end-to-end learning manner is more likely to obtain a better overall solution, since the sub-parts can coordinate with each other. Current methods almost employ the end-to-end manner to solve the image recognition task. Similarly, the end-to-end manner also has advantages compared to the two-step manner of methods for the visual encoding problem. This study is the first to introduce the end-to-end manner to design the visual encoding model and obtain better encoding performance based on better-matched features with voxels.

4.2 How to Encode High-Level Visual ROIs

Regardless of the two-step manner of encoding or the end-to-end manner of encoding, the encoding performance of high-level visual ROIs such as LO is worse compared to the encoding of low-level visual ROIs. High-level visual ROIs are responsible for complex semantic visual representations, which are essentially hard to characterize. In this way, seeking well-matched features with those voxels from the computer vision domain seems hard to realize. Although the proposed method still seems helpless, the encoding results have validated the advantage of the end-to-end manner, and we think that complex high-level ROIs can be encoded with more fMRI data, namely the potential of the end-to-end manner was restricted with the limited amount of fMRI data, compared to big data that has millions of samples in the computer vision domain. The end-to-end manner has led the rapid development with big data at hand in the computer vision domain. Therefore, collecting more data will be the next direction for the visual encoding domain. Although a minority of researchers [23] start to be aware of the problem of data, their volume of data still cannot be called "big data", compared to the classical ImageNet in the computer vision domain. Visual encoding can refer to the development path of the computer vision domain, and the encoding domain might be taking off by combining the end-to-end manner and big fMRI data.

5   Conclusions

In this study, we proposed an ROI-wise visual encoding using an end-to-end CNN regression model. Through selective optimization, we obtained higher encoding performance than the two-step manner-based models in low-level visual areas. From the perspective of effectiveness, the proposed method showed the ability to automatically learn better-matched features with neuron activity from training data. From the perspective of efficiency, the proposed method accomplished the ROI-wise encoding with better performance. Overall, effective and efficient encoding is accomplished based on the proposed method. Besides, one referable way to develop computational neuroscience models from the perspective of computer vision was provided and further give rise to consideration of the potential of end-to-end manner and a large volume of fMRI data for future visual encoding.

References

1. Mitchell, T.M., Shinkareva, S.V., Carlson, A., Chang, K.-M., Malave, V.L., Mason, R.A., et al.: Predicting human brain activity associated with the meanings of nouns. Science **320**(5880), 1191–1195 (2008). https://doi.org/10.1126/science.1152876
2. Naselaris, T., Kay, K.N., Nishimoto, S., Gallant, J.L.: Encoding and decoding in fMRI. Neuroimage **56**(2), 400–410 (2011). https://doi.org/10.1016/j.neuroimage.2010.07.073
3. Liang, Z., Higashi, H., Oba, S., Ishii, S.: Brain dynamics encoding from visual input during free viewing of natural videos. In: International Joint Conference on Neural Networks, pp. 1–8. IEEE Press, Budapest, Hungary (2019)
4. Pinti, P., et al.: The present and future use of functional near-infrared spectroscopy (fNIRS) for cognitive neuroscience. Ann. N. Y. Acad. Sci. **1464**, 1–5 (2020). https://doi.org/10.1111/nyas.13948
5. Ramkumar, P., Hansen, B.C., Pannasch, S., Loschky, L.C.: Visual information representation and rapid-scene categorization are simultaneous across cortex: an MEG study. Neuroimage **134**, 295–304 (2016). https://doi.org/10.1016/j.neuroimage.2016.03.027
6. Bengio, Y., Courville, A., Vincent, P.: Representation learning: a review and new perspectives. IEEE Trans. Pattern Anal. Mach. Intell. **35**(8), 1798–1828 (2013). https://doi.org/10.1109/TPAMI.2013.50

7. Sermanet, P., Eigen, D., Zhang, X., Mathieu, M., Fergus, R., LeCun, Y.: Overfeat: integrated recognition, localization and detection using convolutional networks. arXiv preprint arXiv: 13126229 (2013)

8. He, K., Zhang, X., Ren, S., Sun, J.: Deep residual learning for image recognition. In: Proceedings of the IEEE Conference on Computer Vision and Pattern Recognition, pp. 770–778. IEEE Press, Las Vegas (2016)

9. Felzenszwalb, P., McAllester, D., Ramanan, D.: A discriminatively trained, multiscale, deformable part model. In: Computer Vision and Pattern Recognition, pp. 1–8. IEEE Press, Anchorage, Alaska (2008)

10. Kay, K.N., Naselaris, T., Prenger, R.J., Gallant, J.L.: Identifying natural images from human brain activity. Nature **452**(7185), 352 (2008)

11. Huth, A.G., Nishimoto, S., Vu, A.T., Gallant, J.L.: A continuous semantic space describes the representation of thousands of object and action categories across the human brain. Neuron **76**(6), 1210–1224 (2012)

12. Krizhevsky, A., Sutskever, I., Hinton, G.E.: ImageNet classification with deep convolutional neural networks. In: International Conference on Neural Information Processing Systems, p. 1097–105. NIPS Press, Lake Tahoe, Nevada (2012)

13. Russakovsky, O., Deng, J., Su, H., Krause, J., Satheesh, S., Ma, S., et al.: ImageNet large scale visual recognition challenge. Int. J. Comput. Vision **115**(3), 211–252 (2015). https://doi.org/10.1007/s11263-015-0816-y

14. LeCun, Y., Bengio, Y., Hinton, G.: Deep learning. Nature **521**(7553), 436 (2015). https://doi.org/10.1038/nature14539

15. Goodfellow, I., Bengio, Y., Courville, A., Bengio, Y.: Deep Learning. MIT Press, Cambridge (2016)

16. Agrawal, P., Stansbury, D., Malik, J., Gallant, J.L.: Pixels to voxels: modeling visual representation in the human brain. arXiv preprint arXiv:14075104 (2014)

17. Yamins, D.L., Hong, H., Cadieu, C.F., Solomon, E.A., Seibert, D., DiCarlo, J.J.: Performance-optimized hierarchical models predict neural responses in higher visual cortex. Proc. Natl. Acad. Sci. **111**(23), 8619–8624 (2014)

18. Güçlü, U., van Gerven, M.A.: Deep neural networks reveal a gradient in the complexity of neural representations across the ventral stream. J. Neurosci. **35**(27), 10005–10014 (2015)

19. Eickenberg, M., Gramfort, A., Varoquaux, G., Thirion, B.: Seeing it all: convolutional network layers map the function of the human visual system. Neuroimage **152**, 184–194 (2016). https://doi.org/10.1016/j.neuroimage.2016.10.001

20. Styves, G., Naselaris, T.: The feature-weighted receptive field: an interpretable encoding model for complex feature spaces. Neuroimage **180**, 188–202 (2018)

21. Wen, H., Shi, J., Chen, W., Liu, Z.: Deep residual network predicts cortical representation and organization of visual features for rapid categorization. Sci. Rep. **8**(1), 3752 (2018). https://doi.org/10.1038/s41598-018-22160-9

22. Shi, J., Wen, H., Zhang, Y., Han, K., Liu, Z.: Deep recurrent neural network reveals a hierarchy of process memory during dynamic natural vision. Hum. Brain Mapp. **39**(5), 2269–2282 (2018). https://doi.org/10.1002/hbm.24006

23. Han, K., Wen, H., Shi, J., Lu, K.-H., Zhang, Y., Liu, Z.: Variational autoencoder: an unsupervised model for modeling and decoding fMRI activity in visual cortex. bioRxiv 214247 (2017)

24. Qiao, K., Zhang, C., Wang, L., Chen, J., Zeng, L., Tong, L., et al.: Accurate reconstruction of image stimuli from human functional magnetic resonance imaging based on the decoding model with capsule network architecture. Front. Neuroinform. **12**, 62 (2018)

25. Horikawa, T., Kamitani, Y.: Generic decoding of seen and imagined objects using hierarchical visual features. Nat. Commun. **8**(1), 1–15 (2017). https://doi.org/10.1038/ncomms15037

26. Zhang, C., et al.: A visual encoding model based on deep neural networks and transfer learning for brain activity measured by functional magnetic resonance imaging. J. Neurosci. Methods **325**, 108318 (2019)
27. Chang, N., Pyles, J.A., Marcus, A., Gupta, A., Tarr, M.J., Aminoff, E.M.: BOLD5000, a public fMRI dataset while viewing 5000 visual images. Sci. Data **6**(1), 49 (2019)
28. Needell, D., Vershynin, R.: Signal recovery from incomplete and inaccurate measurements via regularized orthogonal matching pursuit. IEEE J. Sel. Top. Sign. Proces. **4**(2), 310–316 (2010)

Deep Insights into Graph Adversarial Learning: An Empirical Study Perspective

Jintang Li, Zishan Gu, Qibiao Peng, Kun Xu, Liang Chen[✉], and Zibin Zheng

Sun Yat-sen University, Guangzhou, China
{lijt55,guzsh,pengqb3,xukun6}@mail2.sysu.edu.cn,
{chenliang6,zhzibin}@mail.sysu.edu.cn

Abstract. Graph Neural Networks (GNNs) have shown to be vulnerable against adversarial examples in many works, which encourages researchers to drop substantial attention to its robustness and security. However, so far, the reasons for the success of adversarial attacks and the intrinsic vulnerability of GNNs still remain unclear. The work presented here outlines an empirical study to further investigate these observations and provide several insights. Experimental results, analyzed across a variety of benchmark GNNs on two datasets, indicate that GNNs are indeed sensitive to adversarial attacks due to its non-robust message functions. To exploit the adversarial patterns, we introduce two measurements to depict the randomness of node labels and features for a graph, noticing that the neighborhood entropy significantly increased under adversarial attacks. Furthermore, we find out that the adversarially manipulated graphs typically tend to be much denser and high-rank, where most of the dissimilar nodes are intentionally linked. And the stronger the attacks are, such as Metattack, the patterns are more apparent. To sum up, our findings shed light on understanding adversarial attacks on graph data and lead potential advancement in enhancing the robustness of GNNs.

Keywords: Graph adversarial attack · Network robustness · Graph neural networks · Node classification

1 Introduction

Graph structure data is a unique non-Euclidean data structure that is pervasive across different domains in machine learning , ranging from recommendation systems, social networks, knowledge graphs, and many other practical applications [5,6,18,26]. Graph Neural Networks (GNNs), as a class of models that combine deep learning models and methods for structured data, has gained a considerable amount of research attention due to the expressive power in modeling the relationships between nodes or edges in a graph. Naturally, at the meantime, a wide range of techniques on graph analysis have been developed in this field, which has made considerable progress over the last decade.

Despite the great success, recent studies have shown that the well-performed GNNs inevitably inherit the limitations of deep neural networks—they are found

© Springer Nature Singapore Pte Ltd. 2021
Y. Wang (Ed.): HBAI 2020, CCIS 1369, pp. 87–101, 2021.
https://doi.org/10.1007/978-981-16-1288-6_6

to be sensitive to the well-designed inputs, i.e., *adversarial examples*. On this basis, a broad range of techniques on attacking GNNs have been proposed towards this area, revealing the high vulnerability of GNN models [3,8,24,28,29]. Take the node classification task as an example, an attacker can easily enforce the model to make certain misclassification by small, often imperceptible perturbations (e.g., a few edge flips) to the input graph. By exploring the vulnerability of GNNs, Zügner et al. [28] first propose an efficient attack on graph data, which can perform perturbations on both graph structure and node features, while the perturbations are still constrained to ensure the attack's "unnoticeability". Xu et al. [24] present a novel gradient-based approach for attacking the GNNs from an optimization perspective, showing an impressive performance to fool GNNs. Most of the attackers reveal the strong ability on fooling GNNs, however, the adversarial patterns of attacks and the explanations to GNNs' vulnerability are less discussed.

In this work, we conduct comprehensive experiments to provide some insights to graph adversarial learning: We attempt to investigate the adversarial patterns of attacks and the reasons for the intrinsic vulnerability of GNNs. To achieve this, we employ a line of attack methodologies, including state-of-the-arts, and evaluate their performance with several GNNs (target models) on two benchmark datasets. From experimental results, we find that the adversarially manipulated graph is (i) much denser, (ii) high-rank, (iii) higher neighborhood entropy, and (iv) has more dissimilar nodes connected than the original graph statistically.

In conclusion, we make the following contributions whilst exploring this area:

- We analyze the reasons for the intrinsic vulnerability of GNNs, showing that the non-robust message functions would result in a high vulnerability.
- We provide a comparison for different attacks over a line of GNNs on node classification task to explore the adversarial patterns.
- We introduce several measurements to further capture these patterns and support our observations and claims.

2   Related Work

With the rise in the threat of security, researchers evidently have dropped a large amount of attention in studying graph adversarial attack [4,14,20]. As the first work in graph domain, Zügner et al. [28] propose Nettack based on a linear version of Graph Convolution Network (GCN) [15], which generates adversarial perturbations by searching the perturbation space sequentially. In a follow-up study, Zügner et al. [29] study the discreteness of graph data, and solve the bilevel problem of poisoning attacks using meta gradients. Wu et al. [22] introduce integrated gradients that could guide the attack of perturbing certain features or edges while still benefiting from the parallel computations. Additionally, several heuristic methods are also proposed to poison the GNNs [1,8,16], revealing the vulnerability of GNNs in different graph analysis tasks. However, the adversarial patterns of attacks are less explored and the reasons of the success of attacks still remain unclear.

In order to defend the aforementioned attacks, a line of techniques has been used as a practical countermeasure to improve the robustness of GNNs. Zhu et al. [27] derive a robust graph convolution model by learning the hidden representation as a Gaussian distribution and using the attention mechanism to aggregate the messages from node neighborhoods. In addition, it is an intuitive way to pre-process the input data and thus reducing the effects of adversarial examples. Wu et al. [22] inspect the input graph and recover the potential adversarial examples with Jaccard Similarity. Entezari et al. [9] demonstrate that attackers only affect the high-rank singular components of the graph, and further propose a low-rank approximation method to reduce the adversarial effects.

A recent work [23] offers an important insight into the neighborhood aggregation of GNNs, i.e., the neighborhood aggregation is not always necessary and beneficial. Following this insight, we aim to deepen our understanding of the vulnerability of GNNs from an empirical study perspective. Our work reveals the adversarial patterns of attacks and provides the explanation that the aggregation functions have a significant influence on the robustness of GNNs.

3   Analysis of Graph Neural Networks

In this section, we intend to discuss the vulnerability of GNNs, and to further draw attention on the reasons for this. Specifically, we begin with giving some basic notations of graph data and discuss the details of the message passing Graph Neural Networks. What's more, two measurements of the neighborhood entropy are introduced to depict the chaos in node neighborhoods.

3.1   Notation

In line with the focus of this work, we consider the task of semi-supervised node classification in an undirected, unweighted graph. Formally, we follow the widely used notation to represent a graph $G = (V, E)$, where $V = \{v_i\}$ is a finite set of vertices (nodes) and $E = \{e_j\}$ is a finite set of links (edges). The D dimensional node features can be denoted as a matrix $X \in \{0, 1\}^{N \times D}$ where $N = |V|$. Typically, the connections of node pairs in a undirected graph G can be represented as an adjacency matrix $A \in \{0, 1\}^{N \times N}$, where $A_{u,v} = 1$ denotes an edge is present between node u and v while $A_{u,v} = 0$ otherwise. In addition, for the node classification task, a set of class labels Y is given where y_i denotes the ground-truth label of v_i.

3.2   Message Passing Graph Neural Networks

There are several works in studying the expressive power of GNNs [10,17,23,25], including its depth, width, representational properties and limitations. Specifically, most of GNNs follow a neighborhood aggregation scheme, where the hidden

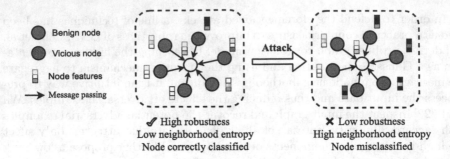

Fig. 1. Neighborhood aggregation of GNN before and after the attack. The darker color indicates the larger values of the node features. A GNN may have a high degree of robustness in predicting the class label of a node if its neighborhood share similar features (messages) with it, as opposed to the low robustness with a neighborhood where the features (messages) of nodes vary greatly from the central node.

representation of a node is computed by recursively aggregating and passing messages from its neighborhood. Based on this work [11], we define message passing graph neural networks as follows:

$$m_i^{(K+1)} = M^{(K)}(\{h_j^{(K)}|v_j \in \mathcal{N}(v_i)\}),$$
$$h_i^{(K+1)} = U^{(K)}(h_i^{(K)}, m_i^{(K+1)}) \tag{1}$$

where $M^{(K)}$ and $U^{(K)}$ denote the message passing function and update function at K-th layer, $m_i^{(K)}$ and $h_i^{(K)}$ are the message and hidden representation of v_i correspondingly. In particular, $h_i^{(0)} = X_i$. $\mathcal{N}(v_i)$ denotes the neighboring nodes adjacent to v_i in the graph G.

From Eq. (1), the hidden representation of a node v_i is overly dependent on the message aggregated and transformed from its neighborhood. If the message function and update function are improperly designed, e.g., sensitive to noisy inputs, the message aggregation will be negatively affected and result in the failure of GNNs. To illustrate why GNNs are vulnerable due to message passing functions, we take GCN as an example and describe its message passing function and update function as follows:

$$M^{(K)}(\{h_j^{(K)}|v_j \in \mathcal{N}(v_i)\}) = \sum_{v_j \in \mathcal{N}(v_i) \cup v_i} \frac{h_j^{(K)} W^{(K)}}{\sqrt{(|\mathcal{N}(v_i)|+1)(|\mathcal{N}(v_j)|+1)}},$$
$$U^{(K)}(h_i^{(K)}, m_i^{(K+1)}) = \sigma(m_i^{(K+1)}) \tag{2}$$

where σ denotes the element-wise activation function.

Following the scheme of message aggregation, the GNNs can learn the hidden representations of a node from its neighborhood. For all of its advantages, message aggregation or neighborhood aggregation is something of a double-edged sword. Notice that the message passing function of GCN can be regarded as a *mean-like* function, which is useful for aggregating the neighborhoods message and is widely adopted in most of GNNs. However, the mean aggregation is sensitive when there are extreme values in the neighborhood's messages, e.g., very distinctive features from the adjacent nodes. This suggests that an attacker can easily affect the message aggregation of a node by injecting some vicious nodes with dissimilar features or labels into its neighborhood. As shown in Fig. 1, a GNN may have a high degree of robustness in predicting the class label of the center node by aggregating the messages from its neighborhood, where the majority share similar features (messages) with it. In comparison to the low robustness with a neighborhood where the features (messages) of nodes vary greatly from the central node. We therefore claim that *the vulnerability of GNNs may be derived from the high dependency on the node neighborhoods*, i.e., they will naturally become vulnerable if the message functions are improperly designed while the node neighborhoods are intentionally changed.

3.3   Neighborhood Entropy Measurements

As we discussed in Sect. 3.2, the vulnerability of GNNs is mainly due to the aggregation layers exploiting the messed-up neighborhoods. So, no matter what the exact procedure is, the outcome of a specific attack method will always wind up making connections between nodes with dissimilar features or different labels, and so is the defense method doing the opposite operations.

In addition, Xie et al. [23] argue that the neighborhood aggregation operation is not always necessary and beneficial when the neighbors of a node are highly dissimilar. In this spirit, we propose two measurements of entropy to depict the chaos in node neighborhoods and use them to represent the predictability of a graph. To obtain the label-diversity for a graph, we compute the Neighborhood Entropy of nodes labels (NE-label) by the following:

$$\text{NE-label}(v_i) = -\sum_c^C P_c(v_i) \log\left(P_c(v_i)\right),$$

$$\text{where } P_c(v_i) = \frac{\sum_{v_j \in \mathcal{N}(v_i) \cup v_i} [y_j = c]}{|N(v_i)| + 1},$$

(3)

where C is the number of classes, and $[y_j = c]$ is the indicator function that equals to 1 if the label of node v_j is c, and equals to 0 otherwise. As for the feature-diversity for one single node, we similarly compute the Neighborhood Entropy of the node features (NE-feature) in its neighborhood including its own:

$$\text{NE-feature}(v_i) = -\sum_d^D P_d(v_i) \log\left(P_d(v_i)\right),$$

$$\text{where } P(v_i) = \frac{p(v_i)}{\sum_d^D p_d(v_i)},$$

(4)

$$p(v_i) = \sum_{v_j \in \mathcal{N}(v_i) \cup v_i} \frac{h_j}{\sqrt{(|\mathcal{N}(v_i)| + 1)(|\mathcal{N}(v_j)| + 1)}},$$

where $p(v_i)$ is an aggregation of all the features for neighbors of v_i including v_i (similar to what GCN do in Eq. (2)) and $P(v_i)$ is normalized $p(v_i)$.

These two measurements indicate how wild the label and feature distributions are in the neighborhood of a single node. For example, within a graph with high predictability, the average value of neighborhood entropy for all of the nodes is expected to be rather low, since two nodes with the same label and similar features are more likely to be linked to [2] (more details will be discussed in Sect. 4.2). As it turns out, just as we expected, the relatively high entropy results in high chaos of nodes neighborhood and low robustness of GNNs.

4   Experiments and Discussions

Dataset. For all experiments, we adopt two commonly used datasets as benchmarks: CiteSeer and Cora [19]. For each dataset, we randomly select 20% of the nodes to make up the training set (half of which are treated as the validation set), and treat the remaining as the test set. We also follow the setting of [28] which only considers the largest connected component of the graph. In addition, we assume that the attackers have full access of the datasets, i.e., the link connections and node features, but the target model is completely unknown to attackers. In our experiments, both the poisoning attack and the non-targeted attack are considered, i.e., the primary goal of attackers is to reduce the overall performance of classifiers, whose weights are retrained after attacks. The study of evasion attack and targeted attack is left for future work. Table 1 is an overview of the datasets.

Target Models. To validate the vulnerability caused by the non-robust message functions, a line of frequently used GNNs are adopted: Graph Convolutional Network (GCN) [15], Simplified Graph Convolution (SGC) [21], Cluster-GCN [7], GraphSAGE [13]. These models primarily use the "mean" message passing function to aggregate the hidden activations of a node from its neighborhoods. In addition to the GNNs using *mean-like* message passing function, we adopt RGCN [27] which enhances the neighborhood aggregation by imposing Gaussian distribution and attention mechanism.

Attacker Models. We concentrate primarily on the structure attack for a fair comparison, as most of the previous works do not consider the feature attack. To better compare the performance of various attacks, we assemble a number of attack methods including state-of-the-arts.

- RAND. The simplest attack that inserts or removes edges from the graph randomly.
- DICE [2]. "Delete Internally, Connect Externally" (DICE) is originally a heuristic algorithm for disguising communities. The core idea is to randomly connect nodes with different labels or remove edges between nodes that share the same label.

Table 1. Dataset statistics. We only consider the largest connected component of the graph for each dataset.

Dataset	#Nodes	#Edges	#Classes	#Features	#Density
CiteSeer	2,110	3,668	6	3703	0.082%
Cora	2,485	5,069	7	1433	0.082%

- Fast Gradient Sign Method (FGSM) [12]. A vanilla gradient-based method that simply generates adversarial examples based on the sign of gradient derived from the partial derivative of classification loss w.r.t. the input graph.
- PGD [24]. A state-of-the-art gradient-based that leverage projected gradient descent (PGD) from a first-order optimization perspective.
- Metattack [29]. A state-of-the-art gradient-based method that solves the bilevel optimization problem of poisoning attacks using meta learning.

Setup. For each target model, we fine-tune the hyperparameters on the original graph and keep them fixed on the perturbed one. Besides, we impose the same perturbation constraint τ (i.e., the attack budget) on different attackers, ranging from 5% to 25% of edges in the graph. We use the classification accuracy as an evaluation metric, with results obtained over 10 runs to minimize the effect of randomness. Specifically, we enforce these adversarial attack methods to a fair situation, i.e., prior knowledge of datasets and target models is the same in order to investigate their performance in more depth.

4.1 Structural Vulnerability of Graph Neural Networks

In order to show the performance of GNNs under different attacks, we use different attack methods separately to poison the input graph and train the target GNNs to evaluate the classification performance using the generated adversarial examples. The classification results of GNNs on CiteSeer and Cora can be seen in Table 2, here we report the mean classification accuracy (in percent) on the clean graph and the perturbed one with increasing perturbation rates.

Performance of Adversarial Attacks. Observed from Table 2, it is clear that GNNs are indeed sensitive to adversarial attacks even with relatively small perturbations. The classification accuracy is easily affected by the attackers. Simple attacks like RAND are expected to have little impact on the poisoning of target models even with larger perturbations (25%). However, based on the core idea—"Delete Internally, Connect Externally", the enhanced randomized DICE attack shows stronger performance in attacking GNNs. This implies that most of the non-robust message functions can be influenced by injecting more edges between dissimilar nodes and removing them between similar nodes in the graph.

Table 2. Mean classification accuracy (in percent) of target models on the clean graph and the perturbed graph with different perturbation rates τ. The best attack performance is boldfaced. Here "Cluster" is short for Cluster-GCN and "SAGE" is short for GraphSAGE.

τ	Attack	CiteSeer					Cora				
		GCN	SGC	Cluster	SAGE	RGCN	GCN	SGC	Cluster	SAGE	RGCN
	Clean	70.8 ± 0.2	68.6 ± 0.3	71.7 ± 0.5	70.9 ± 0.7	70.0 ± 0.6	83.5 ± 0.3	83.2 ± 0.2	82.6 ± 0.5	81.0 ± 0.8	77.9 ± 0.3
5%	RAND	70.7 ± 0.3	67.7 ± 0.1	72.2 ± 1.1	70.7 ± 0.6	68.8 ± 0.7	82.3 ± 0.3	81.0 ± 0.3	80.6 ± 0.8	80.9 ± 0.7	76.8 ± 0.4
	DICE	69.1 ± 0.2	66.4 ± 0.1	70.5 ± 0.8	69.6 ± 0.4	69.6 ± 0.3	82.6 ± 0.3	81.1 ± 0.1	80.8 ± 1.2	80.7 ± 0.8	76.3 ± 0.8
	FGSM	68.8 ± 0.5	66.7 ± 0.2	71.1 ± 0.2	68.8 ± 1.2	69.3 ± 1.3	79.7 ± 0.2	78.2 ± 0.4	79.6 ± 1.1	80.0 ± 0.4	77.2 ± 0.9
	PGD	68.9 ± 0.4	68.2 ± 0.1	69.3 ± 0.6	68.8 ± 0.5	67.6 ± 1.3	79.2 ± 1.0	**74.6 ± 0.4**	79.2 ± 0.9	79.0 ± 0.9	77.1 ± 1.0
	Metattack	**66.0 ± 0.5**	**64.6 ± 0.2**	**68.0 ± 0.5**	**68.0 ± 1.8**	**65.9 ± 0.7**	**78.8 ± 0.2**	78.3 ± 0.2	**77.0 ± 0.6**	**77.1 ± 1.0**	**75.0 ± 1.0**
10%	RAND	70.1 ± 0.6	67.7 ± 0.7	70.8 ± 0.4	70.0 ± 0.7	69.1 ± 0.9	81.2 ± 0.6	79.8 ± 0.1	81.0 ± 1.2	79.7 ± 0.7	76.2 ± 0.6
	DICE	69.6 ± 0.5	67.0 ± 0.1	69.9 ± 0.7	69.2 ± 0.8	68.6 ± 0.3	81.1 ± 0.4	80.7 ± 0.6	80.4 ± 0.3	79.7 ± 0.7	74.8 ± 0.3
	FGSM	63.9 ± 0.7	62.4 ± 0.6	69.6 ± 0.8	67.7 ± 1.8	67.1 ± 1.5	73.6 ± 0.3	73.5 ± 0.3	76.5 ± 0.6	76.1 ± 1.3	75.1 ± 1.1
	PGD	63.5 ± 0.7	62.2 ± 0.3	67.7 ± 1.2	65.8 ± 1.4	63.8 ± 0.5	74.0 ± 0.5	**71.2 ± 1.2**	76.4 ± 0.5	76.2 ± 1.6	**71.6 ± 1.6**
	Metattack	**55.2 ± 0.3**	**52.0 ± 0.5**	**62.0 ± 1.9**	**64.8 ± 1.1**	**57.4 ± 1.7**	**72.3 ± 0.5**	72.6 ± 0.6	**72.4 ± 1.2**	**73.8 ± 1.1**	71.8 ± 0.9
15%	RAND	68.7 ± 0.6	67.1 ± 0.1	70.8 ± 0.6	69.4 ± 0.5	68.5 ± 0.6	82.2 ± 0.4	81.0 ± 0.2	80.8 ± 1.0	80.0 ± 1.2	76.6 ± 0.8
	DICE	67.2 ± 0.2	63.2 ± 0.4	68.1 ± 0.9	68.8 ± 0.9	67.1 ± 2.0	79.5 ± 0.4	79.2 ± 0.2	77.8 ± 1.2	76.4 ± 0.6	72.6 ± 1.1
	FGSM	59.7 ± 0.6	56.8 ± 0.6	68.0 ± 1.0	64.2 ± 2.0	62.3 ± 1.7	68.1 ± 0.7	68.2 ± 0.3	73.5 ± 1.2	74.3 ± 0.7	72.1 ± 1.6
	PGD	60.3 ± 0.5	57.7 ± 0.2	63.0 ± 1.2	65.9 ± 1.5	59.0 ± 1.8	66.0 ± 0.8	**65.4 ± 0.2**	71.5 ± 0.9	73.3 ± 0.8	67.1 ± 1.1
	Metattack	**49.9 ± 0.5**	**47.7 ± 0.6**	**52.4 ± 1.4**	**60.0 ± 2.3**	**48.8 ± 1.7**	**64.1 ± 0.6**	67.7 ± 0.3	**69.9 ± 2.3**	**70.3 ± 0.9**	**62.1 ± 0.7**
20%	RAND	68.3 ± 0.3	64.5 ± 0.2	68.2 ± 0.7	68.1 ± 1.0	65.8 ± 1.2	80.3 ± 0.3	79.2 ± 0.1	78.1 ± 1.1	77.7 ± 0.7	74.9 ± 1.0
	DICE	66.9 ± 0.3	64.6 ± 0.1	67.4 ± 0.8	67.6 ± 0.6	63.0 ± 2.5	77.7 ± 0.1	75.9 ± 0.4	75.2 ± 0.5	76.5 ± 0.4	71.5 ± 0.5
	FGSM	52.4 ± 0.4	49.7 ± 0.7	63.6 ± 1.6	62.8 ± 1.6	58.8 ± 1.2	58.9 ± 0.4	61.5 ± 0.6	71.9 ± 1.6	70.3 ± 1.6	67.2 ± 1.5
	PGD	55.0 ± 0.5	54.0 ± 0.7	57.5 ± 2.7	64.0 ± 1.7	52.8 ± 1.0	62.9 ± 0.7	63.7 ± 0.4	70.7 ± 0.8	70.0 ± 1.5	61.7 ± 1.1
	Metattack	**40.0 ± 0.4**	**38.7 ± 0.4**	**46.0 ± 2.8**	**53.5 ± 0.5**	**40.2 ± 1.7**	**52.3 ± 0.5**	**56.2 ± 0.4**	**60.8 ± 2.9**	**64.6 ± 1.6**	**50.5 ± 0.5**
25%	RAND	67.4 ± 0.3	64.3 ± 0.1	68.7 ± 0.5	68.2 ± 0.5	65.9 ± 1.4	78.9 ± 0.2	77.7 ± 0.2	77.6 ± 0.9	76.4 ± 0.6	73.4 ± 0.3
	DICE	64.8 ± 0.6	60.9 ± 0.1	64.9 ± 0.6	65.6 ± 0.8	62.5 ± 1.8	76.3 ± 0.3	74.7 ± 0.2	73.7 ± 1.1	74.7 ± 1.0	71.0 ± 1.4
	FGSM	41.9 ± 1.3	41.5 ± 0.9	58.6 ± 1.7	61.1 ± 1.8	51.7 ± 2.8	48.3 ± 0.8	50.9 ± 0.7	60.8 ± 1.7	65.8 ± 2.0	59.9 ± 1.2
	PGD	50.2 ± 0.4	49.3 ± 0.5	52.9 ± 1.5	60.8 ± 1.1	48.7 ± 1.4	58.0 ± 0.5	57.7 ± 0.3	67.1 ± 2.7	67.5 ± 1.2	57.9 ± 1.0
	Metattack	**35.4 ± 0.5**	**36.3 ± 1.5**	**41.8 ± 3.3**	**46.4 ± 1.4**	**36.9 ± 1.8**	**44.6 ± 0.8**	**47.6 ± 0.6**	**52.3 ± 1.1**	**59.2 ± 2.0**	**45.3 ± 1.7**

In addition, we can find that the gradient-based attacks, particularly Metattack, have gained dramatic attack performance on both datasets. These attack methods utilize the gradients derived from the surrogate model (GCN), showing the significant performance and transferability in attacking other GNNs as well as GCN. With higher τ, Metattack shows the performance of a strong attacker that decreases the accuracy by more than 30% on Cora dataset. While other gradient-based approaches, FGSM and PGD perform worse than Metattack but are still successful in attacking target GNNs. A possible explanation for the results is that the gradient obtained by meta learning has better approximation on the loss of target models, thus have advantage on exploiting the vulnerability of GNNs sufficiently.

Vulnerability of Graph Neural Networks. From the viewpoint of GNNs, various models display varying levels of robustness to attacks. For GCN and SGC, whose message passing functions are simple mean-like functions, both of them struggle to preserve their robustness against attacks. However, Cluster-GCN and GraphSAGE behave more robustly even in the face of stronger attacks. We are giving the explanations from the aggregation schemes: (i) *Cluster-GCN*. Using a graph clustering algorithm, Cluster-GCN samples a number of subgraphs whose nodes are strongly correlated. In view of this, certain low-correlation edges between subgraphs will be dropped as if the clustering algorithm works functionally. By doing so, some of the effects of the adversarial behaviors can be alleviated. However, the clustering algorithm can also be tricked as the perturbations increase. (ii) *GraphSAGE*. GraphSAGE is a more universal graph convolution network that samples and aggregates the messages from nodes' neighborhoods. Here we adopt the *GraphSAGE-mean* in this experiment. Based on Eq. (1), the message passing of GraphSAGE can be denoted as follows:

$$M^{(K)}(\{h_j^{(K)}|v_j \in \mathcal{N}(v_i)\}) = \sum_{v_j \in \mathcal{N}(v_i)} \frac{h_j^{(K)}W^{(K)}}{|\mathcal{N}(v_j)|},$$

$$U^{(K)}(h_i^{(K)}, m_i^{(K+1)}) = \sigma(m_i^{(K+1)}\|h_i^{(K)}W^{(K)}),$$

$$(5)$$

where $\|$ denotes the concatenate operation.

Despite using the mean aggregation as a message passing function, the higher robustness of GraphSAGE may be derived from the update function with the concatenate operation. The message aggregation of GraphSAGE is less dependent on the neighborhoods but more on the node itself, whose feature is unperturbed in the structure attack setting. This explains the higher robustness of GraphSAGE and it shows a simple but effective way to improve the robustness of message aggregation, which is also useful to enhance the robustness of GNNs.

For RGCN, it uses Gaussian distribution in graph convolution layers to absorb the effects of adversarial attacks and introduces a variance-based attention mechanism to prevent the propagation of unnecessary messages in node neighborhoods. The message functions are designed more robust than mean-like functions, and therefore, it is beneficial for defending such adversarial attacks.

This also indicates the importance of designing more robust message functions for GNNs.

As described in Sect. 3, the message functions of GNNs have high dependencies on the neighborhoods of nodes. Just like a double-edged sword, it is useful to learn the hidden representations of nodes by following a message aggregation scheme. On the other hand, it also results in high vulnerability of GNNs if message function are incorrectly designed. Therefore, an effective way to improve the robustness is to design a more robust message aggregation function against the attacks. To conclude, we argue that the vulnerability of GNNs is on account of the high dependencies on the neighborhoods of nodes (as shown in Fig. 1). If the message functions can be somehow improved to reduce the dependencies (like GraphSAGE and RGCN), the model will be more robust against attacks.

4.2   Adversarial Patterns of Attacks on Graph Data

As stated in Sect. 4.1, the vulnerability of GNNs is observed in Table 2, which is consistent with the previous studies. In this part, we aim to further discover the adversarial patterns of attacks on graph data, which helps researchers to understand the reasons of the success in attacking GNNs and thus considering the countermeasures against such attacks. Indeed, the following adversarial patterns are observed:

High Neighborhood Entropy. Previously, Xie et al. [23] mention that the neighborhood aggregation is not always necessary and beneficial for GNNs. Actually, it is consistent with our claim that the main reason for the vulnerability of GNNs is the non-robust message functions. To better understand this, we plot the distribution of neighborhood entropy under different attacks on Cora dataset in Fig. 2. A clear difference between the neighborhood entropy statistics for the unperturbed versus perturbed nodes can be observed, especially for the stronger attacks FGSM, PGD and Metattack. We can see that the more the neighborhood entropy has increased, the more vulnerable of the GNNs and the stronger of the attacks. This is consistent with the results in Table 2. An attacker always manages to increase the neighborhood entropy to affect the non-robust message functions and hinder the message aggregation of nodes, therefore, it should be more cautious in performing aggregation when the neighborhood entropy is high.

High Rank, Dense and High Distinct Rate. Given that, high neighborhood entropy hinders the message aggregation of nodes, there is a high probability that an attacker will cause the node neighborhoods to become messed up (e.g., Fig. 1) to increase the neighborhood entropy. Following this insight, we aim to explore the characteristics of the perturbed graph, including the changes of rank and edges. Beyond that, we use *Distinct Rate* r to calculate the ratio of edges connected with nodes belonging to different classes in a graph, i.e.,

$$r = \frac{\sum_{u,v}[y_u \neq y_v]}{|E|} \tag{6}$$

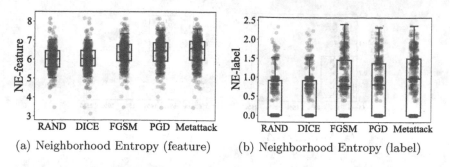

(a) Neighborhood Entropy (feature)   (b) Neighborhood Entropy (label)

Fig. 2. Box plots of neighborhood entropy statistics for the unperturbed graph (green dots) and perturbed graph (red dots, $\tau = 15\%$) on Cora dataset. (Color figure online)

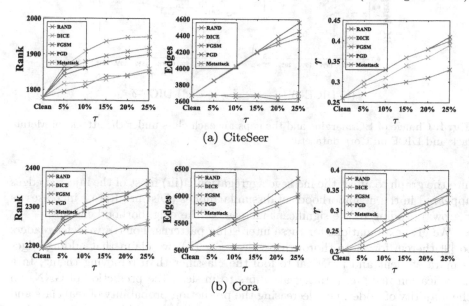

Fig. 3. Statistics (rank, edges, Distinct Rate r) of graph under different attacks on two datasets.

where $[y_u \neq y_v]$ is an indicator that equals 1 if the class of u and v are different, and equals 0 otherwise.

As shown in Fig. 3, the adversarially manipulated graph has the following patterns: **high rank, dense** and **high Distinct Rate** with higher perturbations τ. The adversarial patterns suggest that: (i) the rank of a graph is increasing when being attacked even though the edges are randomly added or removed. A possible explanation is that attackers will affect the high-rank (low-valued) singular components of the graph; (ii) attackers prefer adding edges rather than removing them. The three strongest attacks intentionally add adversarial edges

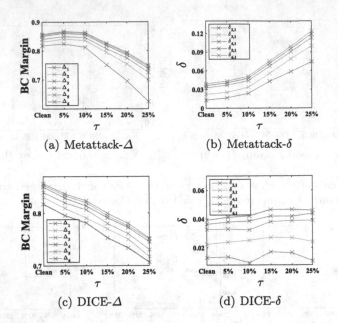

(a) Metattack-Δ (b) Metattack-δ

(c) DICE-Δ (d) DICE-δ

Fig. 4. Change of BC margins and the gaps for each class under the attacks of Metattack and DICE on Cora dataset.

into the graph to affect the message aggregation[1]; (iii) most of the injected edges appeared in the neighborhoods of dissimilar nodes (Distinct Rate r increases as τ grows), leading to the significant increase of the neighborhood entropy.

We give explanations for these interesting patterns. For (i), we refer readers to [9] therein for more thorough reviews. For (ii), we claim that adding edges is more efficient and practical to fool the classifier than removing them[2]. In a classification task, an attacker attempts to mislead the prediction of GNNs on the majority of nodes, i.e., decreasing the prediction probability of real class and increasing that of other classes of nodes. To demonstrate this process, we define the Between-Class (BC) margin Δ as follows:

$$\Delta_j = \frac{\sum_{v_i \in V}(Z_{c_{i,0}} - Z_{c_{i,j}})}{|V|}, \text{ where } j = 1, 2, \cdots, C - 1, \tag{7}$$

where $Z \in R^{N \times C}$ is the prediction matrix of a classifier, $c_{i,j}$ denotes the j_{th} most probable class label of node v_i. Specifically, $c_{i,0}$ denotes the predicted class of v_i. The BC margin represents the confidence of a GNN in predicting the nodes. In other words, a lower Δ_j means the model is less confident with the prediction, which inevitably yields a poorer performance in classification. In addition, we

---

[1] The edges of the graph perturbed by RAND and DICE almost unchanged since they randomly choose to add or remove edges with the same probability.

[2] In fact, removing edges may result in singleton nodes and it is also not beneficial for attacks.

also define $\delta_{i,j} = \Delta_i - \Delta_j$ to capture the gaps between BC margins of a GNN under attacks. The aforementioned measurements of GCN under the attacks of DICE and Metattack are shown in Fig. 4. We omit the statistics of RAND, FGSM and PGD for simplicity since they show similar patterns with the chosen two methods. As it turns out, a strong attack like Metattack (Fig. 4(a)) tends to decrease Δ_1 more dramatically than other BC margins, especially compared with a rather ineffective method like DICE (Fig. 4(c)). This pattern is pictured more clearly in Fig. 4(b) and (d), which shows the gaps $(\delta_{i,1})$ between the rest and the second probable class for Metattack are increasing, but the gaps $(\delta_{i,1})$ for DICE almost unchanged statistically. That is, a stronger attack may followed by dramatically changes of BC margins especially Δ_1. This seems pretty reasonable since we only need one wrong class's probability to surpass that of the ground-truth class. As the attack budget is fixed to a small value, it is relatively more efficient to increase the second most probable class's probability rather than the others. This is why effective methods are always more likely to add edges instead of removing them. For removing an edge with a node of the ground-truth label may increase all the other class's probability simultaneously, while adding one with a node of the second probable class will mainly increase the probability of itself. Accordingly, though adding and removing edges both have the ability to fool the classifier, the former could achieve the same effect with a rather lower budget. We believe this pattern will be even more clear with the targeted attacks, which is not discussed in this paper and shall be covered in future works. For (iii), it's straightforward to follow the core idea of DICE, and the empirical results show the efficiency in attacking GNNs. A stronger attacker will not only choose to add adversarial edges and also consider the ones that connected with dissimilar nodes. Moreover, an interesting phenomenon is observed that DICE has a similar Distinct Rate r with FGSM, PGD, and Metattack but it does not cause a high increase of neighborhood entropy from Fig. 2. Actually, this also suggests that adding adversarial edges is more beneficial for attacks than removing them.

5   Conclusion and Future Work

In this work, we study the vulnerability of GNNs and the adversarial patterns of attacks on graph data. Through a comprehensive study of several widely used GNNs on two real-world benchmark datasets, we draw the following conclusions: (i) GNNs are vulnerable if the message functions are incorrectly designed and maliciously utilized; (ii) high neighborhood entropy of node features and labels will lead to worse performance of GNNs; (iii) most of attacks may lead to a dense and high-rank graph structure. In addition, attackers prefer adding adversarial edges (especially between dissimilar nodes) rather than removing them to mislead the message aggregation in the node neighborhoods, since the former is a relatively more economical way.

This project provides a comprehensive investigation on graph adversarial learning and offers deep understandings on the reasons of GNNs' intrinsic vulnerability. More generally, these basic findings are consistent with previous researches. Future research could fruitfully explore these insights further by studying other types of attacks (e.g., evasion attack). Moreover, the robustness of GNNs could be improved by designing a more robust message function.

Acknowledgements. The work described in this paper was supported by the Key-Area Research and Development Program of Guangdong Province (2020B010165003), the National Natural Science Foundation of China (61702568, U1711267), the Guangdong Basic and Applied Basic Research Foundation (2020A1515010831), the Program for Guangdong Introducing Innovative and Entrepreneurial Teams (2017ZT07X355), and the Key Research and Development Program of Guangdong Province of China (2018B030325001).

References

1. Bojchevski, A., Günnemann, S.: Adversarial attacks on node embeddings via graph poisoning. In: ICML, pp. 695–704 (2019)
2. Cai, D., Shao, Z., He, X., Yan, X., Han, J.: Mining hidden community in heterogeneous social networks. In: Proceedings of the 3rd International Workshop on Link Discovery, pp. 58–65. ACM (2005)
3. Chang, H., et al.: A restricted black-box adversarial framework towards attacking graph embedding models. In: AAAI, pp. 3389–3396. AAAI Press (2020)
4. Chen, L., et al.: A survey of adversarial learning on graph. arXiv preprint arXiv:2003.05730 (2020)
5. Chen, L., Liu, Y., He, X., Gao, L., Zheng, Z.: Matching user with item set: collaborative bundle recommendation with deep attention network. In: IJCAI, pp. 2095–2101 (2019)
6. Chen, L., Liu, Y., Zheng, Z., Yu, P.: Heterogeneous neural attentive factorization machine for rating prediction. In: CIKM, pp. 833–842. ACM (2018)
7. Chiang, W.L., Liu, X., Si, S., Li, Y., Bengio, S., Hsieh, C.J.: Cluster-GCN: an efficient algorithm for training deep and large graph convolutional networks. In: KDD, pp. 257–266 (2019)
8. Dai, H., et al.: Adversarial attack on graph structured data. In: ICML, pp. 1123–1132. PMLR (2018)
9. Entezari, N., Al-Sayouri, S.A., Darvishzadeh, A., Papalexakis, E.E.: All you need is low (rank) defending against adversarial attacks on graphs. In: WSDM, pp. 169–177 (2020)
10. Errica, F., Podda, M., Bacciu, D., Micheli, A.: A fair comparison of graph neural networks for graph classification. In: ICLR (2020)
11. Gilmer, J., Schoenholz, S.S., Riley, P.F., Vinyals, O., Dahl, G.E.: Neural message passing for quantum chemistry. In: ICML, pp. 1263–1272. JMLR. org (2017)
12. Goodfellow, I.J., Shlens, J., Szegedy, C.: Explaining and harnessing adversarial examples. In: ICLR (2015)
13. Hamilton, W., Ying, Z., Leskovec, J.: Inductive representation learning on large graphs. In: NIPS, pp. 1024–1034 (2017)
14. Jin, W., Li, Y., Xu, H., Wang, Y., Tang, J.: Adversarial attacks and defenses on graphs: A review and empirical study. arXiv preprint arXiv:2003.00653 (2020)
15. Kipf, T.N., Welling, M.: Semi-supervised classification with graph convolutional networks. In: ICLR (2017)

16. Li, J., Zhang, H., Han, Z., Rong, Y., Cheng, H., Huang, J.: Adversarial attack on community detection by hiding individuals. In: WWW, pp. 917–927. ACM/IW3C2 (2020)
17. Loukas, A.: What graph neural networks cannot learn: depth vs width. In: ICLR. OpenReview.net (2020)
18. Nickel, M., Rosasco, L., Poggio, T.: Holographic embeddings of knowledge graphs. In: Thirtieth AAAI Conference on Artificial Intelligence (2016)
19. Sen, P., Namata, G., Bilgic, M., Getoor, L., Galligher, B., Eliassi-Rad, T.: Collective classification in network data. AI Mag. **29**(3), 93 (2008)
20. Sun, L., Dou, Y., Yang, C., Wang, J., Yu, P.S., Li, B.: Adversarial attack and defense on graph data: A survey. arXiv preprint arXiv:1812.10528 (2018)
21. Wu, F., de Souza Jr., A.H., Zhang, T., Fifty, C., Yu, T., Weinberger, K.Q.: Simplifying graph convolutional networks. In: ICML, vol. 97, pp. 6861–6871. PMLR (2019)
22. Wu, H., Wang, C., Tyshetskiy, Y., Docherty, A., Lu, K., Zhu, L.: Adversarial examples for graph data: deep insights into attack and defense. In: IJCAI, pp. 4816–4823 (2019)
23. Xie, Y., Li, S., Yang, C., Wong, R.C., Han, J.: When do GNNs work: understanding and improving neighborhood aggregation. In: IJCAI, pp. 1303–1309 (2020)
24. Xu, K., et al.: Topology attack and defense for graph neural networks: an optimization perspective. In: IJCAI, pp. 3961–3967 (2019)
25. Xu, K., Hu, W., Leskovec, J., Jegelka, S.: How powerful are graph neural networks? In: ICLR (2019)
26. Ye, F., Liu, J., Chen, C., Ling, G., Zheng, Z., Zhou, Y.: Identifying influential individuals on large-scale social networks: a community based approach. IEEE Access **6**, 47240–47257 (2018)
27. Zhu, D., Zhang, Z., Cui, P., Zhu, W.: Robust graph convolutional networks against adversarial attacks. In: KDD, pp. 1399–1407. ACM (2019)
28. Zügner, D., Akbarnejad, A., Günnemann, S.: Adversarial attacks on neural networks for graph data. In: KDD, pp. 2847–2856. ACM (2018)
29. Zügner, D., Günnemann, S.: Adversarial attacks on graph neural networks via meta learning. In: ICLR (2019)

Brain-Controlled Robotic Arm Based on Adaptive FBCCA

Dong Zhang, Banghua Yang[✉], Shouwei Gao, and Xuelin Gu

Shanghai University, Shanghai 200072, China
yangbanghua@shu.edu.cn

Abstract. The SSVEP-BCI system usually uses a fixed calculation time and a static window stop method to decode the EEG signal, which reduces the efficiency of the system. In response to this problem, this paper uses an adaptive FBCCA algorithm, which uses Bayesian estimation to dynamically find the optimal data length for result prediction, adapts to the differences between different trials and different individuals, and effectively improves system operation effectiveness. At the same time, through this method, this paper constructs a brain-controlled robotic arm grasping life assistance system based on adaptive FBCCA. In this paper, we selected 20 subjects and conducted a total of 400 experiments. A large number of experiments have verified that the system is available and the average recognition success rate is 95.5%. This also proves that the system can be applied to actual scenarios. Help the handicapped to use the brain to control the mechanical arm to grab the needed items to assist in daily life and improve the quality of life. In the future, SSVEP's adaptive FBCCA decoding algorithm can be combined with the motor imaging brain-computer interface decoding algorithm to build a corresponding system to help patients with upper or lower limb movement disorders caused by stroke diseases to recover, and reshape the brain and Control connection of limbs.

Keywords: BCI · SSVEP · Adaptive FBCCA · EEG

1 Introduction

At the end of the 1990s, the first Brain Computer Interface (BCI) international conference defined BCI: BCI is a special communication system that does not depend on the peripheral nerve and muscle tissue of the human body [1]. In 2012, Wolpaw gave a more strict definition of BCI: BCI can replace, repair, enhance, supplement or improve the normal output of the central nervous system by detecting the activity of the central nervous system and turning it into artificial output, so as to change the interaction between the central nervous system and the internal and external environment [2]. Steady state visual evoked potential [3] (SSVEP) is a commonly used BCI input signal. Compared with event-related potentials, spontaneous EEG signals, P300 and other methods, SSVEP has the advantages of simple operation, fewer electrodes, high information transmission rate, no training, and strong anti-interference ability [4].

© Springer Nature Singapore Pte Ltd. 2021
Y. Wang (Ed.): HBAI 2020, CCIS 1369, pp. 102–112, 2021.
https://doi.org/10.1007/978-981-16-1288-6_7

At present, the basic principle of the BCI system designed based on SSVEP is that when the human eye receives a fixed frequency visual stimulus, the visual cortex of the brain will generate a continuous response signal related to the stimulation frequency (the fundamental frequency or octave band of the stimulation frequency) [5]. By decoding the response signal, the person's intention can be recognized, and then external devices such as computers can be controlled by the brain. In foreign countries, Professor Middendorf of the United States designed the SSVEP-BCI control system in 2000 [6]; Professor Muller-Putz of Austria realized the SSVEP-BCI-based robotic prosthesis control system [7]; Professor Bakardjian used SSVEP- The BCI system designed virtual games and realized the function of playing games using EEG signals [8]; In China, Gao Xiaorong's team at Tsinghua University developed a high-speed BCI speller based on SSVEP technology [9, 10]; Li Yuanqing's team from South China University of Technology The designed SSVEP and P300 hybrid BCI system is suitable for the control of wheelchairs and other equipment [11, 12]. In recent years, SSVEP-BCI technology has been developed by leaps and bounds, and it has demonstrated important value in the fields of rehabilitation engineering, biomedicine [13], virtual reality [14], military, aerospace, and games. At present, almost all SSVEP-BCI systems at home and abroad are using fixed calculation time window static stop decoding method. Few proposed adaptive Filter Bank Canonical Correlation Analysis (FBCCA) dynamic time window cut-off method and applied this method to actual scenes.

The brain-controlled robotic arm grasping life assistance system based on adaptive FBCCA designed in this paper applies the adaptive FBCCA dynamic time window cut-off method to the actual scene, so that the system has good human-computer interaction functions and high accuracy of EEG decoding and recognition According to the designed experimental paradigm, after 20 subjects participated in the experiment, the average brain control grabbing accuracy was 95.5%. The system image recognition speed is fast, and the recognition status and results can be fed back in real time, so that the system can help handicapped people with motor dysfunction such as stroke to grab the objects they need without help, and help them fulfill certain life needs, improve the quality of life.

2 Method

So far, almost all SSVEP-BCI systems are using a statically stopped decoding method with a fixed calculation time window. However, due to individual differences, each person's BCI ability is different, and even the BCI ability of the same subject at different times is also different, because the state of the brain changes at any time. Therefore, an adaptive FBCCA decoding algorithm is adopted to select different size calculation time windows according to the difference of each subject to achieve a dynamic stop decoding method, which can effectively solve the above problems and improve the operation of the SSVEP-BCI system effectiveness.

2.1 CCA Algorithm

The Canonical Correlation Analysis (CCA) algorithm is a multivariate statistical analysis method that uses the correlation between comprehensive variable pairs to reflect the overall correlation between the two sets of indicators. The principle is: in order to grasp the correlation between the two sets of indicators as a whole, two representative comprehensive variables Wx and Wy are extracted from the two sets of variables (respectively the linear combination of the variables in the two variable groups), Use the correlation between these two comprehensive variables to reflect the overall correlation between the two sets of indicators.

When CCA extracts the SSVEP response frequency, the two sets of multivariate are defined as X and Y respectively, where X is the EEG (Electroencephalography, electroencephalogram) multi-channel signal of EEG.

$$X = \begin{bmatrix} channel_i \\ channel_j \\ \dots \\ channel_m \\ channel_n \end{bmatrix} \tag{1}$$

In formula (1), the subscript of *channel* represents the number of different channels, and Y is the reference signal related to the stimulation frequency. In formula (2), N is the number of harmonics of the stimulation frequency, and the number of *channel* in X is also N.

$$Y = \begin{bmatrix} sin(2\pi ft) \\ cos(2\pi ft) \\ \dots \\ sin(2\pi Nft) \\ cos(2\pi Nft) \end{bmatrix} \tag{2}$$

CCA finds a pair of vectors Wx and Wy for the two sets of multidimensional variables X and Y, and maximizes the correlation between the related variables $x = X^T W_X$ and $y = Y^T W_Y$ through Wx and Wy, as shown in formula (3).

$$\max_{w_x, w_y} \rho = \frac{E[x^T y]}{\sqrt{E[x^T x] E[y^T y]}} = \frac{E\left[W_x^T XY^T W_y\right]}{\sqrt{E\left[W_x XX^T W_x\right] E\left[W_y^T YY^T W_y\right]}} \tag{3}$$

The formula (3) derives the maximum value of the correlation coefficient ρ between X and Y. When different frequencies are selected, the calculated ρ is also different. The frequency corresponding to the maximum ρ is considered the response frequency of SSVEP.

2.2 FBCCA Algorithm

FBCCA adds a filter bank on the basis of CCA, so that the harmonic components of the EEG signal that are not fully utilized in the traditional CCA algorithm are used to improve the accuracy of the algorithm. The FBCCA method mainly includes three parts: (1) filter bank analysis of EEG signals; (2) CCA analysis of SSVEP sub-band components and sine and cosine reference signals; (3) target recognition. First, filter bank analysis decomposes the signal into multiple subband signals through multiple different bandpass filters. We use a zero-phase Chebyshev type I IIR filter to extract each subband component (X_{SB_n}, $n = 1, 2, \ldots, N$) from the original EEG signal x. In order to meet the requirement of zero phase, we use the *filtfilt* function in MATLAB for filtering. After the analysis of the filter set, the typical correlation coefficients of the sinusoidal reference signals corresponding to each subband component and each stimulation frequency (Y_{f_k}, $k = 1, 2, \ldots, 12$) are calculated. For the kth stimulation frequency f_k, the correlation vector ρ_k consists of N correlation coefficients:

$$\rho_k = \begin{bmatrix} \rho_k^1 \\ \rho_k^2 \\ \vdots \\ \rho_k^N \end{bmatrix} = \begin{bmatrix} \rho\left(X_{SB_1}^T W_X\left(X_{SB_1} Y_{f_k}\right), Y^T W_Y\left(X_{SB_1} Y_{f_k}\right)\right) \\ \rho\left(X_{SB_2}^T W_X\left(X_{SB_2} Y_{f_k}\right), Y^T W_Y\left(X_{SB_2} Y_{f_k}\right)\right) \\ \vdots \\ \rho\left(X_{SB_N}^T W_X\left(X_{SB_N} Y_{f_k}\right), Y^T W_Y\left(X_{SB_N} Y_{f_k}\right)\right) \end{bmatrix} \tag{4}$$

In formula (4), $\rho(x, y)$ represents the correlation coefficient between x and y. The square of the correlation coefficient corresponding to each subband component is multiplied by the corresponding weight coefficient and added and summed as the feature of target recognition (Fig. 1).

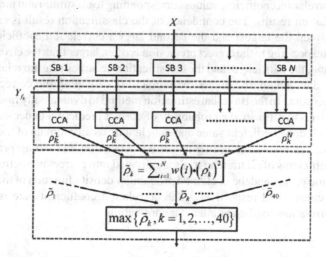

Fig. 1. Schematic diagram of frequency identification process based on FBCCA

$$\widetilde{\rho}_k = \sum_{n=1}^{N} w(n) \cdot (\rho_k^n)^2 \tag{5}$$

In formula (5), n represents the subband index. Since the signal-to-noise ratio of SSVEP harmonic components decreases with the increase of the response frequency, the weight coefficients of each subband component are defined as follows:

$$w(n) = n^{-a} + b, n \in [1 \ N] \tag{6}$$

In formula (6), a and b are constants. In fact, we use the grid search method to find a and b based on offline data to make the system classification performance optimal. Finally, $\widetilde{\rho}_k$ corresponding to each stimulation frequency (i.e. $\widetilde{\rho}_1, \ldots, \widetilde{\rho}_{12}$) is used to determine the frequency of SSVEP, and the frequency of the reference signal corresponding to the maximum correlation coefficient $\widetilde{\rho}_k$ is considered the frequency of SSVEP.

$$f_{target} = \max_{f_k} \widetilde{\rho}_k, k = 1, 2, \ldots, 12 \tag{7}$$

2.3 Adaptive FBCCA Algorithm

The static stop method adopted by the traditional SSVEP decoding algorithm uses a fixed data length for all trials, but due to the variability between trials, the optimal data length for each trial is different. Therefore, in order to improve the operating efficiency of the SSVEP-BCI system, an adaptive FBCCA method is adopted to decode the EEG signal, which is to dynamically find the optimal data length for prediction through Bayesian estimation.

It can be seen from the above FBCCA algorithm that the classification result of the algorithm is the stimulus frequency corresponding to the maximum value of the cumulative correlation coefficient. Therefore, it can be assumed that there is a correlation between the correlation coefficient values corresponding to all stimuli and the correctness of the classification results. The confidence of the classification result is related to the difference between the largest and the second largest correlation coefficient, and the difference corresponding to the correct prediction is often larger than the error prediction. At the same time, the data length and the classification accuracy rate are related, because the longer the data length, the higher the probability of getting the correct prediction result. Then according to the Bayesian estimation method to dynamically find the optimal data length, it tries to estimate the probability of correct prediction under the conditions of a given correlation coefficient value and data length, as an estimate of the confidence of the classification result. According to correct prediction and wrong prediction, the correlation coefficients of all training trials are divided into correct prediction group and wrong prediction group, and the likelihood probability density function of the correlation coefficient is constructed respectively. The correlation coefficient here is the largest cumulative correlation coefficient after standardization.

$$d_m = \frac{\widetilde{\rho}_k}{\sum_{n=1}^{N} \rho_k^n} \tag{8}$$

In formula (8), $\widetilde{\rho}_k$ is the largest cumulative correlation coefficient among all categories. Suppose the correct prediction is written as H_1 and the wrong prediction is written as H_0. Likelihood probability density functions $p(d_m|H_1, t)$ and $p(d_m|H_0, t)$ are generated by Gaussian kernel density estimation, that is, make a histogram of grouped d_m, and then use Gaussian kernel density estimation to expand and Smoothing, where t represents the data length used for classification.

In the online process, for each new data segment, first calculate the standardized cumulative correlation coefficient and obtain the predicted target character, and then estimate the posterior probability of being correctly predicted according to Bayesian inference:

$$P(H_1|d_m, t) = \frac{P(d_m|H_1, t)P(H_1|t)}{P(d_m|H_1, t)P(H_1|t) + P(d_m|H_0, t)P(H_0|t)} \tag{9}$$

In formula (9), $P(H_1|t)$ and $P(H_0|t)$ are the prior probability of correct prediction and wrong prediction under different data lengths. They are estimated based on the classification accuracy rate under different data lengths in offline experiments of. Once the posterior probability reaches the threshold P_{thre}, the predicted result will be output, where the threshold is determined offline by grid search. If the current trial fails to meet the threshold condition, the predicted result is forced to output when the length of the data segment reaches the preset maximum value.

3 Data Collection

Based on the adaptive FBCCA algorithm proposed above by Bayesian estimation to dynamically find the optimal data length for prediction, a brain-controlled robotic arm grasping assisted life system based on adaptive FBCCA is constructed. The algorithm is applied to practical applications to assist the daily life of disabled persons with motor dysfunction such as stroke.

The experimental data of the system is collected by DSI 24 Dry Electrode EEG Headset of Wearable Sensing (USA) Company. The EEG acquisition device is a 24-lead electrode cap, which is convenient, fast and comfortable to use and does not require conductive paste. EEG sensors are arranged in the international 10/20 system Fp1, Fp2, F7, F3, F4, Fz, F8, T3, C3, C4, Cz, T4, T5, P3, P4, T6, O1 and O2 positions, the EEG cap sampling frequency is 300 Hz, and the data is transmitted via Bluetooth. The experimental data processing uses 7 channels in 24 leads, namely P3, P4, Cz, T5, T6, O1 and O2.

The system uses a depth camera for object positioning and a robotic arm for object capture. The depth camera used is Intel's RealSense D435, which has high resolution and fast transmission speed. The manipulator used is a JACO three-finger lightweight manipulator of Kinova, which consists of a 6-degree-of-freedom manipulator and a three-degree-of-freedom finger grip. It has the characteristics of light weight, simple control, high safety, and friendly human-computer interaction. The robotic arm has a compact structure, each joint can be independently controlled, redundant safety control and the use of singularity avoidance algorithms make the robotic arm suitable for this brain control system to meet the basic life needs of the disabled.

The experimental paradigm interface for collecting data contains 12 blocks, 12 blocks representing 12 instructions, apple 1, banana 1, green tea, orange, cola, apple 2, banana 2, mineral water, orange, 7 up, cancel and confirm. 12 blocks correspond to 12 blinking frequencies, 9, 9.25, 9.5, 9.75, 10.25, 10.5, 10.75, 11, 11.25, 11.5, 11.75 and 12 Hz (Fig. 2).

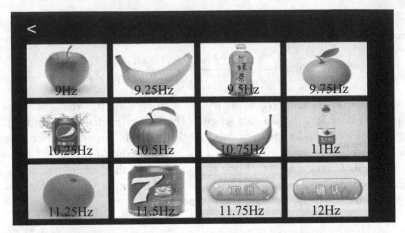

Fig. 2. Data collection experiment paradigm interface

The data collection process of this experiment is shown in Fig. 3, including 4 blocks, corresponding to apples, bananas, green tea, and oranges. Each block includes 5 trials and 1 trial for 20 s.

1 trial includes:

1) Choose visually stimulating objects for 2 s, a total of 10 target objects, and rest for 1 s.
2) 2 s visual stimulus to confirm or cancel the capture, skip to step (1) to cancel the capture.
3) 15 s to grab items by robotic arm.

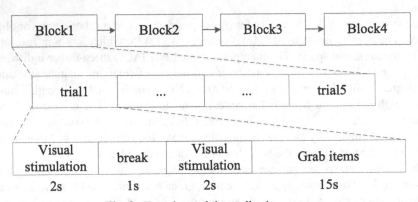

Fig. 3. Experimental data collection process

In this experiment, 20 students from Shanghai University were invited as subjects (12 males, 8 females, age: 20–30 years old) to participate in this experiment. Each subject performed a total of 20 trials and collected a total of 400 trial experiment data.

Before participating in the experiment, the subjects were told whether the experiment harmed the human body, and signed an informed consent form for the experiment. After the experiment, each person was given a certain amount of remuneration. The brain-controlled robotic arm experiment is shown in Fig. 4.

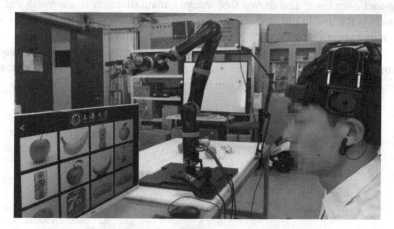

Fig. 4. Brain-controlled robotic arm experiment diagram

4 Results

4.1 EEG Topographic Map

The subject looked at the EEG signal generated by the scintillation stimulus in the Apple 2 block and plotted the EEG topographic map as shown in Fig. 5(b). It can be seen that the subject's brain produces a steady-state visual evoked potential, which reflects the occipital lobe The energy in the occipital region was significantly increased, which also verified the conclusion that SSVEP is mainly related to the occipital region of the brain. Figure 5(a) shows the target lock display after the subject has successfully watched the Apple 2 block.

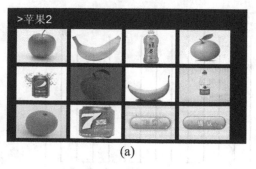 

(a)   (b)

Fig. 5. (a) Subject looks at apple 2 (b) EEG topographic map

4.2 EEG Signal Spectrogram

The collected subjects' original time-domain EEG signals are drawn into frequency-domain maps. The original EEG signal is shown in Fig. 6(a), the ordinate is the EEG channel, and the abscissa is time, showing the amplitude change of the EEG signal of each channel over time. The drawn frequency domain diagram is shown in Fig. 6(b), the ordinate is the amplitude, and the unit is decibel. It can be seen that the peak of the corresponding spectrum map is 12 Hz when the subject fixates the confirmed grasping block in the experimental pattern, which corresponds to the stimulation flicker frequency of the confirmed grasping block. This also verifies that the EEG signals generated by the subject staring at different blocks can be recognized by adaptive FBCCA.

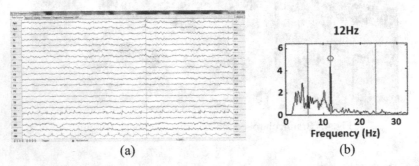

(a)   (b)

Fig. 6. (a) Subject's original EEG signal (b) 12 Hz SSVEP spectrogram

4.3 Accuracy

There are 20 subjects in this experiment, and each subject has 4 blocks, and one block contains 5 trials, that is, one subject has 20 object grabs. The grasping success rate of the robotic arm of this system is 100%, so the grasping success rate of the brain-controlled robotic arm depends on the correct rate of EEG decoding. The correct rate of EEG decoding of 20 subjects is shown in Fig. 7. After calculation, 20 people are obtained. The average accuracy rate of the subjects' brain-controlled grabbing objects was 95.5%.

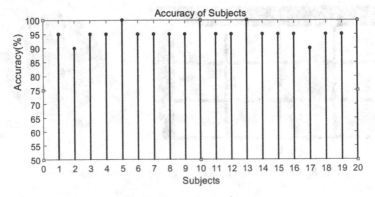

Fig. 7. Accuracy of subjects

Compared with the fixed window FBCCA, the recognition accuracy rate is increased by about 4%, and the recognition speed is increased by about 30%.

5 Conclusion

This paper uses an adaptive FBCCA algorithm based on Bayesian estimation to dynamically find the optimal data length to predict the result, adapt to the differences of different trials and different individuals, and solve the traditional SSVEP-BCI system usually used a fixed calculation time, the static stop of the window leads to the problem that the efficiency of the system decreases. Through this method, an adaptive FBCCA-based brain-controlled robotic arm grasping life assistance system was constructed. The system's robotic arm grasping accuracy rate was 100%, the EEG decoding accuracy rate was 95.5%, and the brain-controlled robotic arm grasping average accuracy rate reached 95.5%, can be used to assist disabled persons with physical disabilities such as stroke to perform some simple tasks to improve the quality of life.

In the future, SSVEP's adaptive FBCCA decoding algorithm can be combined with the motor imaging brain-computer interface decoding algorithm to construct a corresponding BCI system to help patients with upper or lower limb movement disorders caused by stroke diseases to recover and reshape the brain Connect with body control.

Acknowledgment. This project is supported by National Key R&D Program of China (No. 2018YFC1312903), National Natural Science Foundation of China (No. 61976133), Major scientific and technological innovation projects in Shandong Province (2019JZZY021010), National Defense Basic Scientific Research Program of China (Defense Industrial Technology Development Program) (JCKY2019413D002).

References

1. Wolpaw, J., Birbaumer, N., Heetderks, W.J.: Brain-computer interface technology: a review of the first international meeting. IEEE Trans. Rehabil. Eng. **8**(2), 164–173 (2000)
2. Wolpaw, J., Wolpaw, E.W.: Brain-Computer Interfaces: Principles and Practice. Oxford University Press, Oxford (2011)
3. Zhang, Y., Guo, D., Li, F., et al.: Correlated component analysis for enhancing the performance of SSVEP-based brain-computer interface. IEEE Trans. Neural Syst. Rehabil. Eng. **26**(5), 948–956 (2018)
4. Chen, X., Wang, Y., Gao, S., et al.: Filter bank canonical correlation analysis for implementing a high-speed SSVEP-based brain-computer interface. J. Neural Eng. **12**(4), (2015)
5. Nakanishi, M., Wang, Y., Chen, X., et al.: Enhancing detection of SSVEPs for a high-speed brain speller using task-related component analysis. IEEE Trans. Biomed. Eng. **65**(1), 104–112 (2018)
6. Middendorf, M., Mcmillan, G., Calhoun, G., et al.: Brain-computer interfaces based on the steady-state visual-evoked response. IEEE Trans. Rehabil. Eng. **8**(2), 211–214 (2000)
7. Muller-putz, G.R., Pfurtscheller, G.: Control of an electrical prosthesis with an SSVEP-based BCI. IEEE Trans. Biomed. Eng. **55**(1), 361 (2008)
8. Bakardjian, H., Tanaka, T., Cichocki, A.: Optimization of SSVEP brain responses with application to eight-command Brain-Computer Interface. Neurosci. Lett. **469**(1), 34 (2010)

9. Lin, K., Chen, X., Huang, X., Ding, Q., Gao, X.: A hybrid BCI speller based on the combination of EMG envelopes and SSVEP. Appl. Inform. **2**(1), 1–12 (2015). https://doi.org/10.1186/s40 535-014-0004-0

10. Lin, Z., Zhang, C., Wu, W., et al.: Frequency recognition based on canonical correlation analysis for SSVEP-based BCIs. IEEE Trans. Biomed. Eng. **53**(2), 1172–1176 (2007)

11. Li, Y., Pan, J., Wang, F., et al.: A hybrid BCI system combining P300 and SSVEP and its application to wheelchair control. IEEE Trans. Biomed. Eng. **60**(11), 3156 (2013)

12. Li, Y., Yu, T.: EEG-based hybrid BCIs and their applications. In: International Winter Conference on Brain-Computer Interface, pp. 1–4. IEEE (2015)

13. He, B., Baird, R., Butera, R., et al.: Grand challenges in interfacing engineering with life sciences and medicine. IEEE Trans. Biomed. Eng. **60**(3), 589–598 (2013)

14. Horii, S., Nakauchi, S., Kitazaki, M.: AR-SSVEP for brain-machine interface: estimating user. In: Proceedings of the 2015 IEEE Virtual Reality (VR), Arles, France. IEEE (2015)

Automatic Sleep Spindle Detection and Analysis in Patients with Sleep Disorders

Chao Chen[1,2], Xuequan Zhu[2], Abdelkader Nasreddine Belkacem[3], Lin Lu[4(✉)], Long Hao[4], Jia You[1], Duk Shin[5], Wenjun Tan[6], Zhaoyang Huang[7], and Dong Ming[1]

[1] Academy of Medical Engineering and Translational Medicine,
Tianjin University, Tianjin 300072, China
[2] Key Laboratory of Complex System Control Theory and Application,
Tianjin University of Technology, Tianjin 300384, China
[3] Department of Computer and Network Engineering, College of Information Technology,
UAE University, Al Ain 15551, UAE
[4] Zhonghuan Information College Tianjin University of Technology, Tianjin 300380, China
lulin1020@outlook.com
[5] Department of Electronics and Mechatronics, Tokyo Polytechnic University,
Atsugi 243-0297, Japan
[6] School of Computer Science and Engineering, Northeastern University,
Shenyang 110189, China
[7] Department of Neurology, Xuanwu Hospital, Capital Medical University,
Beijing 100088, China

Abstract. Nowadays, Sleep disorder is a common disease, and spindle spindles are important features of the second stage non-rapid eye movement (NREM) sleep. In this paper, we propose an improved automatic detection method of spindles based on wavelet transform. The spindles automatic detector is mainly composed of wavelet transform and clustering. We collected the electroencephalography (EEG) signals of six patients with sleep disorders all night for ten hours, and then preprocessed the data and other operations, and then used our improved method to detect the sleep EEG signals by spindles. By comparing with the previous automatic detection method not improved and another automatic detection method, the results show that the accuracy of sleep spindles detection can be effectively improved. The accuracy of the improved detector is 5.19% higher than before, and 9.7% higher than that of another method based on amplitude threshold. Finally, we made a simple comparison between people with sleep disorders and normal people. We found that there were significant differences in spindle density between people with sleep disorders and people without sleep disorders. The average spindle density in the normal population averaged 2.59 spindles per minute. People with sleep disorders had an average spindle density of 1.32 spindles per minute. In future research, our research direction is to improve the accuracy of spindles automatic detection by improving the spindles detector and study the difference of spindles between patients with sleep disorders and normal people in a large number of samples, so that the difference of spindles can be used as the basis for the diagnosis of sleep disorders.

Keywords: Sleep spindles · EEG · Automatic detection · Sleep disorders · Wavelet transform and clustering

© Springer Nature Singapore Pte Ltd. 2021
Y. Wang (Ed.): HBAI 2020, CCIS 1369, pp. 113–124, 2021.
https://doi.org/10.1007/978-981-16-1288-6_8

1 Introduction

1.1 A Subsection Sample

Sleep spindles are characteristic waves in N2 stage of NREM sleep, and one of the few transient events that is different from the normal sleep. Although its appearance time is very short, it has been found to be related to various sleep diseases, especially playing an important role in the consolidation of human memory [1]. In the clinic, some research scholars have found that various disorders, such as schizophrenia, Parkinson's syndrome, autism, and sleep disorders, are related to changes in the density of the spindles. Sleep spindles are produced in the thalamus of human brain, which are produced by the complex interaction among thalamus, limbic area and cortical area. They are defined as the short period oscillation waves visible on the EEG signal graph, which generally exist in the "non rapid eye movement sleep" state. In the sleep microstructure, spindle is one of the most important elements, which, together with K-complex wave, constitutes a sign to distinguish "non rapid eye movement second sleep stage (N2)". Berger first described the sleep spindles in 1933. Loomis et al. First used 20–40 uV amplitude and 14–15 Hz frequency to define the spindles. The sleep spindle consists of a group of rhythmic waves whose amplitude gradually increases and then decreases. Studies have examined their frequency ranges and methods of analyzing EEG signals visually or computer by medical experts [2–5]. According to the research, the human body produces sleep spindles from the thalamus of the brain in the state of fatigue. Its purpose is precisely to transmit signals to other parts of the brain, so as to prevent external interference signals from stimulating these other parts during sleep, so as to ensure good sleep performance.

The American Academy of sleep medicine (AASM) defines sleep spindles as EEG signals with sinusoidal spindles lasting for 0.5 s–3 s, with a frequency distribution of 11–16 Hz, which has a very obvious central bias in EEG data [6–9]. This definition of sleep spindles will be used throughout this study. Since the American Society of sleep medicine standard does not distinguish between slow (<13 Hz) and fast (>13 Hz) waves, this paper does not make a distinction in the study. It is generally defined that the central frequency of sleep spindle is between 11 and 16 Hz. The duration of sleep spindles is generally defined as at least 0.5 s, and some papers define the maximum limit of spindles as 3 s [10–13]. As shown in Fig. 1.

Experts have been testing spindles to represent the golden rule, but the consistency among experts is only 86%. Visual segmentation is often affected by personal factors, and often miss some spindle that can be detected by automatic algorithm. Because the signal-to-noise ratio of the background wave changes greatly throughout the night, and the characteristics (frequency, duration, amplitude) of the spindles also changes with the individual, sleep stage, sleep cycle, and acquisition point, it is very difficult to ensure the consistency of the spindles [14–18]. In order to solve this problem, it is put forward to let many experts divide the spindle wave independently, but this method is more time-consuming and labor-consuming. Therefore, the development of automatic algorithm has always been the focus of engineering research.

In this paper, our data is from Dr. Huang Chaoyang, sleep monitoring room of Xuanwu Hospital in Beijing. The data collection equipment uses PSG. In addition to EEG, We collected the EEG data of 3 channels on the left and right. F3 and F4 are

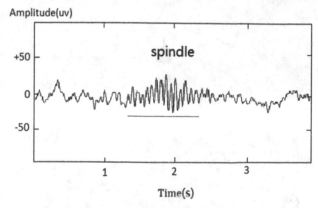

Fig. 1. Sleep spindle.

the frontal brain areas, C3 and C4 are the central brain areas, and O1 and O2 are the occipital areas. These electrode positions have the highest frequency of spindle waves. In general, the central brain area is the largest. Data analysis tools mainly use Matlab 2016a, Python, etc. Based on Morlet wavelet transform, we improved the automatic detection of sleep spindles with cluster. Compared with the method before and another automatic detection method, the accuracy of the improved automatic detection of spindles has been significantly improved. Finally, we compared the difference between the patients with sleep disorders and the normal people, hoping to provide a method for clinical diagnosis and treatment of sleep disorders.

2   Methods

2.1   Data Acquisition

The six data used for the study were collected from Dr. Huang Chaoyang, sleep monitoring room of Xuanwu Hospital in Beijing. The sleep data of six patients with sleep disorders were collected all night for 10 h. The data were obtained by polysomnography, including EEG, eye electricity, mandibular electromyography, oronasal airflow and respiratory motility, ECG, blood oxygen, snoring, limb movement, body position and other parameters. Before sleep monitoring, we will tell patients to pay attention to their eating habits and keep their scalp clean, which is helpful to collect sleep EEG data. Before sleep monitoring, patients should urinate and defecate in advance to ensure that ten hours of sleep data from 9 p.m. to 7 a.m. are collected. The sampling frequency is 512 Hz. Because most of the sleep spindles appear in the second stage of non rapid eye movement, many spindles detector need to be divided into sleep stages in advance. The automatic detector used in this paper can directly detect the spindles of the sleep data of 10 h in the whole night. In this paper, we use F4 channel in EEG channel, The relevant electrode positions we collected are shown in the Fig. 2 below. The analysis tools mainly use Matlab 2016a and Python.

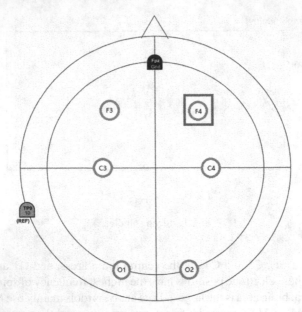

Fig. 2. Related electrodes distribution.

2.2 Automatic Detection of Sleep Spindles

Our improved automatic spindle detection method mainly uses wavelet transform and unsupervised method-K-means clustering. First, we use the traditional wavelet transform method to detect the spindles of the processed EEG signal. After the detection is over, we then use the clustering method to cluster the detected spindle wave extraction frequency and amplitude features. Finally, we can cluster the results of the spindle detection. The flow of the entire experimental method is shown in Fig. 3.

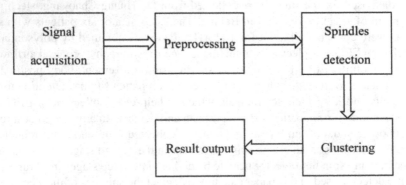

Fig. 3. Sleep spindles automatic detection.

Continue wavelet transform (CWT) is a signal analysis method that projects one-dimensional signal to two-dimensional time-scale plane. This two-dimensional plane form is established by the translation and expansion transform of a parent wavelet [16–19]. The definition of wavelet function is as follows:

$$\int_{-\infty}^{+\infty} \varphi(t)dt = 0 \tag{1}$$

Here, $\|\varphi(t)\| = 1$, the center of the function is at $t = 0$, which is called the mother wavelet function, also called the base wavelet function. The wavelet function generated by the parent wavelet function can be expressed as:

$$\varphi_{\mu,s}(t) = \frac{1}{\sqrt{s}}\varphi(\frac{t-\mu}{s}) \tag{2}$$

Here, μ and s are translation parameters and scale parameters respectively. Changing the translation parameter μ can change the window position and analyze the composition characteristics of $f(t)$ in different time periods. By changing the scale parameter s, the shape and size of the window can be changed, thus the spectrum structure of the parent wavelet can be changed. This also reflects the advantages of wavelet transform in time resolution and frequency resolution.

For any signal function $f(t) \in L^2(R)$, if the signal is decomposed on this wavelet function, its wavelet transform can be obtained as:

$$W\{f(\mu, s)\} = <f, \varphi_{\mu,s}> = \int_{-\infty}^{+\infty} f(t)\frac{1}{\sqrt{s}}\varphi^*(\frac{t-\mu}{s})dt \tag{3}$$

Here, φ^* is the complex conjugate function of φ, W is the result of wavelet transform, and $<a, b>$ is the inner product of variable a and variable b. The concept of inner product can express the similarity of two functions. Wavelet transform shows the similarity of f and $\varphi_{\mu,s}$. When $s > 1$, it is equivalent to stretching the waveform. The global profile of the signal and the similarity of the wavelet function are observed on a large scale. When $s < 1$, it is equivalent to compressing the waveform, and observing the local characteristics of the signal and the similarity of the wavelet function from the details. The mother wavelet function used in this paper is Morlet wavelet. Morlet wavelet has good centralization and symmetry in time and frequency domain, and has certain similarity with spindle wave, so we choose Morlet wavelet as the mother wavelet of wavelet transform [20–24].

Based on Morlet wavelet, the function of automatic selection of spindle wave is defined as:

$$\varphi(x) = (\pi F_B)^{-0.5} \exp(2\pi i F_C x) \exp(-x^2/F_B) \tag{4}$$

Where, $F_B = 2s^2$, $s = n/2\pi F_C$, n is the number of cycles of complex Morlet wavelet. Fc is the center frequency. Set it to 13.5, which is the most accurate frequency target. We first calculate the CWT of the filtered signal according to the center frequency of the complex Morlet wavelet at 13.5 Hz, then select the real part of the wavelet coefficient corresponding to the frequency range of 11 Hz to 16 Hz, and use the 0.1 s moving window to calculate its moving average value. Setting 4.5 times of the accumulated mean moving value of all time periods without artifacts as the threshold value. If the real-time mean moving value > threshold, and the duration of the real-time mean moving value greater than the threshold value is greater than 0.5 s and less than 3 s, it is judged as spindle wave. If the distance between the identified spindles is less than 1 s, the latter spindles will be discarded, and finally the spindles will be merged in the duration range (Fig. 4).

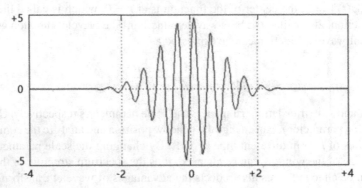

Fig. 4. Morlet wavelet transform.

We propose to improve the method of automatic selection of spindle wave by clustering. Clustering is the process of clustering similar things together and dividing different things into different categories. It is a very important means in data analysis. In terms of data analysis, clustering and classification are two technologies. Classification means that we have known the classification of things and need to learn the classification rules from the samples, which is a kind of guided learning. Clustering is a kind of unsupervised learning, in which we give simple rules to get the classification. First, we determine a k value, that is, we want to cluster the data sets to get k sets. Randomly select k data points from the dataset as the center of mass [25]. For each point in the data set, calculate its distance from each centroid (such as the Euclidean distance).

Euclidean distance:

$$d_{12} = \sqrt{(x_1 - x_2)^2 + (y_1 - y_2)^2} \tag{5}$$

Cosine distance:

$$\cos \theta = \frac{x_1 x_2 + y_1 y_2}{\sqrt{x_1^2 + y_1^2}\sqrt{x_2^2 + y_2^2}} \tag{6}$$

Correlation coefficient:

$$\rho_{XY} = \frac{Cov(X, Y)}{\sqrt{D(X)}\sqrt{D(Y)}} = \frac{E((X - EX)(Y - EY))}{\sqrt{D(X)}\sqrt{D(Y)}} \tag{7}$$

If it is close to any centroid, it will be divided into the set to which that centroid belongs. After putting all the data together, there are k sets. Then recalculate the centroid of each set. If the distance between the newly calculated centroid and the original centroid is less than a set threshold (indicating that the position of the recalculated centroid changes little, tends to be stable, or converges), we can think that the clustering has reached the expected result, and the algorithm is terminated. The process of K-means clustering is shown in Fig. 5. In this paper, we extract the central frequency and amplitude of each spindles as a data set of clustering. Cluster the spindles automatically selected from each sample, and then test the clustering results.

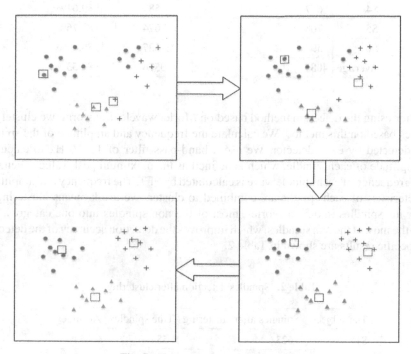

Fig. 5. K-means clustering process.

3 Data Processing and Result

The automatic detection process of spindle wave is shown in the figure above. Our data is from Dr. Huang Chaoyang of Xuanwu Hospital in Beijing. We collected six patients with sleep disorders. The patients were in a quiet sleep monitoring room for 10 h of signal collection from 9 p.m. to 7 a.m. We analyzed the related F4 channel EEG signals. Any standard signal preprocessing includes filtering, down sampling and re reference. We used 0.5–35 Hz band-pass filter to reduce the sampling frequency from 512 Hz to 256 Hz. For the processed signal, we first evaluated six data by experts, and detected the spindle wave using the golden rule. Then we use the Morlet wavelet transform to detect the spindles automatically. We selected 669, 733, 634, 657, 768, 594 spindles during the whole night's sleep. We calculated the accuracy of the true spindles detected by the experts. As shown in Table 1.

Table 1. Spindles detection based on Morlet wavelet

The Subjects	Spindles recognized by detector	True spindles	Accuracy
S1	669	592	88.49%
S2	733	623	84.99%
S3	634	571	90.06%
S4	657	589	89.64%
S5	768	674	87.76%
S6	594	527	88.72%
Average	**4085**	**3576**	**87.53%**

After using the detection method based on Morlet wavelet transform, we cluster the spindles based on this method. We calculate the frequency and amplitude of the spindle wave detected by each detector. We use a band-pass filter of 11–16 Hz to calculate the amplitude of each spindle, which is defined as the maximum peak value. Then, the center frequency of each spindle wave is calculated by FFT. The frequency and amplitude characteristics of each spindle are combined to cluster. We use k-means clustering to cluster the spindles into 5 categories, most of the non spindles into one category. We delete the most of the non spindles, which improves the detection accuracy of the detector. The specific results are shown in Table 2.

Table 2. Spindles detection after clustering

The subjects	Spindles after clustering	True spindles	Accuracy
S1	623	584	93.73%
S2	671	611	91.05%
S3	599	562	93.82%
S4	616	582	94.48%
S5	707	655	92.64%
S6	573	519	90.57%
Average	**3789**	**3513**	**92.72%**

In order to further verify the performance of the improved automatic spindles detector, we use another detection method based on amplitude threshold to detect the spindles. The main operation flow of this method is as follows: firstly, 11–16 Hz band-pass filter is applied to the data firstly, and then the signal envelope is obtained by connecting the local maximum value of the band-pass rectifier signal. In the envelope, we look for peaks and troughs, and construct the top 120 sequence graph based on frequency. We set the minimum threshold to twice the maximum frequency of the envelope amplitude peak. The upper limit of the threshold is 8 times of the mean value of F4 channel filtered absolute value. All points in the envelope that exceed the lower limit of the threshold are marked as the spindle wave boundary. All points in the envelope larger than the upper limit of the threshold are marked as possible spindles. For each peak, find the boundary point before and after it, and calculate the duration. The criterion is 0.5 s–3 s. The results of automatic detection of spindle wave are shown in Table 3.

Table 3. Spindles detection based on amplitude threshold

The subjects	Spindles recognized by detector	True spindles	Accuracy
S1	703	586	83.36%
S2	662	534	80.66%
S3	659	548	83.15%
S4	615	499	81.13%
S5	817	686	83.97%
S6	543	467	86.00%
Average	3999	3320	83.02%

4 Comparison

Sleep spindle is the characteristic wave of the second stage of sleep. Sleep spindle is closely related to sleep quality. The density of the spindles is defined as the number of spindles per minute. In order to study the spindle difference between sleep disorder patients and normal people, we processed and analyzed the spindles of six sleep disorder patients, and calculated the spindle density of these six patients. After that, we processed the sleep EEG data of six normal people. The specific number of detected spindles is not listed here. We calculated and plotted the spindle density of the two populations in Fig. 6. As shown in the figure below, the spindle densities of the six patients were 2.09, 1.39, 0.98, 0.89, 1.59, 1.01, and the average density was 1.32. The spindle densities of the six controls were 2.73, 2.38, 2.92, 1.68, 3.53, 2.28, and the average density was 2.59. We compared the spindle density of these six patients with the spindle density of normal people. It is found that the spindle density of people with sleep disorders is much lower than that of normal people. It can be concluded that the spindle density of most patients with sleep disorders may be lower than normal. Our future research hopes to analyze this phenomenon through more data. In addition, our next goal is to analyze other characteristics of spindles in different populations, such as average amplitude and frequency characteristics.

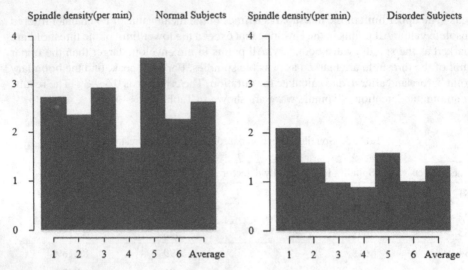

Fig. 6. Sleep spindle density comparison in disorder and normal subjects.

5 Conclusion

At present, sleep disorder has become a universal disease, which is distributed in all ages. However, there are many kinds of sleep disorders. Most of the diagnosis of sleep disorders still depends on the analysis of the scale. Sometimes different doctors rely on experience to make judgments. So sleep disorders need to be judged by a standard. Sleep spindles are proposed as a characteristic index of sleep quality assessment. The detection of sleep spindle mainly depends on manual detection. The number of spindles in a night varies from 200 to 1000. It takes a lot of manpower to detect the spindle manually. In addition, different doctors may have different judgments based on experience. Therefore, the demand for automatic spindle detector is very urgent. At present, there are some spindles automatic detectors. However, the accuracy of some spindles detectors is not ideal, or there are many requirements for data.

In this paper, we propose a clustering method to improve the Morlet wavelet based spindles detector. We carried out the experiment and research on the 10 h sleep data of six patients with sleep disorders. Before the detection of the spindles, only the original data was filtered by a simple band-pass filter. The results show that the improved detector improves the average accuracy by 5.18%. The accuracy of S4 in one sample can reach 94.48%. The average accuracy can reach 92.72%. In addition, we also compared the performance of the improved spindles detector with another detector based on amplitude threshold. According to the comparison between Table 2 and Table 3, we can find that the accuracy of the improved spindles detector is 8.75% higher than that based on the amplitude threshold. This shows that we can improve the spindle wave detector to a certain extent. After that, we compared the difference of spindles density between sleep impaired and normal people. It can be found that the spindles density of sleep impaired people is significantly lower than that of normal people. The average density of spindles in the normal population is 2.59 per minute, while the density of spindles in the patients with sleep disorders we collected is only 1.32 per minute. The main purpose of our article is to propose an improved spindles automatic detector, hoping to improve the performance of spindle detector to a certain extent, so as to reduce the cost of human and material resources in clinical spindles detection. Then through the study of the difference of spindles characteristics between sleep disorder patients and normal people, we found that the spindles density of sleep disorder patients decreased. In the future research, our goal is to find out more differences of spindles between patients with sleep disorders and normal people, so as to provide a method for clinical judgment and treatment of sleep disorders.

Acknowledgment. This work was financially supported by National Key R&D Program of China (2018YFC1314500), National Natural Science Foundation of China (61806146), Natural Science Foundation of Tianjin City (17JCQNJC04200), Tianjin Key Laboratory Foundation of Complex System Control Theory and Application (TJKL-CTACS-201702) and Young and Middle-Aged Innovation Talents Cultivation Plan of Higher Institutions in Tianjin.

References

1. De, G.L., Ferrara, M.: Sleep spindles: an overview. Sleep Med. Rev. **7**(5), 423–440 (2003)
2. Parekh, A., Selesnick, I.W., Rapoport, D.M., et al.: Sleep spindle detection using time-frequency sparsity. In: Signal Processing in Medicine and Biology Symposium, pp. 1–6. IEEE (2015)
3. Loomis, A.L., Harvey, E.N., Hobart, G.A.: Further observations on the potential rhythms of the cerebral corlex during sleep. Science **82**, 452–469 (1935)
4. Fazel, M., Hindi, H., Boyd, S.P.: A rank minimization heuristic with application to minimum order system approximation. In: American Control Conference, 2001. Proceedings of the IEEE, vol. 6, pp. 4734–4739 (2001)
5. Ferrarelli, F., Huber, R., Peterson, M.J., et al.: Reduced sleep spindle activity in schizophrenia patients. Am. J. Psychiatry **164**(3), 483 (2007)
6. Molle, M., Marshall, L., Gais, S., et al.: Grouping of spindle activity during slow oscillations in human non-rapid eye movement sleep. J. Neurosci. **22**(24), 10941–10947 (2002)
7. Matin, N., Lafortune, M., Godbout, J., et al.: Topography of age-related changes in sleep spindles. Neurobiol. Aging **34**(2), 468–476 (2013)
8. Wamsley, E.J., Tucker, M.A., Shinn, A.K., et al.: Reduced sleep spindles and spindle coherence in schizophrenia: mechanisms of impaired memory consolidation. Biol. Psychiatry **71**(2), 154–161 (2012)
9. Wendt, S.L., Christensen, J.A., Kempfner, J., et al.: Validation of a novel automatic sleep spindle detector with high performance during sleep in middle aged subjects. In: International Conference of the IEEE Engineering in Medicine & Biology Society. Conference Proceedings IEEE Engineering in Medicine and Biology Society, p. 4250 (2012)
10. Tsanas, A., Clifford, G.D.: Stage-independent. Single lead EEG sleep spindle detection using the continuous wavelet transform and local weighted smoothing. Front. Hum. Neurosci. **9**, 181 (2015)
11. Hirshkowitz, M.: COMMENTARY - Standing on the shoulders of giants: the Standardized Sleep Manual, after 30 years. Sleep Med. Rev. **4**(2), 169–179 (2000)
12. Gibbs, E.L., Lorimer, F.M., Gibbs, F.A.: Clinical correlates of exceedingly fast activity in the eletroencephalogram. Dis. Nerv. Syst. **11**(11), 323 (1950)

13. Wright, J., Gancsh, A., Rao, S., et al.: Robust principal component analysis: exact recovery corrupted low-rank matrices via convex optimization. J. ACM
14. Wright, J., Peng, Y., Ma, Y., et al.: Robust principal component analysis: exact recovery of corrupted low-rank matrices by convex optimization. In: International Conference on Neural Information Processing Systems. Curran Associates Inc., pp. 2080–2088 (2009)
15. Parekh, A., Selesnick, I.W., Osrio, R.S., et al.: Sleep spindle detection using time-frequency sparsity. In: Signal Processing in Medicine and Biology Symposium, pp. 1–6. IEEE (2015)
16. Parekh, A., Selesnick, I.W., Osorio, R.S., et al.: Multichannel sleep spindle detection using sparse low-rank optimization. J. Neurosci. Methods **1**, 1–16 (2017)
17. Parekh, A., Selesnick, I.W., Rapoport, D.M., et al.: Detection of k-complexes and sleep spindles (DETOKS) using Sparse optimization. J. Neurosci. Methods **251**, 37–46 (2015)
18. Shi, J., Liu, X., Li, Y., Zhang, Q.: Multichannel EEG-based sleep stage classification with joint collaborative representation and multiple kernel learning. J. Neurosci. Methods **254**, 94–101 (2015)
19. Liu, M.Y., Huang, A., Huang, N.E.: Evaluating and improving automatic sleep spindle detection by using multi-objective evolutionary algorithms. Front. Hum. Neurosci. **11**, 261 (2017)
20. Ting, C.M., Shh, S., Zainuddin, Z.M., et al.: Spectral estimation of nonstationary EEG using particle filtering with application to event-related desynchronization (ERD). IEEE Trans. Biomed. Eng. **58**(2), 321–331 (2011)
21. Anderer, P., et al.: Automatic sleep spindle detection validated in 167H of sleep recordings from 278 healthy controls and patients. In: Abstract of the 17th Congress of the European Sleep Research Society, Prague, p. 313, October 2004
22. Blankertz, B., Tomioka, R., Lemm, S., et al.: Optimizing spatial filters for robust EEG single-trial analysis. IEEE Signal Process. Mag. **25**(1), 41–56 (2007)
23. Fish, D.R., Allen, P.J., Blackie, J.D.: A new method for the quantitative analysis of sleep spindles during continuous overnight EEG recordings. J. Sleep Res. **70**, 273–277 (1988)
24. Clemens, Z., Fabo, D., Halasz, P.: Overnight verbal and visual memory retention correlates with the number of sleep spindles. In: 17th Congress of the European Sleep Research Society-Abstract, Prague, October 2004
25. Jain, A.K., Dubes, R.C.: Algorithms for clustering data. Technometrics **32**(2), 227–229 (1988)

Diagnosing Parkinson's Disease Using Multimodal Physiological Signals

Guoxin Guo[1], Shujie Wang[1], Shuaibin Wang[1], Zhiyu Zhou[2], Guangying Pei[1(✉)], and Tianyi Yan[1]

[1] School of Life Science, Beijing Institute of Technology, Haidian District, Beijing, China
pei_guangying@bit.edu.cn
[2] School of Artificial Intelligence, Beijing Normal University, Haidian District, Beijing, China

Abstract. Parkinson's disease (PD) is the second most common neurodegenerative disease after Alzheimer's disease. Due to the complex etiology and diverse clinical symptoms, it's difficult to accurately diagnose PD. In this study, we applied multimodal physiological signals, which include electroencephalography (EEG), electrocardiogram (ECG), photoplethysmography (PPG), and respiratory (RA), to classify PD and healthy control (HC) based on a multimodal support vector machine (SVM). Our experiments achieved an accuracy of 96.03%. Besides, we performed statistical analysis on the four types of physiological data of the PD group and the HC group. Results showed that the EEG of non-dementia PD patients had a significant decrease in high-frequency power, and the high-frequency energy distribution of the normalized PPG signal increased compared with HC. The current study suggests that combining the physiological information of multiple models and machine learning methods could improve the diagnosis accuracy of PD disease and be a potentially effective method of clinical diagnosis.

Keywords: Parkinson's disease · Electroencephalography · Multimodal physiological signals · Machine learning

1 Introduction

Parkinson's disease (PD) is the second most common neurodegenerative disease after Alzheimer's disease and affects two percent to three percent of people over 60 [1, 2]. The motor symptoms of PD are bradykinesia, postural instability, rigidity, and rest tremor [3, 4]. PD is a long-term disease that usually occurs in middle-aged and elderly people, and its average age of onset is about 60 years old. Accompanying the development of the disease a few years later, the self-care ability of patients will be gradually lost or even bedridden for a long time.

In terms of pathophysiology, the characteristic of PD is that the death of dopaminergic neurons in the basal ganglia leads to the loss of dopamine, which affects the processing of information by the cerebral cortex. Due to the complex etiology and diverse clinical symptoms of PD, it's difficult to accurately diagnose PD, especially in the early stage [5]. The clinical diagnosis of PD is completed by clinical scales and combined with clinical

© Springer Nature Singapore Pte Ltd. 2021
Y. Wang (Ed.): HBAI 2020, CCIS 1369, pp. 125–136, 2021.
https://doi.org/10.1007/978-981-16-1288-6_9

symptoms, neuroimaging data, and other diagnostic criteria [5]. The physiological signal can be obtained efficiently with low cost and is associated with the disease characteristics of PD patients. Building a machine learning classification model based on physiological signals is an excellent auxiliary method to improve the certainty of the clinical diagnosis of PD disease [6].

Electroencephalography (EEG) is a widely used examination method for clinical neurological diseases, and it can detect dynamic changes in the brain activity of PD patients. The high time resolution of EEG allows it to be used to study sub-second dynamic changes in brain neural activity [7]. The quantitative EEG technology (QEEG) is widely used for EEG analysis. The increase of delta and theta relative power and decrease of alpha and beta relative power of EEG appear in the early stages of PD, and the main changes are the slowing of EEG and the reduction of dominant frequency [8, 9]. Neurofeedback training of sensorimotor rhythm (SMR) can effectively improve PD symptoms and clinical scale scores, which suggests that the sensory-motor rhythm (SMR) may have a significant correlation with PD motor dysfunction [10]. In addition to motor dysfunction, autonomic nerve dysfunction quite possibly occurs in PD at an early stage. Electroencephalography (ECG) can detect the innervation effect of the heart sympathetic and parasympathetic nerves. Studies have shown that people with low heart rate variability (HRV) have a 2–3 times higher risk of PD that's than people with normal HRV [11]. The changes in electrocardiographic may be earlier than the appearance of PD [12]. However, current research has not yet determined the value of ECG in the early diagnosis of PD. The dysfunction of the cardiovascular system is one of the common non-motor symptoms of PD, which can be detected by the PPG signal [13]. Autonomous muscle activity of PD patients is affected by motor dysfunction and may lead to lung dysfunction, such as shortness of breath, repeated coughing, etc. [14]. Above all, we can improve the accuracy of the clinical diagnosis of PD by combining the differences of various physiological signal characteristics.

From the view of physiological signal processing, data-driven machine learning methods are becoming more powerful and widely used. Machine learning methods can be applied to multimodal physiological data analysis due to the advantages of their multivariate property. Additionally, unlike traditional signal processing methods, machine learning methods can ensure the optimal use of a large amount of information that exists in heterogeneous data from multiple sources. Moreover, the multivariate pattern analysis method can discover potential biomarkers based on multimodal physiological signals to distinguish patients from normal controls at the individual level and further highlight the physiological mechanism of PD behavioral symptoms. Recently, many researchers combine multimodal physiological data with machine learning methods and have obtained many valuable results [15–18]. Kyle Ross et al. used ECG and galvanic skin response (GSR) signals to classify professional trauma patients and novices at a professional level and achieved an accuracy of 79.84% [15]. Rong L et al. used EEG and ECG signals combined with the SVM model to classify cognitive load, which yielded an accuracy of 97.2% [16]. Sara et al. used electromyogram (EMG) and ECG data combined with feature selection and machine learning algorithms to detect the psychological stress of healthy people, and the four levels of pressure recognition accuracy reached 96.2% [17]. Wei et al. recognized emotions by using four modal physiological signals (EEG,

ECG, respiratory (RA), and GSR) combined with a weight fusion strategy, successfully improved the accuracy rate of 74.52% in single-mode to 84.62% in multi-mode [18].

In our study, we analyzed multimodal physiological signals of early and mid-term PD with cognitively normal and healthy controls by using machine learning methods. Considering the heterogeneity between different modal physiological data, we employed a multimodal kernel SVM to improve model accuracy and provide multiple analysis perspectives. The purpose of our research is: 1) to construct a multi-modal auxiliary diagnosis model and compare the performance with the single-modal model. 2) to analyze the characteristic differences between EEG, ECG, PPG, and RA signals between HC and PD patients.

2 Materials and Methods

2.1 Subjects

18 participants were recruited from November 2019 to January 2020 in the present study. 9 nondemented Parkinson's disease patients were recruited from the Neurological Rehabilitation Center of Beijing Rehabilitation Hospital Affiliated to Capital Medical University and 9 healthy controls were recruited from the Physical Examination Center of Aerospace Central Hospital in Beijing, China. Demographic and clinical details are summarized in Table 1. This study was approved by the Ethics Committee of the Beijing Rehabilitation Hospital Affiliated to Capital Medical University and Aerospace Central Hospital following the Declaration of Helsinki, and all participants were given informed written consent before the experiment.

Table 1. Demographic data.

	PD	HC	P-value
N (sex ratio M/F)	9 (3/6)	9 (0/9)	0.058[a]
Age (SD), y	55.22 (6.25)	52.11 (4.98)	0.287[b]
H&Y (SD)	2.28 (0.71)	–	–
UPDRS III (SD)	25.89 (7.32)	–	–
MMSE (SD)	28.11 (0.99)	28.77 (0.92)	0.182[b]
MoCA (SD)	25.00 (4.12)	–	–

H&Y, Hoehn & Yahr stage; UPDRS III, Movement Disorders Society-Unified Parkinson's Disease Rating Scale-Part III (severity of motor symptoms); MMSE, Mini-Mental State Examination; MoCA, Beijing version of the Montreal Cognitive Assessment.
[a]χ^2 test
[b]Two-sample t-test.

2.2 Multimodal Physiological Data Recording and Processing

Participants were instructed to sit comfortably, stay awake, and keep eyes open and in a quiet room during the 15-min Multimodal physiological signals (including EEG, ECG, photoplethysmography (PPG), and respiratory (RA) signals) synchronous recording. The EEG was recorded with an ActiCHamp amplifier system using an electrode cap with 32 Ag/AgCl electrodes placed according to the standard international 10–20 system (LiveAmp, Brain Products GmbH, Gilching, Germany). The reference was the Left Mastoid Process. Synchronous acquisition of ECG, photoplethysmography, and respiratory signals by using the external AUX port of the ActiCHamp amplifier system. The sampling rate was 1,000 Hz, and the EEG electrode impedances were kept below 5 KΩ. An online bandpass filter with 0.1–100 Hz and an offline bandpass filter with 0.1– 45 Hz was used to improve the signal-noise ratio. Multimodal physiological data were pre-processed by MATLAB R2014a (Mathworks Inc., Natick, MA, United States) with the open-source toolbox EEGLAB (Swartz Center for Computational Neuroscience, La Jolla, CA, United States). To remove artifacts, such as electrooculogram artifacts, muscle artifacts, an independent component analysis was used on EEG data within all channels. The voltage of EEG data segments exceeding 150 μV was removed, and the other modal signal segments were removed at the same time. Then, the pre-processed multimodal physiological data were divided into 60 s for each epoch to extract features. Finally, to ensure that the number of epochs is the same between subjects, fourteen valid epochs without artifacts were selected from each subject.

For each epoch of EEG data, a fast Fourier transform was used to calculate spectral power for EEG data within all channels. The selected frequency bands were: delta (2– 4 Hz), theta (4–8 Hz), alpha (8–13 Hz), beta (13–30 Hz), and SMR (12–15 Hz), absolute powers, and relative powers of the delta, theta, alpha, and beta band were computed for each scalp electrodes. The relative power was the ratio of the absolute power in a frequency band to the power of the entire frequency spectrum from 2 to 30 Hz. Then, the ratio of the alpha spectrum to theta spectrum was calculated.

For each epoch of ECG data, we first detected the R peaks and computed the R-R intervals which are the time between every two consecutive peaks [19]. The ECG waveform is shown in Fig. 1. Then, we computed the Heart Rate (HR) values, the standard deviation of normal R-R interval (SDNN), the Heart Rate Variability (HRV), the root mean square of successive R-R interval (RMSSD), and the proportion of NN50 divided by the total number of R-R intervals (PNN50). In addition to the heart rate features, we computed the power spectra of the R-R interval using Fast Fourier Transformation (FFT). We got the following frequency-domain features: very-low-frequency power (VLF, 0–0.04 Hz), low-frequency power (LF, 0.04–0.15 Hz), high-frequency power (HF, 0.15–0.4 Hz), normalized low-frequency power (nLF), normalized high-frequency power (nHF), the ratio between the power on LF and HF bands of the ECG and the total power (TP). The normalized calculation for LF and HF is shown in Eq. (1) and (2).

$$nLF = 100 * LF/(TP - VLF) \tag{1}$$

$$nHF = 100 * HF/(TP - VLF) \tag{2}$$

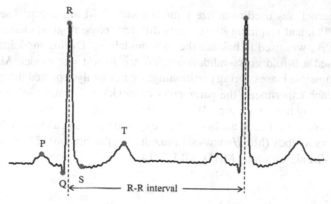

Fig. 1. ECG and QRS waveform. P, the peak of P; Q, the peak of Q; S, the peak of S; T, the peak of T.

After an offline bandpass filter with 0.1–30 Hz for PPG and respiratory signals, we normalized the data by subtracting the mean and dividing by the standard deviation. Then we calculated the pulse rate variability (PRV) [20], mean, and the standard deviation of pulse intervals, pulse rate, and respiratory. We calculated the spectral power of the normalized PPG signals and respiratory signals.

2.3 Feature Selection

We employed the elastic network method for our feature selection on the subset of the original features. The elastic network was proposed by Hui Zou's team in 2005 [21], which is used the L1 penalty and L2 penalty. Elastic net is similar to lasso but with fewer limitations and more widely used. To find the optimal norm regularization parameters L1 and L2, we employed two circulations in the code.

2.4 Multimodal SVM Algorithm

SVM is a classic supervised learning algorithm and has been successful in many fields. Multimodal SVM have shown more benefits for data from multiple heterogeneous sources, it can choose a suitable kernel function for each modality's data. When each modality's data matched the suitable kernel function, the decision function and kernel function as shown in Eq. (3) and (4),

$$\hat{y}(x) = \sum_{i=1}^{n} \alpha_i y_i K(x_i, x) + b \tag{3}$$

$$K(x_i, x_j) = \sum_{m=1}^{M} \beta_m k_m(x_i^m, x_j^m), \sum_m \beta_m = 1 \tag{4}$$

where n is the number of training samples and α_i is the weight coefficient. y_i is the label of the training sample. x_i is the input data of the training sample. $k_m(x_i^m, x_j^m)$ is the kernel function of the mth modality. β_m is the modality weight of the mth modality. And b is a constant coefficient.

A linear kernel was used to utilize a multimodal SVM algorithm. The feature of EEG, ECG, PPG, and respiratory represents different physiological characteristics of the body. The β_m was used to balance the four modalities. During model training and testing, we used a 9-fold cross-validation approach to test our model. Moreover, to further avoid possible biases during partitioning, we randomly repeated the experiments 10 times. In each experiment, the parameters of model and feature selection and β_m were determined by inner iterations. When model-training was finished, the frequency of the selected feature for each modality in all experiments was calculated. We used the LIBSVM library toolbox (http://www.csie.ntu.edu.tw/cjlin/libsvm) [22] to construct the multimodal SVM algorithm by MATLAB R2014a.

3 Results

3.1 Classification Model Comparison

The comparison results of multi-modal and single-modal methods were shown in Table 2. With single-modal methods, we obtained a cross-validated accuracy of 87.54% for EEG modality, 62.10% for ECG modality, 71.5% for PPG modality, and 73.3% for respiratory modality. We got a significant increase in accuracy, 96.06% for Multimodal, by using multi-modal methods. Moreover, we compared the receiver operating characteristic (ROC) curves and the area under the curve (AUC) values between single-modal and multi-modal (Fig. 2).

Table 2. The performance of classification for multimodal and single-modal methods

Model	Accuracy	Sensitivity	Specificity
EEG	87.54 ± 13.46%	86.19 ± 15.14%	88.89 ± 19.75%
ECG	62.10 ± 23.83%	72.22 ± 25.28%	51.98 ± 28.51%
PPG	71.50 ± 18.57%	74.84 ± 21.95%	68.17 ± 29.27%
RA	73.37 ± 15.38%	76.43 ± 16.78%	70.32 ± 24.23%
Multimodal	96.03 ± 6.30%	94.44 ± 9.30%	97.62 ± 5.10%

The plus-minus gives the standard deviation; EEG, electroencephalogram; ECG, electrocardiogram; PPG, photoplethysmography; RA: respiratory; Multimodal: EEG + ECG + PPG + RA.

3.2 Feature Statistical Analysis

Before feature selection, the two-sample t-tests were performed on the features of each modality's data to test the significant differences ($p < 0.05$). The characteristic statistical results (top 10) of the four modal physiological signals were shown in Table 3. There were 10 significant differences in the characteristics of EEG modalities, all of which were listed in Table 3. Among them, the frontal lobe high-frequency power (SMR, alpha, and

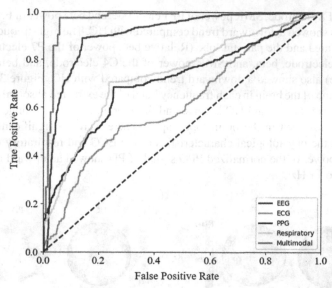

Fig. 2. ROC curves of single-modal and multi-modal. The AUC values in this experiment are as follows: EEG, 0.9075; ECG, 0.6192; PPG, 0.7103; Respiratory, 0.7351; and Multimodal, 0.9712.

Table 3. The results of statistical analysis for multimodal physiological signal

EEG		ECG		PPG		RA	
Feature	P-value	Feature	P-value	Feature	P-value	Feature	P-value
FP1-SMR	**0.040**[b]	PNN50	0.091[b]	P.S.0.5	0.127[b]	RA.rate	0.319[a]
F3-Beta	**0.027**[b]	HR	0.176[a]	P.S.0.8	0.083[b]	R.S.0.8	0.284[a]
P7-rBeta	**0.009**[b]	M.RR	0.250[b]	P.S.5.3	**0.019**[a]	R.S.1.3	0.291[b]
P3-SMR	**0.020**[b]	VLF	0.240[b]	P.S.5.5	**0.005**[a]	R.S.2.0	0.449[b]
CP2-Beta	**0.025**[b]	TP	0.242[b]	P.S.6.5	**0.038**[a]	R.S.2.3	0.220[b]
C4-Beta	**0.007**[b]	nLF	0.376[b]	P.S.6.8	**0.018**[a]	R.S.2.5	0.218[b]
C4-SMR	**0.028**[b]	LF	0.408[b]	P.S.7.8	**0.018**[a]	R.S.3.0	0.377[b]
F8-Alpha	**0.031**[b]	HRV	0.434[b]	P.S.8.0	**0.018**[a]	R.S.3.3	0.231[b]
F8-Beta	**0.010**[b]	LF/HF	0.424[b]	P.S.11.5	**0.047**[a]	R.S.3.5	0.335[b]
F8-SMR	**0.005**[b]	SDNN	0.674[b]	P.S.11.8	0.062[a]	R.S.3.8	0.445[b]

EEG, electroencephalogram; ECG, electrocardiogram; PPG, photoplethysmography; RA, respiratory; r, relative power; M.RR, mean of R-R interval; LF/HF, the ratio between the power on LF and HF bands; P.S., Spectral power of PPG signal; RA.rate, respiratory rate; R.S., Spectral power of the respiratory signal.

The bolded text indicated a significant difference in the two groups(p < 0.05).

[a]mean of the feature of PD > mean of the feature of HC

[b]mean of the feature of PD < mean of the feature of HC

beta power of F8 electrode, SMR power of FP1 electrode, and beta power of F3 electrode) of PD patients showed a downward trend compared with HC. The high-frequency power of the central area and the parietal lobe (Relative beta power of the P7 electrode, SMR power of P3 electrode, beta, and SMR power of the C4 electrode, and beta power of CP2 electrode) also showed a downward trend compared with HC. Figure 3 shows the topographic map of the brain in each frequency band of the extracted absolute energy and relative energy of the PD and HC groups, and these brain electrical changes described above can be observed in the brain topography. There were no significant statistical differences in the physiological characteristics of the ECG and respiratory modalities. The spectral power of the normalized PPG signal of PD showed an upward trend in the interval of 5 to 11 Hz.

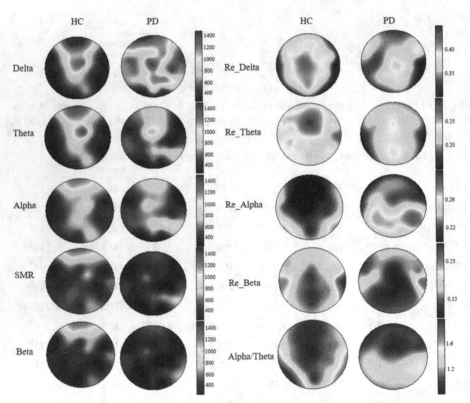

Fig. 3. The topography of the distribution of mean power in the different frequency bands. The warmer colors indicate higher relative power (scaled from minimum to maximum values of the total group). Re, relative power.

4 Discussion

Here we constructed a single-modal classification model and a multi-modal classification model respectively for early and mid-stage PD patients and HC based on multimodal support vector machine (SVM) and compared the classification performance of two types of models. The results showed that the classification performance of the multi-modal model had greatly improved classification performance compared with the single-modal model. Based on the multi-kernel learning method, the multi-modal fusion model can fully combine the information between different modal data. Compared with one-dimensional physiological information, multi-dimensional physiological information can more comprehensively reflect the truly pathological state of the PD patients. Moreover, we found that the high-frequency power of EEG in PD patients decreased in the frontal, parietal and central areas. For the PPG signal, the spectral power increased at 5–11 Hz of the normalized PPG signal of PD patients. While there were no significant differences in characteristic indicators in ECG and respiratory modalities.

EEG is an important marker of cognitive decline, and the study of PD patients showed that a decrease of EEG spectrum power above 8 Hz and an increase of spectrum power below 8 Hz compared with the healthy [23–25]. The bradykinesia of PD is inversely proportional to the power of β oscillations in the basal ganglia (BG) and frontal cortex [26, 27]. Moreover, the decrease in alpha background activity also occurs in non-dementia patients [28]. In our study, patients in our PD group are cognitively normal, accompanies with dyskinesia symptoms such as bradykinesia, and we detected significantly increased beta and SMR power in the frontal, parietal, and central regions. Sensorimotor rhythm (12–15 Hz) originates from the sensorimotor cortex [29], most of which belong to the range of beta band (13–30 Hz). Moreover, alpha power decreased in the right frontal lobe, and there was no significant increase in delta and theta power, which may be related to our patient with non-dementia.

In patients with cardiovascular diseases, the frequency spectrum energy distribution decreases in the low frequency (below 5 Hz) of the pulse signal, while the frequency spectrum energy distribution increases at the high frequency (above 5 Hz) compared to HC [30]. Our results showed that an increase in the 5–11 Hz spectrum of the normalized PPG signal, but there was a downward trend with no significant below 5 Hz. Besides, PD patients are always accompanied by autonomic dysfunction and respiratory dysfunction [31, 32] (with symptoms such as shortness of breath and cough). And we can know that the time-domain indicator of heart rate variability PNN50 has a downward trend from Table 3, although there were no statistical differences in ECG and respiratory signals may due to the limited number of samples.

Above all, our results showed the reduction of EEG power at high-frequency of non-dementia PD patients and the increase in high-frequency energy of PPG signals. Considering there is a high probability that PD patients will be accompanied by cardiovascular diseases, respiratory characteristics, and heart rate variability indexes deserve further study. By constructing the multi-modal model to identify early and mid-stage PD patients and HC based on the physiological signals of the four modalities, we got an accuracy rate of 96.03%. To enhance the stability and practicality of the model, future research will increase the sample size.

To avoid errors caused by randomness and the overfitting effect of the model, we used a 9-fold cross-validation approach to test our model 10 times. Several limitations need to be noted regarding the present study, the sample size was relatively small and the gender and age were not exactly matched. Currently only a preliminary exploration of Parkinson's auxiliary diagnosis by using multimodal physiological signals, the results proved higher classification for multi-modal diagnosing than any single-modal. In future research, we will increase the sample size and further improve the accuracy and stability of the multi-modal.

5   Conclusion

In our study, we constructed a single-modal and a multi-modal classification model respectively based on multi-modal physiological data and compared the classification performance of the two types of models. The results showed that the multi-modal classification model has a great improvement in accuracy compared with the single-modal classification model. However, our study just demonstrated that the multi-modal classification model is better than any of the single-modal classification models. Besides, we found that the reduction of EEG at high-frequency power and the increase of PPG signals at high-frequency energy in the PD group. Our preliminary investigation suggests that multi-modal physiological signal fusion analysis can effectively improve the accuracy of PD patients different from the healthy, and as a potential diagnose method in PD clinical research.

Acknowledgment. We gratefully acknowledge all the participants in this experiment for their cooperation. We thank the clinical doctors and researchers at the Neurological Rehabilitation Center of Beijing Rehabilitation Hospital Affiliated to Capital Medical University and the Physical Examination Center of Aerospace Central Hospital. We thank all the members of our lab for their suggestions and support for this project.

References

1. Lees, A.J., Hardy, J., Revesz, T.: Parkinson's disease. Lancet **373**(9680), 2055–2066 (2009)
2. Poewe, W., Seppi, K., Tanner, C.M., et al.: Parkinson disease. Nat. Rev. Dis. Primers **3**, 21 (2017)
3. Vu, T.C., Nutt, J.G., Holford, N.H.G.: Progression of motor and nonmotor features of Parkinson's disease and their response to treatment. Br. J. Clin. Pharmacol. **74**(2), 267–283 (2012)
4. Sveinbjornsdottir, S.: The clinical symptoms of Parkinson's disease. J. Neurochem. **139**, 318–324 (2016)
5. Serrano, J.I., Castillo del, D., Cortés, V.: EEG microstates change in response to increase in dopaminergic stimulation in typical Parkinson's disease patients. Front. Neurosci. **12** (2018)
6. VallsSolé, J., Valldeoriola, F.: Neurophysiological correlate of clinical signs in Parkinson's disease. Clin. Neurophysiol. **113**(6), 792–805 (2002)
7. Schumacher, J., Peraza, L., Firbank, M.: Dysfunctional brain dynamics and their origin in Lewy body dementia. Brain **142**(6), 1767–1782 (2019)

8. Han, C.X., Wang, J., Yi, G.S., et al.: Investigation of EEG abnormalities in the early stage of Parkinson's disease. Cogn Neurodyn. **7**(4), 351–359 (2013)
9. Geraedts, V.J., Boon, L.I., Marinus, J., et al.: Clinical correlates of quantitative EEG in Parkinson disease a systematic review. Neurology **91**(19), 871–883 (2018)
10. Philippens, I.H.C.H.M., Wubben, J.A., Vanwersch, R.A.P., Estevao, D.L., Tass, P.A.: Sensorimotor rhythm neurofeedback as adjunct therapy for Parkinson's disease. Ann. Clin. Trans. Neurol. **4**(8), 585–590 (2017)
11. Alonso, A., Huang, X., Mosley, T.H., Heiss, G., Chen, H.: Heart rate variability and the risk of Parkinson disease: the atherosclerosis risk in communities study. Ann. Neurol. **77**, 877–883 (2015)
12. Akbilgic, O., Kamaleswaran, R., Mohammed, A., et al.: Electrocardiographic changes predate Parkinson's disease onset. Sci Rep. **10**(1), 11319 (2020)
13. Sabino-Carvalho, J.L., Cartafina, R.A., Guimarães, G.M.N., Brandão, P.R.P., Lang, J.A., Vianna, L.C.: Baroreflex function in Parkinson's disease: Insights from the modified-Oxford technique. J. Neurophysiol. (2020). https://doi.org/10.1152/jn.00443.2020
14. Neu, H.C., Connolly Jr., J.J., Schwertley, F.W., Ladwig, H.A., Brody, A.W.: Obstructive respiratory dysfunction in Parkinsonian patients. Am. Rev. Respir. Dis. **95**, 33–47 (1967)
15. Ross, K., Sarkar, P., Rodenburg, D., et al.: Toward dynamically adaptive simulation: multimodal classification of user expertise using wearable devices. Sens. (Basel) **19**(19), 4270 (2019)
16. Xiong, R., Kong, F., Yang, X., Liu, G., Wen, W.: pattern recognition of cognitive load using EEG and ECG signals. Sens. (Basel) **20**(18), E5122 (2020)
17. Pourmohammadi, S., Maleki, A.: Stress detection using ECG and EMG signals: a comprehensive study. Comput. Methods Programs Biomed. **193**, (2020)
18. Wei, W., Jia, Q., Feng, Y., Chen, G.: Emotion recognition based on weighted fusion strategy of multichannel physiological signals. Comput. Intell. Neurosci. **2018**, 5296523 (2018)
19. Clifford, G., Azuaje, F., McSharry, P.: Advanced Methods and Tools for ECG Data Analysis. Artech House, Inc. (2006)
20. Yuda, E., Shibata, M., Ogata, Y., et al.: Pulse rate variability: a new biomarker, not a surrogate for heart rate variability. J. Physiol. Anthropol. **39**(1), 21 (2020)
21. Zou, H., Hastie, T.: Regularization and variable selection via the elastic net. J. R . Stat. Soc.: Ser. B (Stat. Methodol.) **67** (2005)
22. Chang, C.C., Lin, C.J.: LIBSVM: a library for support vector machines. ACM Trans. Intell. Syst. Technol. (2011)
23. Caviness, J.N., Hentz, J.G., Belden, C.M., et al.: Longitudinal EEG changes correlate with cognitive measure deterioration in Parkinson's disease. J. Parkinsons Dis. **5**(1) (2015)
24. Aarsland, D., Creese, B., Politis, M., et al.: Cognitive decline in Parkinson disease. Nat. Rev. Neurol. **13**(4), 217 (2017)
25. Babiloni, C., Del Percio, C., Lizio, R., Noce, G., Lopez, S., Soricelli, A., et al.: Functional cortical source connectivity of resting state electroencephalographic alpha rhythms shows similar abnormalities in patients with mild cognitive impairment due to Alzheimer's and Parkinson's diseases. Clin. Neurophysiol. **129**, 766–782 (2018)
26. Jenkinson, N., Brown, P.: New insights into the relationship between dopamine, beta oscillations and motor function. Trends Neurosci. **34**, 611e618 (2011)
27. Litvak, V., Jha, A., Eusebio, A., Oostenveld, R., Foltynie, T., Limousin,P., et al.: Resting oscillatory cortico-subthalamic connectivity in patients with Parkinson's disease. Brain **134**, 359e374 (2011)
28. Stoffers, D., Bosboom, J.L.W., Deijen, J.B., Wolters, E.C., Berendse, H.W., Stam, C.J.: Slowing of oscillatory brain activity is a stable characteristic of Parkinson's disease without dementia. Brain **130**, 1847–1860 (2007)

29. Roth, S.R., Sterman, M.B., Clemente, C.D.: Comparison of EEG correlates of reinforcement, internal inhibition and sleep. Electroencephalogr. Clin. Neurophysiol. **23**, 509–520 (1967)
30. Abugroun, A., et al.: Cardiovascular risk among patients ≥65 years of age with Parkinson's disease (from the national inpatient sample). Am. J. Cardiol. 14 Sep 2020. https://doi.org/10.1016/j.amjcard.2020.09.021
31. Farrell, M.C., Shibao, C.A.: Morbidity and mortality in orthostatic hypotension. Auton Neurosci. **229**, (2020)
32. Tandon, M., Ahmad, F.M.H., Narayanan, S., Mohan, C., Yadav, S.: Impact of Levodopa in Lung functions in patients with Parkinson Disease. Ann. Indian Acad. Neurol. **23**(3), 338–341 (2020)

Emotion Recognition Using Multi-core Tensor Learning and Multimodal Physiological Signal

Hongyan Xu[1,2], Jiajia Tang[1,2], Jianhai Zhang[1,2]([envelope]), and Li Zhu[1,2]

[1] School of Computer Science, Hangzhou Dianzi University, Hangzhou, China
{xuhongyan,jhzhang}@hdu.edu.cn, hdutangjiajia@163.com
[2] Key laboratory of Brain Machine Collaborative Intelligence of Zhejiang Province, Hangzhou, China

Abstract. Emotion recognition based on multimodal physiological signal has attracted a bunch of attention. Tensor learning helps to extract effective shared features from multi-modal high-dimensional data. However, in tensor decomposition, the determination of the core size has always been a difficult problem, resulting in the loss of effective feature information. In this paper, we propose a multi-core voting tensor learning method, namely MCVTL, for multimodal emotion analysis, which try to improve the results of emotion recognition by fusing multi-core information of various scales. Especially, through fusing the knowledge with 4 cores, the performance is improved by nearly 5% in valence and 6% in arousal compared with the single-core case. The empirical results demonstrate the effectiveness of the proposed method.

Keywords: Physiological signal · Emotion recognition · Tensor learning

1 Introduction

Emotion is a spontaneous psychological performance of humans (animals) in response to certain interpersonal relationships or related events [16]. In recent years, with the development of human-computer interaction technology, emotion recognition has attracted more and more attention. However, human emotions are affected by many factors [11,17], and there are usually no clear boundaries between different emotions, which makes automatic emotion recognition a huge challenge. Existing studies have shown that emotional changes can cause corresponding changes in a variety of physiological signals in the human body [18], such as electrocardiogram (ECG) [13], electroencephalogram (EEG) [12], muscle electrogram (EMG) [1], blood pressure (BVP), galvanic skin response (GSR), etc. Therefore, research on emotion recognition based on physiological signals has become a hot topic. In addition, in order to obtain richer emotional information, many studies have tried to fuse multi-modal physiological information to obtain more accurate emotional states.

© Springer Nature Singapore Pte Ltd. 2021
Y. Wang (Ed.): HBAI 2020, CCIS 1369, pp. 137–148, 2021.
https://doi.org/10.1007/978-981-16-1288-6_10

Multi-modal physiological signal data naturally have tensor characteristics, that is, there are multiple dimensions such as channel, time, and frequency band. Therefore, this kind of data is suitable for organizing into high-dimensional tensor form, and tensor decomposition is helpful to discover the characteristic patterns shared between different modal data. [4] reviewed the application of tensor in EEG signal analysis and proved its effectiveness. [14] described in detail the tensor decomposition calculation process, and achieved effective results in image classification and motor imagery (MI) experiments. At the same time, the paper gives an objective evaluation performance of the tensor decomposition algorithm and points out that computational complexity is the key issue of tensor decomposition. Fortunately, although it is not completely solved, lraSNTD [19] algorithm has significantly improved the computational efficiency. Due to the lack of a method to determine the optimal kernel size, the current feature extraction methods based on single-core tensor decomposition may lose a lot of effective information. In this paper, for the problem of emotion recognition based on multimodal physiological signals, we propose MCVTL method, which aims to improve the accuracy of emotion recognition by fusing multi-core information of different scales.

The organization structure of this paper is as follows: the second section depicts our method. The third section is given the experiment processing, including preprocessing, parameter settings, etc. The fourth section is results and analysis. Finally, we give our conclusion.

2   Methods

It is difficult to exploit multi-scale complex characteristics only with a single core. Hence, through similar ensemble learning, MCVTL is proposed to fuse multi-scale information from the data.

The framework of our method is given in Fig. 1. Therein, the left part is feature extraction procedure. We tensorized the original data first. Multiple tensor cores with different sizes are obtained by tensor decomposition from the original tensor respectively. Since the feature extraction is independent and sizes are different, all cores have rarely shared information. The right part is classification process. The classification result is obtained through the same classifier with similar ensemble learning strategy.

2.1   Tensor Decomposition

A tensor is a multidimensional or N-way array, covering multi-linear and multi-aspect structural information, usually represented by $\mathbf{Y}$. The representation of a tensor is composed of the product of different modes, which are also called modes (different modes can refer to time, frequency, space, transparency, color, theme, experiment, category, etc.). The specific representation of tensor and the calculation operations involved can refer to [14]. For feature extraction, tensor decomposition models are usually divided into two categories, CP decomposition

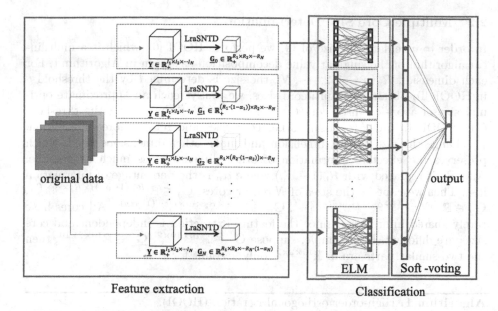

Fig. 1. Structure diagram of MCVTL

and Tucker decomposition [14]. In our paper, we employ Tucker decomposition to extract features. The main idea of Tucker decomposition is to decompose the original tensor $\underline{\mathbf{Y}} \in \mathbb{R}^{I_1 \times I_2 \times \cdots \times I_N}$ data into a tensor core and a series of principal component matrices, usually using the tensor core as the extracted features [14]. The formula is shown as follows,

$$\underline{\mathbf{Y}} = \underline{\mathbf{G}} \times_1 \mathbf{A}^{(1)} \times_2 \mathbf{A}^{(2)} \cdots \times_N \mathbf{A}^{(N)} \qquad (1)$$

$\underline{\mathbf{G}} \in \mathbb{R}^{R_1 \times R_2 \times \cdots \times R_N}$ is the tensor core, and $\mathbf{A}^{(N)} \in \mathbb{R}^{I_n \times R_n} (n = 1, 2, \cdots, N)$ is the principal component matrix. Tucker decomposition is performed based on the original tensor data, which is usually very large, leading to high computational complexity.

To solve this problem, low-rank NMF (lraNMF) is applied to obtain the tensor core and factor matrix in the form of low-rank approximation, so that the original tensor does not need to be loaded into the memory, only its low-rank factors need to be loaded. lraSNTD [19] does not need to expand the original large tensor in each dimension, reducing the computational loss. lraSNTD runs lraNMF on the expansion matrix corresponding to each mode to obtain approximate non-negative factor matrices for all modes, which are employed to update the tensor core. Therefore, the tensor core $\underline{\mathbf{G}}$ can be calculated efficiently.

2.2 Multiple Core Size Determination

In order to calculate the size of $\underline{\mathbf{G}}$, we perform HOOI [6], which is a multilinear algorithm of the singular value decomposition as shown in Algorithm 1. For each dimension $R_n(n = 1, 2, \cdots, N)$, the size is determined by the threshold θ in HOOI. To obtain the multi-core sizes, we firstly reach an approximate optimal size of a basic tensor core $\underline{\mathbf{G}}_0 \in \mathbb{R}^{R_1 \times R_2 \times \cdots \times R_N}$ by setting the threshold θ in HOOI. In order to obtain other core sizes and retain more information, we change the size of one dimension and make other dimensions fixed, which preserves the effective information of other dimensions as much as possible. And R_n is replaced with $R_n(1 - \alpha_n)$ where α_n is the percentage of information loss. Then we capture the sizes of N tensor cores, $\underline{\mathbf{G}}_1 \in \mathbb{R}^{(R_1 \cdot (1 - \alpha_1)) \times R_2 \times \cdots \times R_N}$, $\underline{\mathbf{G}}_2 \in \mathbb{R}^{R_1 \times (R_2 \cdot (1 - \alpha_2)) \times \cdots \times R_N}$, $\cdots$, $\underline{\mathbf{G}}_N \in \mathbb{R}^{R_1 \times R_2 \times \cdots \times (R_N \cdot (1 - \alpha_N))}$. All cores have rarely shared information since the feature extraction is independent and core sizes are different. For example, suppose $\underline{\mathbf{G}}_1 \in \mathbb{R}^{10 \times 10 \times 2}$, $\underline{\mathbf{G}}_2 \in \mathbb{R}^{10 \times 2 \times 10}$, then the two similar parts are in $\mathbb{R}^{10 \times 2 \times 2}$, only account for 20%.

Algorithm 1. High-order orthogonal iteration (HOOI).

Input: Nth-order $\underline{\mathbf{Y}} \in \mathbb{R}^{I_1 \times I_2 \times \cdots \times I_N}$(usually in Tucker format);
Output: Improved Tucker approximation using Alternating Least Square (ALS) approach, with orthogonal factor matrices $\mathbf{U}^{(n)}$;
1: Initialzation via the Tucker decomposition;
2: **repeat**
3:    **for** $n = 1$ to N **do**
4:        $\underline{\mathbf{Z}} \leftarrow \underline{\mathbf{Y}} \times_{q \neq n} \left\{ \mathbf{U}^{(q)T} \right\}$;
5:        $\mathbf{X} \leftarrow \mathbf{Z}_{(n)} \mathbf{Z}_{(n)}^T \in \mathbb{R}^{R \times R}$;
6:        $\mathbf{U}^{(n)} \leftarrow$ leading R_n eigenvectors of $\mathbf{X}$;
7:    **end for**
8:    $\underline{\mathbf{G}} \leftarrow \underline{\mathbf{Z}} \times_N \mathbf{U}^{(N)T}$;
9: **until** the cost function ($\|\underline{\mathbf{Y}}\|_F^2 - \|\underline{\mathbf{G}}\|_F^2$) cases to decrease;
10: **return** $[\![\underline{\mathbf{G}}; \mathbf{U}^{(1)}, \mathbf{U}^{(2)}, ..., \mathbf{U}^{(N)}]\!]$;

2.3 Classification

As shown in Fig. 1, $N + 1$ tensor cores $(\underline{\mathbf{G}}_0, \underline{\mathbf{G}}_1, \cdots, \underline{\mathbf{G}}_N)$ are obtained through lraSNTD from the original tensor $\underline{\mathbf{Y}}$. Then each core is put into the Extreme learning machine (ELM) [7] network separately. ELM is a shallow network framework for capturing effective information and obtaining predicted probabilities. For M classes, the predicted probability is denoted as P_{m_n} ($n = 0, 1, 2, \cdots, N, m = 1, 2, \cdots, M$). Through the soft voting method, we receive the max of the predicted probability P_{m_n}. According to $P_{pre} = \max\limits_{1 \leq m \leq M} \sum_{n=0}^{N} P_{m_n}$, we find the corresponding predicted class.

2.4   Performance Meatures

We use accuracy and F1-score as performance meatures.

Accuracy is the correct proportion of the entire sample judged by the classifier.

$$accuracy_k = \frac{TP+TN}{TP+TN+FP+FN}, \tag{2}$$

where TP (True Positive) is the numbers that positive sample is correctly predicted as a positive sample, and TN (True Negative) is the numbers that negative sample is correctly predicted as a negative sample, and FP (False Positive) is the numbers that negative sample is wrongly predicted as a positive sample, and FN (False Negative) is the numbers that positive sample is wrongly predicted as a negative sample.

F1-score is a measure of a test's accuracy, reflecting the balance between the precision and recall, obtained as follows:

$$\text{F1-score} = (\frac{1}{n}\sum \frac{2 \cdot precision_k \cdot recall_k}{precision_k + recall_k})^2, \tag{3}$$

where $precision$ is the proportion of TP in all cases that are predicted to be positive and $recall$ is the proportion of TP in the actual positive cases, obtained by

$$precision_k = \frac{TP}{TP+FP}, recall_k = \frac{TP}{TP+FN}. \tag{4}$$

2.5   Deap Database

Our paper is conducted in the publicly available emotion database DEAP [8], which consists of multimodal information for the analysis of human emotional states. A total of 32 EEG channels and eight peripheral physiological signals of 32 subjects (aged between 19 and 37) were recorded whilst watching music videos. The 40 one-minute video clips were carefully selected to elicit different emotional states in valence-arousal emotion model. In DEAP, each video clip is rated from 1 to 9 for valence and arousal by each subject after the viewing, and the discrete rating value can be used as a classification label in emotion recognition [15]. In this paper, Two emotional states (high valence: valence ≥ 5; low valence: valence < 5; high arousal: arousal ≥ 5; low arousal: arousal < 5) are classified to verify the effectiveness of our method. The experimental procedure is shown as Fig. 2.

3   Experiment

In our work, 16-channel [2] EEG (FP1, FP2, AF3, AF4, F3, F4, T7, T8, C3, C4, CP1, CP2, P3, P4, O1, O2) and 8 physiological signals (2 EOG, 2 EMG, skin electricity, respiration, blood pressure and skin temperature) are used for

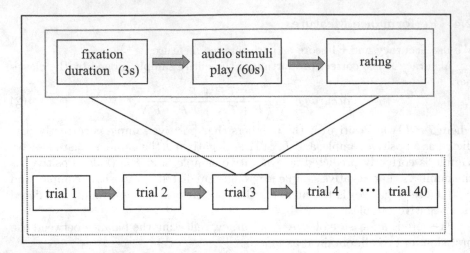

Fig. 2. The procedure of experiment in DEAP

emotion recognition. In the preprocessing procedure, 4.0–44 Hz, 0.1–12 Hz, 50–63 Hz, 0–2.4 Hz, 0–2.4 Hz, 0–2.4 Hz, 0–0.2 Hz band pass filters were employed to EEG, EOG, EMG, skin electricity, respiration, blood pressure and skin temperature signals respectively. [9] reported that the effective window size for valence recognition using the DEAP was between 3–12 s. Therefore, in our paper, each 60 s trial is segmented into 20 3 s samples with non-overlapping for the purpose of increasing the number of samples. Finally, we get a total of 800 (40 trials × 20 samples) samples for each subject. All the samples are derived from the same trial share the same category label. In order to organize physiological signals data into a tensor, the discrete wavelet transform (DWT) is applied to obtain the time-frequency information. EEG signals and other physiological signals have different frequency ranges, so the frequency domain scale in DWT is set to 10. To valid performance of the MCVTL model, all 32 subjects' data are used. The data are organized into 25600 (800 * 32, samples * subjects) 3rd-order tensors with the size 10 (frequency bins) ×384 (time frames) ×24 (channels). In addition, all data of each channel has been normalized separately.

To capture the multiple cores sizes, we set the threshold $\theta = 99\%$ in HOOI, finding that the size of the basic tensor core $\underline{\mathbf{G}}_0 \in \mathbb{R}^{frequency\ bins \times time\ frames \times channels}$ of each subject is around $6 \times 80 \times 10$, so we obtain the suitable size of tensor core $\underline{\mathbf{G}}_0 \in \mathbb{R}^{6 \times 80 \times 10}$. For obtaining other core sizes, we set the value $\alpha_1 = 0.17$, 0.33, 0.5, $\alpha_2 = 0.25$, 0.5, 0.75, $\alpha_3 = 0.2$, 0.4, 0.6, and explore the sizes of other 9 tensor cores, $\underline{\mathbf{G}}_1 \in \mathbb{R}^{5 \times 80 \times 10}$, $\underline{\mathbf{G}}_2 \in \mathbb{R}^{4 \times 80 \times 10}$, $\underline{\mathbf{G}}_3 \in \mathbb{R}^{3 \times 80 \times 10}$, $\underline{\mathbf{G}}_4 \in \mathbb{R}^{6 \times 60 \times 10}$, $\underline{\mathbf{G}}_5 \in \mathbb{R}^{6 \times 40 \times 10}$, $\underline{\mathbf{G}}_6 \in \mathbb{R}^{6 \times 20 \times 10}$, $\underline{\mathbf{G}}_7 \in \mathbb{R}^{6 \times 80 \times 8}$, $\underline{\mathbf{G}}_8 \in \mathbb{R}^{6 \times 80 \times 6}$, $\underline{\mathbf{G}}_9 \in \mathbb{R}^{6 \times 80 \times 4}$.

lraSNTD is employed to decompose the training data to obtain three factor matrices referring to frequency bins, time frames and channels. The training data and the testing data are projected onto the feature subspace composed of the three factor matrices to obtain the training features and testing features. Then, through the classification system of MCVTL, we receive the prediction result.

To compare the performance of multi-core and single-core models, we verify 10 models (MCV-$n(n = 1,2,\cdots,10)$) on the task where each MCV-n includes n cores. Specifically, $\underline{\mathbf{G}}_0$ is employed to MCV-1 ([14] proves the basic tensor core has the best performance with $\theta = 99\%$), but the cores of other model MCV-n are selected from these 10 cores, $\underline{\mathbf{G}}_0$ to $\underline{\mathbf{G}}_9$. The number of the different options for each model MCV-$n(n = 2,\cdots,10)$ is full combination C_{10}^n. However, there will be reduplicate sequences if we randomly select cores. Therefore, we traverse all the different cases and grasp the average results.

To validate the effectiveness of our methods, the average classification accuracy is computed using a scheme of three 10-fold cross-validations to increase the reliability of our results for each subject. In a 10-fold cross validation, all the validation samples are divided into 10 subsets. Nine subsets are used for training, and the remaining one is applied for testing. Furthermore, the results are statistically evaluated by a paired t-test method to further support and validate our conclusion.

4   Results and Analysis

4.1   Comparison Between Multi-core and Single-Core Models

The performance of the single-core model (MCV-1) and the multi-core models (MCV-2 to MCV-10) in the valance dimension are demonstrated in the Fig. 3. It is found that the average classification accuracy and F1-score of MCV-1 are 0.7614 (point A1) and 0.7532 (point A2), and the results of the multi-core models are higher than MCV-1 (paired t-test, $p < 0.05$). At the same time, it is observed that with the increase in the number of cores, its performance showed an upward trend, reaching 0.8206 (point C1) in accuracy and 0.8154 (point C2) in F1-score on MCV-10, an increase of nearly 5% compared to MCV-1 (paired t-test, $p < 0.05$).

Similarly, the performance of the single-core model (MCV-1) and the multi-core models (MCV-2 to MCV-10) in the arousal dimension are shown in the Fig. 4. It is observed that the accuracy and F1-score of MCV-1 are 0.7865 (point A1) and 0.7717 (point A2), and the results of the multi-core models are higher than MCV-1 (paired t-test, $p < 0.05$). Moreover, it shows that with the number of cores increasing, the performance is improved, reaching 0.8466 (point C1) in accuracy and 0.8354 (point C2) in F1-score on MCV-10, an increase of nearly 6% compared to MCV-1 (paired t-test, $p < 0.05$). More importantly, the accuracy and F1-score curves become almost stable on MCV-4 (with a slight reduction of 1% compared to MCV-10, point B1 and B2) both in valence and arousal.

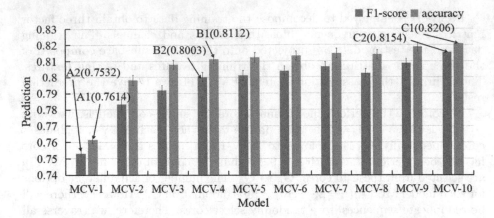

Fig. 3. Results of MCV-1 to MCV-10 in valence dimension

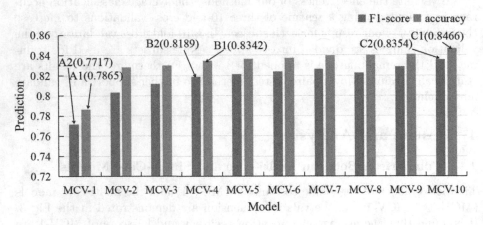

Fig. 4. Results of MCV-1 to MCV-10 in arousal dimension

It is seen that the performance of MCVTL has been greatly improved on the single-core model and it indicates the fact that 4 cores are enough to exploit multi-lever characteristics. We could infer that multi-core model can efficiently integrate multi-scale information.

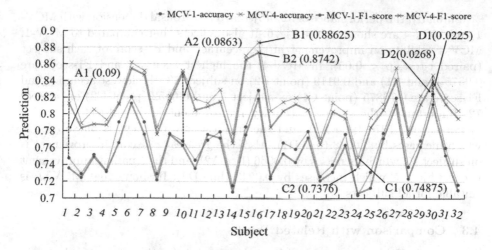

Fig. 5. Results of 32 subjects with MCV-1 and MCV-4 in valence dimension

4.2 Intra-subject Classification Performance with MCVTL Model

The performance of 32 subjects in the valence dimension with MCV-1 and MCV-4 are shown in the Fig. 5. We found that compared to MCV-1, MCV-4 exhibits an improvement in the accuracy across subject (paired t-test, $p < 0.05$). In MCV-4, the highest accuracy and F1-score are 0.88625 (point B1) and 0.8742 (point B2) on subject 16, the lowest accuracy and F1-score are 0.74875 (point C1) and 0.7376 (point C2) on subject 24. Importantly, the greatest accuracy improvement is on subject 1, which increases by 0.09 (line A1), and the smallest improvement is on subject 30, which increases by 0.0225 (line D1). Also, the greatest F1-score improvement is on subject 10, which increases by 0.0863 (line A2), and the smallest improvement is on subject 30, which increases by 0.0268 (line D2).

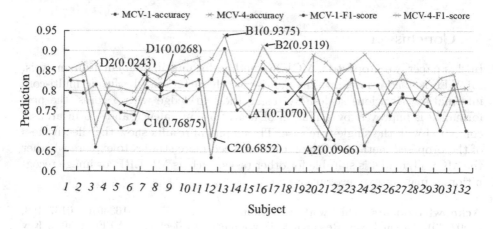

Fig. 6. Results of 32 subjects with MCV-1 and MCV-4 in arousal dimension

Similarly, the performance of 32 subjects in the arousal dimension with MCV-1 and MCV-4 are shown in the Fig. 6. It also reflects that compared to MCV-1, MCV-4 exhibits an improvement in the accuracy and F1-score of each subject (paired t-test, $p < 0.05$). In MCV-4, the highest accuracy and F1-score are 0.9375 (point B1) and 0.9119 (point B2) on subject 13, the lowest accuracy and F1-score are 0.76875 (point C1) on subject 5 and 0.6852 (point C2) on subject 12. Importantly, the greatest accuracy improvement is on subject 20, which increases by 0.1070 (line A1), and the smallest improvement is on subject 8, which increases by 0.0268 (line D1). Also, the greatest F1-score improvement is on subject 20, which increases by 0.0966 (line A2), and the smallest improvement is on subject 7, which increases by 0.0243 (line D2). It shows that MCVTL is suitable for all subjects.

4.3 Comparison with Related Works

As shown in Table 1, our method has a better classification accuracy than previous studies. For instance, our result is improved by 9% in arousal and 10% in valence compared with [10].

Table 1. Comparison on DEAP dataset with related works.

Ref.	Methods	Accuracy (%)	
		Valence	Arousal
[10]	MEMD-based features, ICA, k-NN	67	51
[10]	MEMD-based features, ICA, A-NN	72	75
[3]	Multiband Feature Matrix, CapsNet	66	68
[5]	DT-CWPT, SVM	65	66
[20]	Time series, SVM	71	69
This study	MCV-10, ELM	**82**	**84**

5 Conclusion

In this paper, we proposed a MCVTL method for multimodal emotion analysis. MCVTL is able to integrate the multi-scale characteristics by fusing multi-core information of various scales. By fusing the knowledge with 4 cores, the performance is improved by a margin of nearly 5% in valence and 6% in arousal compared with the single-core case. The empirical results show the effectiveness of the proposed method. In the future, we need more studies to explore whether the MCVTL model is suitable for other tasks, such as MI, ERP, or image recognition, semantic text recognition, etc.

Acknowledgments. This work was supported by NSFC (61633010, 61671193, 61602140), National Key Research & Development Project (2017YFE0116800), Key Research & Development Project of Zhejiang Province (2020C04009, 2018C04012).

References

1. Abtahi, F., Ro, T., Li, W., Zhu, Z.: Emotion analysis using audio/video, EMG and EEG: a dataset and comparison study. In: 2018 IEEE Winter Conference on Applications of Computer Vision (WACV), pp. 10–19. IEEE (2018)
2. Candra, H., et al.: Investigation of window size in classification of EEG-emotion signal with wavelet entropy and support vector machine. In: 2015 37th Annual international conference of the IEEE Engineering in Medicine and Biology Society (EMBC), pp. 7250–7253. IEEE (2015)
3. Chao, H., Dong, L., Liu, Y., Lu, B.: Emotion recognition from multiband EEG signals using CapsNet. Sensors **19**(9), 2212 (2019)
4. Cong, F., Lin, Q.H., Kuang, L.D., Gong, X.F., Astikainen, P., Ristaniemi, T.: Tensor decomposition of EEG signals: a brief review. J. Neurosci. Methods **248**, 59–69 (2015)
5. Daimi, S.N., Saha, G.: Classification of emotions induced by music videos and correlation with participants' rating. Expert Syst. Appl. **41**(13), 6057–6065 (2014)
6. De Lathauwer, L., De Moor, B., Vandewalle, J.: On the best rank-1 and rank-$(R_1, R_2,..., R_N)$ approximation of higher-order tensors. SIAM J. Matrix Anal. Appl. **21**(4), 1324–1342 (2000)
7. Huang, G.B., Zhu, Q.Y., Siew, C.K.: Extreme learning machine: a new learning scheme of feedforward neural networks. In: 2004 IEEE International Joint Conference on Neural Networks (IEEE Cat. No. 04CH37541), vol. 2, pp. 985–990. IEEE (2004)
8. Koelstra, S., et al.: DEAP: a database for emotion analysis; using physiological signals. IEEE Trans. Affect. Comput. **3**(1), 18–31 (2011)
9. Lin, Y.P., Wang, C.H., Wu, T.L., Jeng, S.K., Chen, J.H.: EEG-based emotion recognition in music listening: a comparison of schemes for multiclass support vector machine. In: 2009 IEEE International Conference on Acoustics, Speech and Signal Processing, pp. 489–492. IEEE (2009)
10. Mert, A., Akan, A.: Emotion recognition from EEG signals by using multivariate empirical mode decomposition. Pattern Anal. Appl. **21**(1), 81–89 (2018). https://doi.org/10.1007/s10044-016-0567-6
11. Mill, A., Allik, J., Realo, A., Valk, R.: Age-related differences in emotion recognition ability: a cross-sectional study. Emotion **9**(5), 619 (2009)
12. Mohammadi, Z., Frounchi, J., Amiri, M.: Wavelet-based emotion recognition system using EEG signal. Neural Comput. Appl. **28**(8), 1985–1990 (2017). https://doi.org/10.1007/s00521-015-2149-8
13. Nikolova, D., Mihaylova, P., Manolova, A., Georgieva, P.: ECG-based human emotion recognition across multiple subjects. In: Poulkov, V. (ed.) FABULOUS 2019. LNICST, vol. 283, pp. 25–36. Springer, Cham (2019). https://doi.org/10.1007/978-3-030-23976-3_3
14. Phan, A.H., Cichocki, A.: Tensor decompositions for feature extraction and classification of high dimensional datasets. Nonlinear Theory Appl. IEICE **1**(1), 37–68 (2010)
15. Posner, J., Russell, J.A., Peterson, B.S.: The circumplex model of affect: an integrative approach to affective neuroscience, cognitive development, and psychopathology. Dev. Psychopathol. **17**(3), 715 (2005)
16. Verma, G.K., Tiwary, U.S.: Multimodal fusion framework: a multiresolution approach for emotion classification and recognition from physiological signals. NeuroImage **102**, 162–172 (2014)

17. Vogt, T., André, E.: Improving automatic emotion recognition from speech via gender differentiation. In: LREC, pp. 1123–1126 (2006)
18. Zheng, W.L., Zhu, J.Y., Lu, B.L.: Identifying stable patterns over time for emotion recognition from EEG. IEEE Trans. Affect. Comput. **10**, 417–429 (2017)
19. Zhou, G., Cichocki, A., Xie, S.: Fast nonnegative matrix/tensor factorization based on low-rank approximation. IEEE Trans. Signal Process. **60**(6), 2928–2940 (2012)
20. Zhuang, N., Zeng, Y., Tong, L., Zhang, C., Zhang, H., Yan, B.: Emotion recognition from EEG signals using multidimensional information in EMD domain. BioMed Res. Int. **2017**, 1–9 (2017)

A Review of Transfer Learning for EEG-Based Driving Fatigue Detection

Jin Cui[1,2], Yong Peng[1], Kenji Ozawa[2], and Wanzeng Kong[1(✉)]

[1] School of Computer Science and Technology,
Hangzhou Dianzi University, Hangzhou 310018, Zhejiang, China
{cuijin50057,yongpeng,kongwanzeng}@hdu.edu.cn
[2] Department of Computer Science and Engineering, University of Yamanashi, Kofu, Japan
ozawa@yamanashi.ac.jp

Abstract. Driver mental state detection has been playing an increasingly significant role in safe driving for decades. Electroencephalogram (EEG)-based detection methods have already been applied to improve detection performance. However, numerous problems still have not been addressed in practical applications. Specifically, most of the existing traditional methods require a large number of training data, caused by differences in cross-subject samples and cross-time of the same subject, resulting in enormous calculations and time consumption. To overcome the above limitations, transfer learning, which applies data or knowledge from the source domain to the target domain, has been widely adopted in EEG processing. This article reviews the current state of mainstream transfer learning methods and their application based on driver mental state detection. To the best of our knowledge, this is the first comprehensive review of transfer learning methods for driving fatigue detection.

Keywords: Transfer learning · Electroencephalogram · Driver mental state detection

1 Introduction

Fatigue driving refers to the physiological and psychological disorders caused by the driver's long continuous driving [1–4]. Due to lack of sleep, long continuous driving, and other factors, the driver is easily fatigued, in turn resulting in inattentive driving, decreased judgment, improper driving operation, and increasing the potential for traffic accidents [5, 6]. Effective driver mental state detection reduces the probability of unsafe driving and property loss [7].

Currently, there are three main driver mental state detection methods: computer vision-based [8–10], human physiological signal-based [11, 12], and information integration technology-based [13, 14] methods. Previous methods typically collect images of the driving process, establishing appropriate criteria for judgement and using image processing techniques to analyze the driver's facial expressions to determine if the driver is fatigued. Human physiological signal-based methods usually collect data such as

© Springer Nature Singapore Pte Ltd. 2021
Y. Wang (Ed.): HBAI 2020, CCIS 1369, pp. 149–162, 2021.
https://doi.org/10.1007/978-981-16-1288-6_11

the subject's electroencephalogram (EEG), eye motion, electrocardiogram (ECG), heart rate, and blood pressure to analyze the driver's physical state and predict its mental state. Information integration technology-based methods mainly establish an integration model of a variety of factors that may contribute to the driver's mental state, so as to perform the driver mental state detection and analysis. Among them, EEG [15], as an objective signal, is capable of quickly reflecting the process of human physiological and mental changes and is widely considered as the most readily available and effective driver mental state detection method.

However, the following problems are inevitably encountered when using EEG signals for analysis.

1. The EEG signal is particularly weak and susceptible to noise.
2. EEG is spontaneous and highly individualized, with varying data distributions across subjects and time periods.
3. EEG data samples are precious, and the collection of large amounts of data entails high time and financial costs.

Accordingly, it is extremely important to obtain desirable detection results from a small number of cross-subject sample features. Transfer learning [16] can address the problem of sparse data labels by transferring knowledge from the learned source domain to an unlabeled target domain. It differs from traditional machine learning methods in two aspects: (1) Transfer learning approaches forbid the premise that data from different domains obey the same distribution and are applicable to cases where data distributions are inconsistent; (2) Transfer learning approaches attempt to solve unsupervised problems based on only a few samples.

A growing number of studies have used transfer learning for driver state detection as transfer learning continues to progress in EEG data processing. Among current review articles [17–19] addressing driver mental state and fatigue, to the best of our knowledge, this is the first review article that focuses on the transfer learning approach.

The remainder of this paper is organized as follows. Section 2 provides a simple introduction to transfer learning. Section 3 describes the transfer learning-based driver fatigue detection methods. Finally, our conclusions are outlined in Sect. 4.

2   Transfer Learning

Transfer learning is the ability to systematically identify and apply knowledge and skills learned in a previous domain to a new domain.

There are two very important terms in transfer learning: domain and task. In EEG-based driver fatigue state detection, a domain usually represents the EEG observations obtained when a subject performs the same learning task. The EEG observations of different subjects under the same task are defined as their own domains. Furthermore, the domain can be divided into the source domain (D_S) and the target domain (D_T), depending on whether the domain has knowledge or not. Specifically, the source domain with label information is defined as $\{X_S, Y_S\}$, and the target domain without label information is recorded as $\{X_T\}$. Additionally, a learning task consists of labels and the corresponding function, in which labeled spaces are represented by Y and the function is represented by $f(\cdot)$. For instance, sentiment analysis and driver state analysis are two different tasks.

2.1 Definition of Transfer Learning

Definition 1. As described in [16], there are two important parts in domain D, namely, feature space X and marginal probability distribution $P(X), X = \{x_1, x_2, \ldots, x_n\}$. Obviously, various domains have various feature spaces or obey various marginal probability distributions. Furthermore, given a source domain D_S, a learning task T_S, a target domain D_T, and a learning task T_T, the goal of transfer learning is to improve the learning performance of the target prediction function $f_T(\cdot)$ in D_T by effectively employing the knowledge learned by D_S and T_S, in which the following formula must be obeyed: $D_S \neq D_T$ or $T_S \neq T_T$.

The condition $D_S \neq D_T$ implies that the source and target domain instances are various, i.e., $X_S \neq X_T$, or that the source and target domain marginal probability distributions are various, $P_S(X) \neq P_T(X)$. Specifically, for each task, $T = \{Y, f(\cdot)\}$, where $f(\cdot)$ represents the conditional probability distribution $P(Y|X)$. Furthermore, $T_S \neq T_T$ means that the source labels are unequal to target domain labels, i.e., $Y_S \neq Y_T$, or that the source and target conditional probability distributions are unequal, $P(Y_S|X_S) \neq P(Y_T|X_T)$. It is worth noting that the current problem becomes a traditional machine learning problem if the source and target domains are equal, $D_S = D_T$, and the source and target tasks are also equal, $T_S = T_T$.

Domain Adaptation. As described in [20], Given a marked source domain $D_S = \{X_i, Y_i\}_{i=1}^n$ and an unmarked target domain $D_T = \{X_j\}_{j=1}^m$, it is assumed that their eigenspaces are the same, i.e., $X_S = X_T$, and their class spaces are also the same, i.e., $Y_S = Y_T$. However, the marginal and conditional distributions of both domains are different, i.e., $P_S(X) \neq P_T(X)$ and $P(Y_S|X_S) \neq P(Y_T|X_T)$. Then, the goal of transfer learning is to use marked data D_S to train a classifier $f : x_S \rightarrow y_S$ to classify the label $y_T \in Y_T$ of the target domain D_T.

2.2 A Brief Introduction of Transfer Learning Methods

Instance-Based Transfer Learning. To efficiently use the similarity with the target domain, some source domain data samples are reused according to weight generation rules to carry out the transfer learning [21–24]. The instance-based weight method has rich theoretical achievements and is easily deduced and used. However, this type of method is usually effective only when the distribution difference between fields is small.

Feature-Based Transfer Learning. This type of method mine the correlation between the source and target domains through feature transformation, so as to decline the variation between the two domains [25]; or merge the data features of the source and target domains into a unified feature space, so that the improved traditional method is able to complete the related task [26–31]. Currently, this is the most important and common transfer learning method, which is extensively employed for the cross-subject transfer of EEG in fatigue driving.

Model (Parameter)-Based Transfer Learning. Let the data in the source and target domains share certain model parameters, then the goal of transfer learning is to discover the shared relevant parameters from the source and target domains. Presently, methods involved in deep neural networks [32–35] are also among the model-based transfer learning methods. In addition, models combining domain adaptation and deep neural networks are commonly used methods, which are not only model-based but also feature-based methods.

Relationship-Based Transfer Learning [36]. Most of this type of method emphasize on identifying the relationship between the source and target domain samples, but with only a few related studies. Furthermore, most of them are based on Markov logic net to mine the commonality between various domains.

Over the past decades, to tackle the non-linear, unstable, and high-dimensional characteristics of EEG data, an abundance of effective EEG feature extraction methods further upgraded the extraction effectiveness. In the current EEG-based application, instance-based, feature-based, and model (parameter)-based methods have mostly drawn the attention of researchers. Therefore, Sect. 3 focuses on introducing the development of these three methods.

3   Transfer Learning-Based Driver Fatigue Detection Methods

Transfer learning has been proposed to address the small sample problem and the adaptation of different domains. Transfer learning is capable of providing more effective solutions to the EEG transfer classification problem across subjects. Accordingly, it has been applied in driver fatigue detection.

In the application of transfer learning in driver fatigue detection, most existing detection systems (framework) have the same construction processes, in which several general characteristics can be summarized. Therefore, the first part of this chapter summarizes the characteristics of driver fatigue detection systems based on transfer learning methods. Presently, the transfer learning pattern recognition methods for driver fatigue detection are mainly feature- and model-based, and to a lesser proportion instance-based. These methods are summarized next.

3.1   System Features

Driver fatigue detection systems collect EEG signals during driving, process EEG signals either online or offline, feedback and control the results.

A complete driver fatigue detection system [18, 37] usually includes signal acquisition, signal preprocessing, feature extraction, pattern recognition, and feedback.

Signal acquisition: The weak EEG signal is detected by an electrode placed on the subject's scalp, then amplified and digitized, and finally recorded by the matching recording system. It is mainly collected by the EEG cap and other EEG devices, including 64- and 32-electrode EEG caps.

Signal preprocessing: Used to remove common noise, interference, and artifacts, in order to improve signal quality. Commonly used preprocessing methods are digital filtering and independent component analysis (ICA).

Feature extraction: Used to reduce the dimensionality of EEG data and extract relevant features for pattern recognition. Common feature extraction methods are in temporal, frequency, and spatial domains as well as a combined analysis of the two in three domains Frequency domain analysis: autoregressive (AR) model and power spectrum estimation (PSD); temporal-frequency analysis: wavelet transform and wavelet packet transform; spatial domain analysis: principal component analysis (PCA) and common spatial pattern (CSP).

Pattern recognition model (PRM): The existing transfer learning pattern recognition driver fatigue detection model is mainly based on classification (C) and regression (R) models. The classification model usually sets the category information for the driver's mental state from the EEG data according to a certain threshold. Then, the transfer learning model outputs the fatigue category, which is a discrete value. The regression model predicts the specific sleepiness state through the model, and the output is a continuous value.

Explore transferability in transfer learning: Many existing methods [38–40] consider how to select the optimal auxiliary source domains in order to further reduce the transfer learning cost and error. The appropriate auxiliary data is often more effective for transfer learning with less effort.

In the literature, feature extraction methods and pattern recognition models have some characteristics that can be summarized. In the following sections we summarize them according to different pattern recognition methods.

3.2 Instance-Based Transfer Learning Methods

The processing of instance-based transfer learning method is simple. In order to fully utilize the existing source domain data in EEG-based fatigue detection, it is necessary to perform similarity matching with the target domain according to weight generation rules to complete the data alignment and transfer learning. Table 1 summarizes this approach.

Wu *et al.* [38] proposed an online weighted adaptation regression regularization (OwARR) algorithm used to decrease the amount of data required for a given subject calibration. A source domain selection (SDS) method was also proposed to reduce the computational cost of OwARR by 50%. The online classification/regression task means that there is not enough labeled data for calibration. In the literature, each subject performing the same driving task is considered a distinct source domain. Initially, OwARR is applied to each source domain, then the final regression model is constructed as a weighted mean of these basic models. Together, the final regression models are applied to future unlabeled data. Specifically, SDS is employed to reduce the clustering error of multiple source domains before domain adaptation. By selecting the best first Z source domains, SDS maintains model performance with less computation cost. On average, the training time for OwARR-SDS is approximately half of that for OwARR.

Table 1. Instance-based transfer learning methods.

Ref.	Year	Task	Dataset	Signal	Feature extraction	Pattern recognition method	Performance	PRM
Wu *et al.* [38]	2017	Simulated driving	[41]	EEG	Power spectral density (PSD)	OwARR	Calibration time reduced by ~50%	R
Wei *et al.* [39]	2015	Lane-keeping driving	–	EEG	Welch's fast Fourier transform	Selective transfer learning	–	R
Wei *et al.* [40]	2018	Lane-keeping driving	–	EEG	Multi-channel EEG powers	Hierarchical cluster analysis and Subject-transfer framework	Calibration time reduced by 90%	R

As EEG correlations between individuals are stable, there are existing auxiliary subject data to improve EEG performance. Wei *et al.* [39] proposed a framework for selective transfer learning that effectively utilizes the large amount of training data from other subjects to improve the recognition efficiency of unlabeled target domain data. This theoretical finding is a good reference for cross-subject transfer.

In an effort to improve system performance with minimal personalized calibration data, Wei *et al.* [40] used hierarchical clustering methods to evaluate inter- and intra-subject variability in a wide-scale EEG dataset of a simulated driving task. In addition, based on the existing data collected from the source subject, a model source pool was constructed. Furthermore, the framework carries out the design of an adjustment mechanism for ordering and fusing the source models of each target subject. In terms of time cost, the calibration time of the self-decoding (SD) method was 89.91 min, and that of the subject-transfer (ST) method was 1.48 min, the calibration time required for new users was reduced by 90%.

3.3 Feature-Based Transfer Learning Methods

The largest proportion of EEG-based driver fatigue detection methods are feature-based transfer learning methods due to its better feature alignment effect. This method tends to find source and target domain data based on two common mapping spaces, either optimization based on probability distribution alignment, or a combination of both. It is not difficult to train and the training effect is significant. Furthermore, compared to deep learning methods, training time and training data costs are low, therefore, it is extensively used in EEG-based tasks. Table 2 summarizes this approach.

An online multi-view and transfer Takagi–Sugeno–Kang (TSK) fuzzy system [42] is proposed to estimate the driver's sleepiness, which represents the source and target domain characteristics from multiple perspectives. In this algorithmic framework, the domain EEG data are characterized in terms of multiple perspectives. The multi-angle setting is injected into the transfer learning framework to enhance the consistency of the

Table 2. Feature-based transfer learning methods.

Ref.	Year	Task	Signal	Dataset	Feature extraction	Pattern recognition method	Performance	PRM
Jiang et al. [42]	2020	Lane-keeping driving	EEG	–	Time, frequency and time-frequency features	O-MV-T-TSK-FS	–	R
Chen et al. [43]	2019	Real driving	EEGEOG	Dataset A [49]	Time, frequency wavelet domains features.	Domain transfer learning (ARTL, TCA, JDA, TJM)	94.15% on dataset A	C
				Dataset B [50]			88.43% on dataset B	
Zhang et al. [44]	2017	Simulated driving	EEG	–	Fuzzy mutual information-based wavelet- packet transform	KSR and TDDR (3 classes)	KSR+TDDR+SVM/KSR+TDDR+KNN achieved the same highest G-mean of 79.00%	C
Liu et al. [45]	2020	Simulated driving	EEG	–	Spectral band power	MIDA	73.01% of thirty channels	C
Zhang et al. [48]	2015	Simulated driving	EEG	–	DE	TCA	TCA-SVM (77.02%)	C

different angles. This online fuzzy system is more flexible and controllable than offline training.

Chen *et al.* [43] proposed an automatic detection system based on cross-subject feature selection and transfer classifiers to identify different driving mentalities. Considering the negative effects of noise and irrelevant information on transfer learning, they designed the class separation and domain fusion (CSDF) and utilized a hybrid feature choice methodology to combine different types of filtering methods in one framework. Additionally, they adopted a common adaptation regularization-based transfer learning (ARTL) as the pattern recognition method, which simultaneously optimizes the structural risk, the joint distribution, and the manifold consistency of two domains. This optimization method is based on the structural risk minimization principle and regularization theory.

The kernel spectral regression (KSR) with transformable discriminant dimension reduction (TDDR) method was proposed by Zhang *et al.* [44]. This method uses the reduced feature vector dimensionality to achieve the transfer of the classifier model cross-subjects. However, considering only low-dimensional source space discrimination is undesirable, as this would poorly generalize to the target domain of traditional dimensions. In this work, knowledge transfer using TDDR rewards the separation of domain merge data and penalizes the distance between the source and target domains by defining an objective function that rewards domain merge data. A low-dimensional latent space can be found, ensuring both discriminability and transferability, which addresses the problem of traditional dimension reduction methods only considering low dimension recognition. Furthermore, KSR is capable of overcoming the linear discriminant analysis (LDA) limitation to detect nonlinear components when reducing the EEG feature dimension. In the literature, detection results on two datasets show that the framework improves the performance of multi-class and multi-bandwidth identification.

Liu *et al.* [45] proposed a transfer learning-based cross-subject EEG fatigue recognition algorithm without correction. They also explored the influence of the number of EEG signal channels on algorithm accuracy and compared single and multi-channel situations. Specifically, the random forest algorithm was used to select the channel with the highest characteristic resolution. Their experimental results demonstrated that the occipital lobe channel has a better effect when considering only one channel. In this paper, two classical transfer learning strategies, namely, transfer component analysis (TCA) and maximum independence domain adaptation (MIDA) [46], are used. Among them, TCA is employed to alleviate the classification accuracy decline problem resulting from the distribution mismatch between the source and target data. The goal of TCA is to seek a potential mapping subspace where the maximum mean difference (MMD) between the source and target data is reduced in the Reproducing Kernel Hilbert Space (RKHS) [47]. The distance between these measures is empirically averaged. MIDA enables data from different domains into a potential domain invariant space, where the projected samples are independent of domain features. The accuracy was determined to be 73.01% for all thirty channels using MIDA and 68.00% for one selected channel using TCA, which was better than the baseline and deep learning methods.

3.4 Model-Based Transfer Learning Methods

A parametric model-based transfer learning method in driver fatigue detection usually addresses how to find a common parameter or prior distribution between the spatial model of the source and target domains in order to transfer knowledge through further processing. Deep transfer learning methods also belong to this category. Table 3 summarizes this approach.

Wu *et al.* [51] proposed a combined method based on transfer learning, active class selection (ACS), and a mean squared difference user-similarity heuristic and selects the best sample. Specifically, collaborative filtering is used to combine training data from a solitary subject with external training data from other similar subjects. In addition, in order to improve learning performance by combining a limited number of training samples with a substantial number of supplementary training samples from other similar topics, ACS optimizes class selection to generate individual user-specific training samples. It can boost recognition accuracy by not increasing the number of training samples.

Wu *et al.* [41] proposed an online EEG-based sleep estimation method based on adaptive model fusion. In this framework, only a few subjects require correction to achieve satisfactory results. Specifically, for each domain in Z auxiliary source domains, it combines with the target domain to implement the ridge regression-based domain adaptation operation and Z different models are obtained, which are fused into the final model.

In [52], a deep neural network-based transfer learning driver fatigue detection system is proposed, which increased system availability by relying solely on EEG channels. First, the signal is preprocessed and filtered, then transformed into two-dimensional spectrum. Then, the two-dimensional spectrum is classified by using AlexNet, the final normal and fatigue classification is carried out by using a transfer learning method. The FP1 and T3 channels have been shown experimentally to be the most effective channels for reflecting the driver's fatigue state. Furthermore, with the improved AlexNet convolutional neural network (CNN) model, an efficient driver fatigue detection system can be obtained using only one channel. This method makes the driver fatigue detection system flexible, which is a major advantage.

In [53], two kinds of domain adaptive neural network (DaNN) and adverse discriminative domain adaptation (ADDA), based on the SEED-VIG dataset [50], are used to classify electrooculogram (EOG) and EEG signals. Compared with traditional domain adaptation methods, this method significantly improves the data. The experimental results show that the Pearson correlation coefficients of both domain adaptation networks are improved by more than 10% compared to the baseline. Therefore, the use of adversarial networks for EEG driver fatigue classification is a promising experiment.

Due to the continuous development of deep networks, EEG data could also be processed using model-based transfer learning methods. Moreover, parameter-based methods could be combined with feature-based methods to achieve better experimentation performance. However, there are not many deep network-based methods for fatigue detection and classification, which are necessary to further adopt efficient methods and achieve better experimental results.

Table 3. Model-based transfer learning methods.

Ref.	Year	Task	Dataset	Signal	Feature extraction	Pattern recognition method	Performance	PRM
Wu et al. [41]	2015	Lane-keeping driving	–	EEG	PSD	DAMF	–	R
Wu et al. [51]	2013	Virtual Reality Stroop Task	Virtual reality Stroop task [54]	EEG EDA RSP ECG	Spectral power	Combining transfer learning (TL) and Active Class Selection (ACS)	56.76%–95.82% for one subject	C
Shalash et al. [52]	2019	Simulated driving	–	EEG	–	Modified AlexNet CNN model	T3: 91% FP1: 90%	C
Li et al. [53]	2018	Simulated driving	SEED-VIG [50]	EEG, EOG	ICA	Adversarial Discriminative Domain Adaptation (ADDA)	PCC: 0.8442	R

4 Conclusion

With the continuous improvement of EEG acquisition devices, EEG-based driver mental state detection methods have become objective and accurate. Presently, traditional machine learning- and deep learning-based methods effectively achieve remarkable results on inter-subject experiments. However, EEG data distribution is complex and unstable. In practice, samples are precious, and more powerful models are needed to address the problem of monitoring cross-subject and cross-time EEG signals. The cross-subject problem may be addressed more effectively with the on-going transfer learning research. However, there are still certain limitations, which could be overcome in the future with the development of a large number of transfer learning algorithms.

Acknowledgment. This work was supported by National Key R&D Program of China for Intergovernmental International Science and Technology Innovation Cooperation Project (2017YFE0116800), National Natural Science Foundation of China (U20B2074, U1909202), Science and Technology Program of Zhejiang Province (2018C04012), and supported by Key Laboratory of Brain Machine Collaborative Intelligence of Zhejiang Province (2020E10010).

References

1. Coetzer, R.C., Hancke, G.P.: Eye detection for a real-time vehicle driver fatigue monitoring system. In: 2011 IEEE Intelligent Vehicles Symposium (IV), pp. 66–71 (2011)
2. Lal, S.K., Craig, A.: A critical review of the psychophysiology of driver fatigue. Biol. Psychol. **55**, 173–194 (2001)
3. Sikander, G., Shahzad, A.: Driver fatigue detection systems: a review. IEEE Trans. Intell. Transp. Syst. **20**, 2339–2352 (2019)
4. May, J.F., Baldwin, C.L.: Driver fatigue: The importance of identifying causal factors of fatigue when considering detection and countermeasure technologies. Transp. Res. Part F: Traffic Psychol. Beh. **12**(3), 218–224 (2009)
5. Lal, S.K.L., Craig, A.: Driver fatigue: electroencephalography and psychological assessment. Psychophysiology **39**(3), 313–321 (2002)
6. Lewis, I., Watson, B., Tay, R., White, K.M.: The role of fear appeals in improving driver safety: a review of the effectiveness of fear-arousing (threat) appeals in road safety advertising. Int. J. Behav. Consultation and Therapy **3**(2), 203 (2007)
7. Azam, K., Shakoor, A., Shah, R.A., Khan, A., Shah, S.A., Khalil, M.S.: Comparison of fatigue related road traffic crashes on the national highways and motorways in Pakistan. J. Eng. Appl. Sci. **33**(2), 47–54 (2014)
8. Chellappa, R., Charles, L.W., Saad, S.: Human and machine recognition of faces: a survey. Proc. IEEE **83**(5), 705–741 (1995)
9. Mandal, B., Li, L., Wang, G.S., Lin, J.: Towards detection of bus driver fatigue based on robust visual analysis of eye state. IEEE Trans. Intell. Transp. Syst. **18**(3), 545–557 (2016)
10. Yao, K.P., Lin, W.H., Fang, C.Y., Wang, J.M., Chang, S.L., Chen, S.W.: Real-time vision-based driver drowsiness/fatigue detection system. In: 2010 IEEE 71st Vehicular Technology Conference, pp. 1–5 (2010)
11. Eoh, H.J., Chung, M.K., Kim, S.H.: Electroencephalographic study of drowsiness in simulated driving with sleep deprivation. Int. J. Ind. Ergon. **35**(4), 307–320 (2005)
12. Kong, W., Zhou, Z., Jiang, B., Babiloni, F., Borghini, G.: Assessment of driving fatigue based on intra/inter-region phase synchronization. Neurocomputing **219**, 474–482 (2017)

13. Jung, S.J., Shin, H.S., Chung, W.Y.: Driver fatigue and drowsiness monitoring system with embedded electrocardiogram sensor on steering wheel. IET Intel. Transport Syst. **8**(1), 43–50 (2014)
14. Brandt, T., Stemmer, R., Rakotonirainy, A.: Affordable visual driver monitoring system for fatigue and monotony. In: 2004 IEEE International Conference on Systems, Man and Cybernetics (IEEE Cat. No.04CH37583), vol. 7, pp. 6451–6456 (2004)
15. Chai, R., et al.: Improving EEG-based driver fatigue classification using sparse-deep belief networks. Frontiers Neurosci. **11**, 103 (2017)
16. Pan, S.J., Qiang, Y.: A survey on transfer learning. IEEE Trans. Knowl. Data Eng. **22**, 1345–1359 (2010)
17. Wang, P., Lu, J., Zhang, B., Tang, Z.: A review on transfer learning for brain-computer interface classification. In: 2015 5th International Conference on Information Science and Technology (ICIST) (2015)
18. Monteiro, T.G., Skourup, C., Zhang, H.: Using EEG for mental fatigue assessment: a comprehensive look into the current state of the art. IEEE Trans. Hum. Mach. Syst. **49**(6), 599–610 (2019)
19. Lotte, F., et al.: A review of classification algorithms for EEG-based brain–computer interfaces: a 10 year update. J. Neural Eng. **15**(3), (2018)
20. Patel, V.M., Gopalan, R., Li, R., Chellappa, R.: Visual domain adaptation: a survey of recent advances. IEEE Signal Process. Mag. **32**, 53–69 (2015)
21. Khan, M.N., Heisterkamp, D.R.: Adapting instance weights for unsupervised domain adaptation using quadratic mutual information and subspace learning. In: 2016 23rd International Conference on Pattern Recognition (ICPR), vol. 21, pp. 1560–1565 (2016)
22. Dai, W., Yang, Q., Xue, G.R., Yu, Y.: Boosting for transfer learning. In: Proceedings of the 24th International Conference on Machine Learning, pp. 193–200 (2007)
23. Zhao, Z., Chen, Y., Liu, J., Shen, Z., Liu, M.: Cross-people mobile-phone based activity recognition. In: Twenty-Second International Joint Conference on Artificial Intelligence (2011)
24. Wei, Y., Zhu, Y., Leung, C., Song, Y., Yang, Q.: Instilling social to physical: co-regularized heterogeneous transfer learning. In: Proceedings of the AAAI Conference on Artificial Intelligence, vol. 30, no. 1 (2016)
25. Hu, D., Yang, Q.: Transfer learning for activity recognition via sensor mapping. In: International Joint Conference on IJCAI. DBLP (2011)
26. Pan, S.J., Tsang, I.W., Kwok, J.T., Yang, Q.: Domain adaptation via transfer component analysis. IEEE Trans. Neural Netw. **22**(2), 199–210 (2010). https://doi.org/10.1109/tnn.2010.2091281
27. Long, M., Wang, J., Ding, G., Sun, J., Yu, P.S.: Transfer feature learning with joint distribution adaptation. In: Proceedings of the IEEE International Conference on Computer Vision, pp. 2200–2207 (2013)
28. Satpal, S., Sarawagi, S.: Domain adaptation of conditional probability models via feature subsetting. In: Kok, J.N., Koronacki, J., Lopez de Mantaras, R., Matwin, S., Mladenič, D., Skowron, A. (eds.) PKDD 2007. LNCS (LNAI), vol. 4702, pp. 224–235. Springer, Heidelberg (2007). https://doi.org/10.1007/978-3-540-74976-9_23
29. Gong, M., Zhang, K., Liu, T., Tao, D., Glymour, C., Schölkopf, B.: Domain adaptation with conditional transferable components. In: International Conference on Machine Learning, pp. 2839–2848 (2016)
30. Fernando, B., Habrard, A., Sebban, M., Tuytelaars, T.: Unsupervised visual domain adaptation using subspace alignment. In: Proceedings of the IEEE International Conference on Computer Vision, pp. 2960–2967 (2013)
31. Sun, H., Shuai, L., Shilin, Z.: Discriminative subspace alignment for unsupervised visual domain adaptation. Neural Process. Lett. **44**(3), 779–793 (2016)

32. Long, M., Wang, J., Cao, Y., Sun, J., Philip, S.Y.: Deep learning of transferable representation for scalable domain adaptation. IEEE Trans. Knowl. Data Eng. **28**(8), 2027–2040 (2016)
33. Tan, C., Sun, F., Kong, T., Zhang, W., Yang, C., Liu, C.: A survey on deep transfer learning. In: Kůrková, V., Manolopoulos, Y., Hammer, B., Iliadis, L., Maglogiannis, I. (eds.) ICANN 2018. LNCS, vol. 11141, pp. 270–279. Springer, Cham (2018). https://doi.org/10.1007/978-3-030-01424-7_27
34. Litjens, G., et al.: A survey on deep learning in medical image analysis. Med. Image Anal. **42**, 60–88 (2017)
35. Ganin, Y., et al.: Domain-adversarial training of neural networks. J. Mach. Learn. Res. **17**(1), 2030–2096 (2016)
36. Mihalkova, L., Mooney, R J.: Transfer learning by mapping with minimal target data. In: Proceedings of the AAAI-2008 Workshop on Transfer Learning for Complex Tasks (2008)
37. Wu, D., Xu, Y., Lu, B.: Transfer learning for EEG-based brain-computer interfaces: a review of progresses since 2016. arXiv preprint arXiv:2004.06286 (2020)
38. Wu, D., Lawhern, V.J., Gordon, S., Lance, B.J., Lin, C.T.: Driver drowsiness estimation from EEG signals using online weighted adaptation regularization for regression (OwARR). IEEE Trans. Fuzzy Syst. **25**(6), 1522–1535 (2016)
39. Wei, C.S., Lin, Y.P., Wang, Y.T., Jung, T.P., Bigdely-Shamlo, N., Lin, C.T.: Selective transfer learning for EEG-based drowsiness detection. In: 2015 IEEE International Conference on Systems, Man, and Cybernetics, pp. 3229–3232 (2015)
40. Wei, C.S., Lin, Y.P., Wang, Y.T., Lin, C.T., Jung, T.P.: A subject-transfer framework for obviating inter-and intra-subject variability in EEG-based drowsiness detection. NeuroImage **174**, 407–419 (2018)
41. Wu, D., Chuang, C.H., Lin, C.T.: Online driver's drowsiness estimation using domain adaptation with model fusion. In: 2015 International Conference on Affective Computing and Intelligent Interaction (ACII), pp. 904–910 (2015)
42. Jiang, Y., Zhang, Y., Lin, C., Wu, D., Lin, C.T.: EEG-based driver drowsiness estimation using an online multi-view and transfer TSK fuzzy system. IEEE Trans. Intell. Transp. Syst. **22**, 1752–1764 (2020)
43. Chen, L.L., Zhang, A., Lou, X.G.: Cross-subject driver status detection from physiological signals based on hybrid feature selection and transfer learning. Expert Syst. Appl. **137**, 266–280 (2019)
44. Zhang, J., Wang, Y., Li, S.: Cross-subject mental workload classification using kernel spectral regression and transfer learning techniques. Cogn. Technol. Work **19**(4), 587–605 (2017)
45. Liu, Y., Lan, Z., Cui, J., Sourina, O., Müller-Wittig, W.: Inter-subject transfer learning for EEG-based mental fatigue recognition. Adv. Eng. Inform. **46**, (2020)
46. Yan, K., Kou, L., Zhang, D.: Learning domain-invariant subspace using domain features and independence maximization. IEEE Trans. Cybern. **48**(1), 288–299 (2017)
47. Gretton, A., Borgwardt, K., Rasch, M., Schölkopf, B., Smola, A.: A kernel method for the two-sample-problem. Adv. Neural. Inf. Process. Syst. **19**, 513–520 (2006)
48. Zhang, Y.Q., Zheng, W.L., Lu, B.L.: Transfer components between subjects for EEG-based driving fatigue detection. In: Arik, S., Huang, T., Lai, W.K., Liu, Qingshan (eds.) ICONIP 2015. LNCS, vol. 9492, pp. 61–68. Springer, Cham (2015). https://doi.org/10.1007/978-3-319-26561-2_8
49. Healey, J.A., Picard, R.W.: Detecting stress during real-world driving tasks using physiological sensors. IEEE Trans. Intell. Transp. Syst. **6**(2), 156–166 (2005)
50. Zheng, W.L., Lu, B.L.: A multimodal approach to estimating vigilance using EEG and forehead EOG. J. Neural Eng. **14**(2), (2017)
51. Wu, D., Lance, B.J., Parsons, T.D.: Collaborative filtering for brain-computer interaction using transfer learning and active class selection. PLoS ONE **8**(2), (2013)

52. Shalash, W.M.: Driver fatigue detection with single EEG channel using transfer learning. In: 2019 IEEE International Conference on Imaging Systems and Techniques (IST), pp. 1–6 (2019)

53. Li, H., Zheng, W.L., Lu, B.L.: Multimodal vigilance estimation with adversarial domain adaptation networks. In: 2018 International Joint Conference on Neural Networks (IJCNN), pp. 1–6 (2018)

54. Parsons, T.D., Courtney, C.G., Dawson, M.E.: Virtual reality stroop task for assessment of supervisory attentional processing. J. Clin. Exp. Neuropsychol. **35**(8), 812–826 (2013)

Author Index

Belkacem, Abdelkader Nasreddine   113
Bouneffouf, Djallel   14

Cecchi, Guillermo   14
Chen, Chao   113
Chen, Jian   72
Chen, Liang   87
Cui, Jin   149

Gao, Daiheng   1
Gao, Shouwei   102
Gu, Xuelin   102
Gu, Zishan   87
Guo, Guoxin   125

Hao, Long   113
Huang, Zhaoyang   113

Kong, Wanzeng   149

Li, Guoqi   1
Li, Jintang   87
Lian, Qi   56
Lin, Baihan   14
Liu, Yunzhu   56
Lu, Lin   113

Ming, Dong   113

Ozawa, Kenji   149

Pei, Guangying   125
Pei, Jing   1
Peng, Qibiao   87
Peng, Yong   149

Qi, Yu   56
Qiao, Kai   72

Reinen, Jenna   14
Rish, Irina   14

Shin, Duk   113

Tan, Wenjun   113
Tang, Jiajia   137
Tong, Li   72

Wang, Linyuan   72
Wang, Shuaibin   125
Wang, Shujie   125
Weng, Juyang   34
Wu, Yujie   1
Wu, Zhenzhi   1

Xu, Hongyan   137
Xu, Kun   87

Yan, Bin   72
Yan, Tianyi   125
Yang, Banghua   102
You, Jia   113

Zhang, Chi   72
Zhang, Dong   102
Zhang, Jianhai   137
Zhao, Yu   56
Zheng, Zibin   87
Zhou, Zhiyu   125
Zhu, Li   137
Zhu, Xuequan   113

Printed in the United States
by Baker & Taylor Publisher Services